# AN INTRODUCTION TO POLITICAL COMMUNICATION

*An Introduction to Political Communication* critically explores the relationship between politics, the media and democracy in the United Kingdom, America and other contemporary societies. In this accessible textbook Brian McNair examines how politicians, trade unions, pressure groups and terrorist organisations make use of the media.

Separate chapters look at political media and their effects, the work of political advertising, marketing and public relations, and the communicative practices of organisations at all levels, from grassroot campaigning through to governments and international bodies.

This new edition is revised and updated and draws on a range of contemporary examples to show how politicians and political groups communicate:

- the rise of New Labour under Tony Blair and the failure of the Conservative general election strategy in 1997;
- the scandals surrounding the Clinton presidency and the perceived dumbing down of American media;
- the Good Friday peace agreement in Northern Ireland and the shift in tactics by para-military organisations;
- the liberalising power of the Internet and concerns about threats to the standards of democracy.

**Brian McNair** is Reader in the Department of Film and Media Studies at Stirling University. He is the author of *News and Journalism in the UK*, *Glasnost, Perestroika and the Soviet Media* and *Images of the Enemy*.

# COMMUNICATION AND SOCIETY
## General Editor: James Curran

# AN INTRODUCTION TO POLITICAL COMMUNICATION

## Second edition

## *Brian McNair*

London and New York

First published 1995
by Routledge
11 New Fetter Lane, London EC4P 4EE

Simultaneously published in the USA and Canada
by Routledge
29 West 35th Street, New York, NY 10001

Second edition 1999

© 1995, 1999 Brian McNair

Typeset in Sabon by RefineCatch Limited, Bungay, Suffolk
Printed and bound in Great Britain by
TJ International Ltd, Padstow, Cornwall

*British Library Cataloguing in Publication Data*
A catalogue record for this book is available from the British Library

*Library of Congress Cataloguing in Publication Data*
McNair, Brian, 1959–
An introduction to political communication / Brian McNair. – 2nd
ed.
p.    cm. – (Communication and society)
Includes bibliographical references and index.
1. Communication in politics.  I. Title.  II. Series:
Communication and society (Routledge (Firm))
JA85.M36   1999
324.7′3 – dc21          98–45946

ISBN 0–415–19921–2 (hbk)
ISBN 0–415–19922–0 (pbk)

The significant revolution of modern times is not industrial or economic or political, but the revolution taking place in the art of creating consent among the governed . . . Within the life of the new generation now in control of affairs, persuasion has become a self-conscious art and a regular organ of popular government. None of us begins to understand the consequences, but it is no daring prophecy to say that the knowledge of how to create consent will alter every political premise.

(Walter Lippmann, *Public Opinion*)

FOR RAYMOND AND JANINE

# CONTENTS

# ILLUSTRATIONS

# PREFACE AND
# ACKNOWLEDGEMENTS

More than seventy years ago Walter Lippmann observed that the practice of democracy had 'turned a corner' (1954, p.248). The democratic process, it seemed to him four years after the end of the First World War had, to an extent unprecedented in human history, come to incorporate self-conscious strategies of *persuasion* by political actors. The gradual extension since the early nineteenth century of voting rights to wider and wider sections of the population, combined with the emergence of media of mass communication, had fundamentally transformed the nature of the political process, for better or worse. No longer could it be assumed that political action derived from the collectively arrived at will of rational, enlightened men (for men they exclusively were, of course) of property and education. Henceforth, the masses would decide, through their exercise of the vote, and the influence of *public opinion* on the political process.

But public opinion, Lippmann recognised even in 1922, was a constructed, manufactured thing, which could be shaped and manipulated by those with an interest in doing so. To that end, he noted the rise of a new professional class of 'publicists', or 'press agents', standing between political organisations and media institutions, whose job it was to influence press coverage of their clients, and thus, they hoped, public opinion.

Now, as we approach the end of the twentieth century, these trends have accelerated and deepened, until not only 'the practice of democracy' but politics in all its forms is played out before a mass, sometimes global audience, through electronic and print media which have made McLuhan's metaphor of the planet as a shrinking 'global village' into a truism. As the role of the media in mediating between politicians and public has increased, so has the importance of those publicists, press agents and others in what we may refer to as the political public relations industry. Brave (and probably doomed to failure) is the organisation which ventures into the contemporary political arena without a more or less sophisticated understanding of how the media work and the professional public relations machinery capable of putting that knowledge to good use. For all political actors, from presidents and prime ministers to trade union leaders and terrorists, this is now recognised to be a major prerequisite of successful intervention in public debate and governmental decision-making.

If these trends are generally acknowledged to be real, they have not been greeted with unanimous approval outside the offices of the political public relations agencies themselves. For many, the growing centrality of the media in the political process degrades the latter, undermining its democratic characteristics and transforming it into meaningless, empty spectacle. Others point with distaste to the use of the media by avowedly undemocratic organisations, such as the Provisional IRA in Northern Ireland, to influence public opinion in directions favourable to their political objectives. More optimistic voices welcome the media's heightened political role as signalling a long overdue extension of democratic participation. Others still resign themselves and their organisations to the reality of an age when politics and the media are intimately and forever bound together. Rather than complaining about the increasing 'mediatisation' of the political process, these groups strive to get in on the act.

This book is intended as both an introduction and a modest contribution to that debate, which has become so prominent an element of contemporary political discourse throughout the advanced capitalist world. It will be of value, I hope, to the growing numbers of students, researchers, teachers and concerned citizens with an interest, professional or otherwise, in the relationship between communication and politics.

My own interest in the subject derives from many years of research and teaching in the field of journalism studies, in the course of which it has become abundantly clear that what the media do is as much the product of external factors – in the particular context of this book, the activities of the political communications industry – as with such intra-media considerations as journalistic bias, proprietorial interference, or the routine practices of newsgathering. In previous work I have examined the relationship between the political public relations activities of, for example, the British Campaign for Nuclear Disarmament (CND), the British Labour Party, and the

Soviet government (McNair, 1988, 1989, 1991) and the media coverage received by them. These discussions were marginal, however, in the context of work concerned chiefly with how journalists thought and behaved. This study of political communication will concentrate to a much greater extent on the nature of the interface between politicians and the media, the extent of their interaction, and the dialectic of their relationship. It will probe the limits on the actions of politicians on the one hand and journalists on the other, and the influence of both on what citizens think and do.

Such an emphasis owes much to those who, over the last two decades, have developed what has become known in communication studies as the *source-centred* approach (Goldenberg, 1984; Tiffen, 1989; Schlesinger and Tumber, 1994). The term focusses attention on the active role in shaping media content played by those who provide the source material, rather than the producers of journalistic output themselves. The shift is one of emphasis, and this book does not seek to replace the notion of an all-powerful media with that of the all-powerful 'spin doctor' or media manipulator. It will, however, add to a growing literature in communication and political studies concerned with locating the media's agency and effectivity in a wider social – in this case political – environment, characterised by greater levels of uncertainty, risk and arbitrariness than some perspectives within communication studies have acknowledged.

Structurally, the book is organised into two parts. In Part I, we examine what is meant by the term 'political communication', and who precisely are the communicators. We describe the normative principles of liberal democracy and consider how political communication relates, in theory, to the democratic process. A complete chapter is devoted to outlining the contexts in which modern mass media communicate politically, and another to the 'effects' of political communication on behaviour, attitudes and social processes.

Part II places this introductory and theoretical material in the context of the political communication practices of a variety of actors, including governments and party politicians, both domestically and in the international arena; business and trade union leaders; and marginalised political actors such as pressure groups and terrorist organisations.

A short conclusion makes a tentative effort to answer the question: is the increasing role of mass communication in the political process a 'good' or a 'bad' thing for democracy?

The structure and content of the book owe much to lectures in political communication developed for students of media and public relations at the University of Stirling between 1990 and 1994. My ability to think and write clearly about the subject of political communication has benefited substantially from their comments and feedback. I trust that, were they beginning their studies anew, they would find this book a useful and accessible introduction. Time to write was greatly enhanced by a period of sabbatical leave provided by the University of Stirling. My colleagues in the Department of Film and Media Studies at Stirling provided, as always, valuable support and encouragement.

*Brian McNair*
*March 1995*

# PREFACE TO THE SECOND
# EDITION

Since the first edition of this book was completed and sent to the printer in the autumn of 1994, the trends it identified have continued to provoke contentious debate wherever politics is taken seriously. In both Britain and the United States, from which societies the majority of my examples and illustrations are drawn, communication continues to grow in visibility and importance as a factor in the management and organisation of the political process. The 'spin doctors' and other categories of communication professional have become, to an extent that was not true even as recently as 1995 when the first edition of this book was published, key players not just in the tactical presentation of political messages, but in their strategic design. The names of some of those players have changed, as has the composition of the political elites for whom they work, but across the advanced capitalist world, and wherever mediated politics has become the dominant mode of democratic organisation, the enhanced role of communication constitutes a common feature. In the United States in 1996, Bill Clinton won a second term, largely due to effective political communication. In Britain in 1997, on the other hand, John Major failed to do so, and eighteen years of Conservative government came to an end, in large part due to poor political communication. This edition is fully updated to reflect these developments, and includes discussion of the communications-driven rise of New Labour in the UK, the political impact of the Monica Lewinsky scandal in the USA, the resurgence of conflict between the Western powers and Saddam Hussein in 1998, and the 'ending' of the thirty-year sectarian conflict in Northern Ireland which was signalled by the Good Friday peace agreement of April 1998.

If the names of some of the key players in the practice of political communication have changed, the central arguments and themes of the first edition remain valid, and have not required major revision here. Mediated politics, I continue to argue in this edition, is neither the threat to normative standards of democracy suggested by cultural pessimists, nor the panacea to the traditional limitations of democratic representation identified by some of the more optimistic commentators. Its benefits are huge, and its weaknesses many. On balance, however, the time elapsed between the first and second editions strengthens my belief – and my *feeling*, as a reasonably well-informed citizen and an enthusiastic consumer of mediated politics – that the vast quantity of political communication now in circulation and accessible to anyone who wants it, and the increasingly irreverent, often subversive, unpredictably chaotic character of much of that communication towards politicians and other elite members amounts on balance to an improvement in the quality of the public sphere; an increase in its value as a democratic resource, the full significance which we are still striving to understand and assess. To that extent I take issue with the more apocalyptic hypotheses of 'dumbing down', 'tabloidisation' and 'infotainment' which have driven recent debates in the communication studies field, and which I critique more fully elsewhere in my work on journalism (McNair 1998b, 1999). The resignation as trade and industry secretary of Peter Mandelson in December 1998, amid accusations of 'cronyism', reinforces the argument of the first edition that spin doctors are not all-powerful in the face of a competitive and unpredictable media. Mandelson's resignation was only the most spectacular of a series of presentational failures experienced by New Labour in government, and regardless of the detail of each case, the fact that such misfortune could befall the most communicatively adept political party in Europe must cast doubt on the more pessimistic assessments of the spin doctors' power to dictate to and manipulate the political media.

The researching and writing of this edition have benefited greatly from my involvement in the ESRC-funded *Political Communication and Democracy* project (reference number: L126251022), carried out at Stirling University between 1996 and 1998. Although this volume is not the place for the presentation of detailed empirical findings, my work on that project – still in progress as this edition goes to press – and the period of sabbatical leave which it funded, has greatly assisted and informed my updating and revision of this book, and I am grateful to research assistants Will Dinan and Deirdre Kevin for their help in assembling some of the new data contained here.

*Brian McNair, April 1999*

# Part I

# POLITICS IN THE AGE OF MEDIATION

# 1
# POLITICS IN THE AGE OF MEDIATION

Any book about political communication should begin by acknowledging that the term has proved to be notoriously difficult to define with any precision, simply because both components of the phrase are themselves open to a variety of definitions, more or less broad. Denton and Woodward, for example, provide one definition of political communication as

> public discussion about the allocation of public resources (revenues), official authority (who is given the power to make legal, legislative and executive decision), and official sanctions (what the state rewards or punishes).
>
> (1990, p.14)

This definition includes verbal and written political rhetoric, but not symbolic communication acts which, as we shall see in this book, are of growing significance for an understanding of the political process as a whole.

The American writer Doris Graber advances a more all-encompassing definition of what she terms 'political language', suggesting that it comprises not only rhetoric but paralinguistic signs such as body language, and political acts such as boycotts and protests (1981).

Elsewhere in the work cited above, Denton and Woodward characterise political communication in terms of the *intentions* of its senders to influence the political environment. As they put it

> the crucial factor that makes communication 'political' is not the source of a message [or, we might add, referring

back to their earlier emphasis on 'public discussion', its
*form*], but its content and purpose.

(Ibid., p.11)

This book will follow Denton and Woodward by stressing
the *intentionality* of political communication, which I will define
here simply as *purposeful communication about politics*. This
incorporates:

1  all forms of communication undertaken by politicans and other
   political actors for the purpose of achieving specific objectives;
2  communication addressed *to* these actors by non-politicians
   such as voters and newspaper columnists, and
3  communication *about* these actors and their activities, as contained in news reports, editorials, and other forms of media
   discussion of politics.

In short, *all* political discourse is included in our definition. By political communication, therefore, I, like Graber, have in mind not only
verbal or written statements, but visual means of signification such
as dress, make-up, hairstyle and logo design, i.e., all those elements
of communication which might be said to constitute a political
'image' or identity.

Absent from the book (if not from our definition) is any substantial discussion of the subject of *interpersonal* political communication. It need hardly be stressed that the political discussions of
people in public bars or at dinner parties, the behind-closed-doors
negotiations of governments, and the information gleaned by
journalists from face-to-face meetings with high-level sources, are
highly significant for the political process. By their nature, however,
they are hidden from the analyst, requiring methodologically
difficult and costly empirical research to uncover their secrets. Conducting and reporting such research is beyond the scope of this
volume. Throughout, however, we will bear in mind the potential
gap between the public and the private in political rhetoric.

The book also lacks, in the sections dealing with governmental
communication, substantial discussion of local (i.e., city and dis-
trict, regional and town) politics. As Bob Franklin and others have
described, local government is a sphere of political activity in which
communication is of growing importance (Franklin and Murphy,
1991; Franklin, 1994).

## THE SCOPE OF THE BOOK

The study of political communication directs our attention to the relationship between three elements in the process by which political action is conceived and realised.

### Political organisations

Firstly, there are the *political actors*, narrowly defined: those individuals who aspire, through organisational and institutional means, to influence the decision-making process (see Figure 1.1). They may seek to do this by attaining institutional political power, in government or constituent assemblies, through which preferred policies can be implemented. If in opposition their objectives will

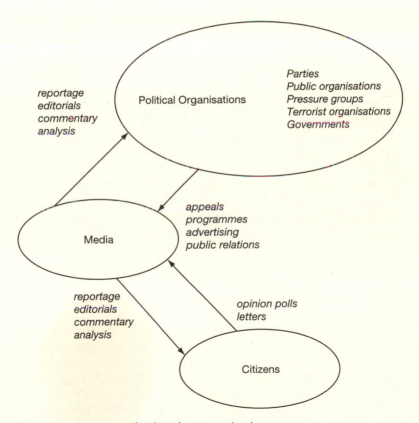

*Figure 1.1* Elements of political communication

be to obstruct existing power-holders, and have them replaced by alternatives.

## Political parties

This category of political actor includes, most obviously, the established political parties: aggregates of more or less like-minded individuals, who come together within an agreed organisational and ideological structure to pursue common goals. These goals will reflect the party's underlying value system, or ideology, such as the British Conservative Party's adherence to 'individual freedom' and the supremacy of the market; or their Labour opponents' preference for 'capitalism with a human face' and the principles of social justice and equality. In the United States the Democrats have historically been associated with relative liberalism in social policy, and an interventionist approach to the economy, while the Republicans aspire to reduce state involvement in all aspects of socio-economic life.

Despite the ideological differences which may exist between political parties in modern democracies they share a commitment to constitutional means of advancing their objectives, attempting to convince a population as a whole of their correctness, and putting their policies to the test of periodic elections. Once mandated (or rejected, as the case may be) they agree to abide by the constitutional rules of the political system in which they operate, respecting the limitations it puts on their power to implement or oppose policy, until such time as another electoral opportunity comes along.

For parties, clearly, the smooth functioning of the process described above is dependent primarily on their ability to communicate with those who will vote for and legitimise them. When, until relatively recently, voting rights in capitalist countries were restricted to small elites of propertied, educated men, it was enough for parties to use various forms of interpersonal communication, such as public meetings and rallies, aided by newspaper coverage, to reach their constituencies. But in an age of universal suffrage and a *mass* electorate parties must use *mass* media. Chapters 6 and 7 examine the many communication strategies and tactics which have been developed by political parties in recognition of this fact. These include techniques which originated in the world of corporate and business affairs, such as marketing – the science of 'influencing mass behaviour in competitive situations' (Mauser, 1983, p.5). Political marketing is analogous to commercial marketing in so far as political organisations, like those in the commercial sector, must *target* audiences from whom (electoral) support is sought, using channels of mass communication, in a competitive environment where the citizen/consumer has a choice between more than one 'brand' of product. While there are obvious differences in the nature of the political and commercial marketplaces, and political parties measure success not in terms of profit but in voting share and effective power, political marketing employs many of the principles applied by the manufacturers of goods and services as they strive for commercial success.

Political advertising, the subject of Chapter 6, is also founded on principles originally worked out by the business sector to exploit the presumed persuasive potential of mass media. This form of political communication uses mass media to 'differentiate' political products (i.e., parties and candidates) and give them meaning for the 'consumer', just as the soap manufacturer seeks to distinguish a functionally similar brand of washing powder from another in a crowded marketplace.

A third commercially influenced category of political communication activity is that of *public relations* – media and information management tactics designed to ensure that a party receives maximum favourable publicity, and the minimum of negative. Activities contained within the rubric of 'public relations' include *pro-active* devices such as party conferences which, as we shall see, are in contemporary politics designed principally to attract positive media coverage of an organisation; news conferences, which permit parties to (attempt to) set political agendas, particularly during election campaigns; and the employment of image managers to design a party's (and its public leaders') 'look'.

*Re-active* political public relations techniques, in which parties strive for damage-limitation, include the lobbying of journalists and the 'spinning' of potentially damaging stories; the suppressing of potentially damaging information, such as was attempted by the Conservative government of John Major on numerous occasions in the early 1990s (the Iraq arms scandal, the Pergau dam affair, etc.); and disinformation tactics such as 'leaking', a device particularly favoured by the Conservative government of Margaret Thatcher.

The design and execution of these forms of political communication is the province of that new professional class referred to in the Preface – nowadays known variously as media or political consultants, image-managers, 'spin-doctors' and 'gurus' which has emerged in the course of the twentieth century and is now routinely employed by political parties.

## Public organisations

If parties are at the constitutional heart of the democratic political process they are not, of course, the only political actors. Surrounding the established institutions of politics are a host of non-party organisations with political objectives. Some, like the British trade unions, have clear organisational links with one or more of the parties (the trade unions, indeed, gave birth to the Labour Party as the organised political expression of workers' interests).

Others, such as consumers' associations and lobby groups, will be more peripheral, dealing as they do with relatively narrow constituencies and issues. Others will, by virtue of the tactics which they adopt, be excluded from constitutional politics altogether, and may have the status of criminal organisations.

We may divide these non-party actors into three categories. Firstly, trade unions, consumer groups, professional associations and others may be defined as *public organisations*. They are united not by ideology, but by some common feature of their members' situation which makes it advantageous to combine, such as work problems (trade unions), or the weakness of the individual citizen in the face of large corporations (consumer groups).

In such organisations individuals come together, not just to help each other in the resolution of practical problems associated with their common situation, but to campaign for change or to raise the public profile of a particular problem, often through enlisting the help of elected politicians. These organisations have, to a greater or lesser degree, institutional status and public legitimacy, as reflected in their access to policy-makers and media, receipt of charitable donations, and official funding. Chapter 8 will examine the techniques used by such organisations to influence the political process, such as 'lobbying', advertising, and the organisation of public demonstrations.

## Pressure groups

Chapter 8 will also consider the political communication practices of a second category of non-party actor: the *pressure group*. Pressure groups (or single-issue groups, as they are also known) may be distinguished from the public organisations listed above in that they

8

are typically less institutionalised and more overtly 'political' in their objectives, being concerned with such issues as the conservation of the natural environment, and the prevention of cruelty to animals being reared for human food consumption, or for use in the testing of drugs and cosmetics. They tend to campaign around *single issues*, such as the anti-nuclear movement in the early 1980s, and the British anti-poll tax campaign of the late 1980s and early 1990s (Deacon and Golding, 1994). They are unlike the established parties, however, in drawing their support and membership from a more diverse social base. While the Labour and Conservative parties in Britain (and the US Democratic and Republican parties) are traditionally associated with 'labour' and 'business' respectively (given that these associations are much looser now than was once the case) an organisation such as the Campaign for Nuclear Disarmament, and its equivalent in other countries, at the height of its influence drew support and active membership from the entire spectrum of social classes in Britain. The environmental movement of the 1990s, likewise, has found support across classes, age groups, and religious and ideological affiliations.

The environmental movement, it should be noted, is an example of a pressure group which sought to break into the mainstream of the political process by establishing 'Green' parties throughout Europe. As a political party the Greens have not succeeded in establishing themselves in the British Parliament, although they have many elected representatives in Germany and other European countries. Even in Britain, however, the environmental movement has had a major impact on the political agenda, requiring both Conservative and Labour governments to develop at least the appearance of pro-environmental policies.[1]

Pressure group politics, like that of parties and public organisations, is about communication, using the variety of advertising and public relations techniques now available. Some groups, like Friends of the Earth, have proved themselves to be skilled exponents of these techniques. But because of their non-institutional, more or less marginal character, they are frequently deprived of the financial and status resources which accrue to more established political actors, and must therefore devise less expensive means of communicating their political messages, such as symbolic forms of protest and demonstration designed to attract the attentions of journalists. Chapter 8 will explore these techniques and assess their effectiveness in some detail.

### Terrorist organisations

The third category of non-party political actor to which we shall refer in Chapter 8 is the *terrorist* organisation. Although the term 'terrorist' is value-laden, and may be rejected by groups whose members may prefer to see themselves as 'freedom fighters' in 'national liberation' or 'resistance' movements, we shall use the term here to refer to groups which use terror tactics – urban bombing, hi-jacking, assassination, and kidnapping, to list the most common – to achieve their political objectives. In this sense, many of the world's governments, including those of South Africa, Israel, France, and the United States, have at one time or another committed acts of (state) terrorism.

More commonly associated with terrorism, however, are such organisations as the Irish Republican Army in Northern Ireland (until the 1998 peace agreement ended 'the war', at any rate), Hamas and Hezbollah in the Middle East, and ETA in the Spanish Basque country. All share a readiness to work for their goals outside of the constitutional process, which they regard as illegitimate, and to use violence as a means of 'persuasion'. Unlike state-sponsored terrorists, who seek to avoid identification and publicity, these organisations actively court media attention, striving to make their 'target publics' aware of their existence and their objectives, often by illegal or violent means.

As Chapter 8 argues, therefore, even acts of random violence directed against civilians may be viewed as a form of political communication, intended to send a message to a particular constituency, and capable of being decoded as such. Modern terrorist organisations also use the public relations and media management techniques of more mainstream political actors, such as news conferences, press releases and leaks, to the oft-expressed chagrin of the latter.

## The audience

The purpose of all this communication is, as has been noted, to persuade. And the target of this persuasion – the audience – is the second key element in the political communication process, without which no political message can have any relevance.

The audience for a particular political communication may be broad, as in a British party political broadcast (PPB) or a US election 'spot', where the objective is to persuade an entire nation of voters.

It may be narrow, as when the editorial of a leading newspaper 'of record', such as the *Sunday Times*, calls on the Conservative party to change its leadership (or to retain it, as the case may be). The audience may be both broad and narrow, as in the case of the IRA bombing of a Manchester shopping mall in 1995. Such a 'communication' has at least two levels of meaning, and is intended for at least two audiences. One, the British people as a whole, are being told that they should not view the Northern Irish conflict as something of irrelevance to them. A second, more selective audience, the government, are being warned that the IRA has the ability and the will to carry out such acts, and that appropriate changes to policy should be forthcoming (as, with the election of a Labour government in 1997, they were).

Whatever the size and nature of the audience, however, all political communication is intended to achieve an effect on the receivers of the message. From US presidential campaigns to the lobbying of individual MPs and senators, the communicator hopes that there will be some positive (from his or her point of view) impact on the political behaviour of the recipient.

As every student of the media knows, the effects issue is one of great complexity and unending controversy. In political communication, as in Hollywood cinema or pornography, the audience's relationship to the message is ambiguous, and extremely difficult to investigate empirically. Attempts have been made to so do none the less, and Chapter 3 will examine the evidence for and against the efficacy of political communication (as measured against the intentions of the communicators), including such issues as the importance of a politician's visual image in shaping voters' perceptions; the impact of 'biased' media coverage on election outcomes; and the relationship between 'public opinion' and attempts (by both politicians and media organisations) to set agendas. We also examine the broader effects issue: what 'effect' has the rise of political communication had on the democratic process?

## The media

Which brings us to the third element in the political communication process – media organisations. In democratic political systems media function both as transmitters of political communication which originates outside the media organisation itself, and as senders of political messages constructed by journalists. As Figure 1.1 indicates, the role of the media in both respects is crucial.

Firstly, and most obviously, political actors must use the media in order to have their messages communicated to the desired audience. Political programmes, policy statements, electoral appeals, pressure group campaigns, acts of terrorism, have a political existence – and potential for communicative effectiveness – only to the extent that they are reported and received as messages by the media audience. Consequently, all political communicators must gain access to the media by some means, whether legislative, as in the rules of political balance and impartiality which govern British public service broadcasting, or by an appreciation of the workings of the media sufficient to ensure that a message is reported.

In Chapter 4 we examine the regulations and conventions which typically govern access to the media for political actors. We also describe the organisational features of media production which may work for or against political communicators in their efforts to obtain coverage. This will lead us into a discussion of the constraints and pressures within which news is selected and produced, and the implications of these for the choices routinely made by media workers.

The media, of course, do not simply report, in a neutral and impartial way, what is going on in the political arena around them. Despite protestations to the contrary by some journalists, there are more than enough analyses of the media in the communication studies literature to show that their accounts of political events (as of any other category of 'reality') are laden with value judgments, subjectivities and biases. Kaid *et al.* suggest that we may view political 'reality' as comprising three categories (1991):

- Firstly, we may speak of an *objective* political reality, comprising political events as they actually occur.
- There is then a *subjective* reality – the 'reality' of political events as they are perceived by actors and citizens.
- Thirdly, and crucial to the shaping of the second category of subjective perceptions, is *constructed* reality, meaning events as covered by the media.

While arguments about the precise efficacy of the media's political output continue, there is no disagreement about their central role in the political process, relaying and interpreting objective happenings in the political sphere, and facilitating subjective perceptions of them in the wider public sphere. For this reason, media 'biases' are of key political importance.

This is true of both print and broadcast media, in all capitalist societies. Some 'biases' may be attributed, as Chapter 4 shows, to constraints and limitations on the newsgathering process. Others are the product of choices made to support this or that political party or idea. Newspapers in Britain and most other capitalist societies are relatively open about which political parties they support (though some seek to maintain the appearance of neutrality). Broadcasters are generally more reticent, although, in many political debates, such as those which have occupied the UK media around such issues as industrial relations and the future of Northern Ireland, clear preferences have been on display.[2]

While the extent and direction of media bias will vary in a modern democracy, the fact that it exists entitles us to view the media organisations as important actors in the political process. Between the sending of a political message and its reception by an audience, something happens to it. It gets altered in various ways, consciously or as a consequence of the media production process, so that its meaning and hence impact on an audience may change.

The media – and the print media in particular – are important to the political process in more direct ways. While analysts may argue about the bias of reportage, all newspapers take pride in their 'public voice'[3] – the editorials in which they articulate political opinions. Sometimes these are presented as the 'voice of the reader', and directed at policy-makers. Alternatively, they may be constructed as the calm, authoritative voice of the editor, viewing the political scene from a detached distance. In both cases, the editorial is intended as a political intervention, and often read as such by a government or a party. Commentaries, analyses, and other forms of 'authored' journalism are also interventionist in intention. Chapter 5 will consider how the journalists' messages interact with the political process as a whole.

The media are important in the political process, finally, as transmitters of messages from citizens to their political leaders. In their coverage of opinion polls, for example, the media may claim to represent 'public opinion', which takes on the status of a real thing by which to understand or evaluate the political situation, often in terms critical of or admonitory to individual politicians. In this way, the views of the citizen are communicated upwards, often with observable effects on parties' behaviour. Newspapers also publish readers' letters, providing a forum for public discussion of political issues. In some newspapers, notably *The Times*, the letters page is likely to be read by politicians as indicative of public opinion (or some significant portion of it), and may be a significant consideration in policy-making. Broadcasting is now awash with political debate and public access programmes, in which members of the public are brought together to discuss the burning issues of the day, and to express their opinions on those issues. In January 1997, for example, Britain's ITV broadcast *Monarchy: the nation decides*. Advertised as the biggest live debate ever broadcast on British TV, the programme allowed 3,000 citizens, egged on by a panel of pro- and anti-monarchy experts, to express their views on the past and present performance of the British monarchy, and its future role, in unprecedentedly critical terms, which both the British royal family, and any government responsible for stewarding the country's constitutional development, would have been foolish to ignore.[4]

For all these reasons, then, an understanding of the contemporary political process is inconceivable without an analysis of the media, and a substantial part of this book will be devoted to that task.

## The international stage

We turn, finally, to a category of political actor of growing importance in the study of communication.

The progress of the twentieth century has seen the political arena become more international, as the media have extended their reach, geographically and temporally. In the modern world media audiences are the targets of political communication not only from domestic sources, but foreign ones. Foreign governments, business organisations, and terrorist groups, all use the global information system to further their political objectives. Traditional forms of interpersonal international diplomacy persist, but modern wars, liberation struggles, and territorial disputes are increasingly fought out in the media, with global public opinion as the prize (since the protagonists – governments and international bodies like the United Nations – are presumed to be responsive to public opinion). As Walter Lippmann recognised in the early 1920s, 'governments today act upon the principle that it is not sufficient to govern their own citizens well and to assure the people that they are acting wholeheartedly on their behalf. They understand that the public opinion of the entire world is important to their welfare' (quoted in Bernays, 1923, p.44).

Efforts to influence international public opinion and policy are clearly political communication as we have defined it in this introduction, and Chapter 9 is devoted to analyses of some prominent examples of such efforts, including the Falklands, Gulf, and Yugoslavian wars, and the broader propaganda campaigns which accompanied the seventy years of East–West conflict, the Cold War.

## CONCLUSION

This book, then, is about political communication in the very broadest sense, incorporating the communicative practices of all kinds of political organisations (and some, such as British public service broadcasting, which are not supposed to be 'political' at all), in both domestic and international arenas.

Throughout, I have referred to the form of polity with which the book is chiefly concerned as 'democratic', although the discussion, particularly of international political communication, will necessarily include societies, such as the former Soviet Union and Iraq, which could not be so described. By 'democracies' I mean, simply, societies in which governments rule primarily through consent rather than coercion; where political leaders have popular legitimacy, if not necessarily always popularity, and where the views of the citizen as expressed through the ballot box and elsewhere are declared to be meaningful. In the next chapter we examine how such societies are supposed to work, and the role played in them by political communication.

# 2

# POLITICS, DEMOCRACY AND THE MEDIA

This chapter outlines the ideal type of society and polity postulated by liberal democratic theory and how the media of mass communication may contribute to the smooth functioning of such societies. We then consider how this ideal has been realised in practice, a discussion which inevitably requires a critique, both of actually existing democratic systems, and of the media's role within them.

## THE THEORY OF LIBERAL DEMOCRACY

The principles of liberal democracy as we understand them today grew out of the bourgeois critique of autocracy in early modern Europe, beginning in the sixteenth century and culminating in the French Revolution of 1789, with its slogan of 'Liberty, Equality, Fraternity'. In the political structures of autocratic societies, such as those typical of the absolutist monarchies of European feudalism, power resided in the king or queen, whose right to rule was divinely ordained by God. Subordinate classes – the peasantry and artisans – were subject to divine order, lacking political rights of any kind. Even the aristocracy, 'lording' it over the lower classes in society, owed unquestioning allegiance to the monarch. The institutions of state were directed primarily to the maintenance of this hierarchical system, and to the suppression of dissent, from wherever it came.

The emergence of the bourgeoisie (or capitalist class) as the dominant economic force in Europe and America required the overthrow of autocracy and its monopolisation of political power. For capitalism to develop freely there had to be freedom of thought and action for those with entrepreneurial skills and the wealth to use them. There had, therefore, to be freedom from the arbitrariness of absolute power, an end to the ideology of divine right, and recognition of the status of capital, earned in the marketplace rather than inherited. Consequently, bourgeois philosophers such as Locke and Milton worked out a critique of autocratic power, replacing it with a theory of representative democracy and individual, or citizenship rights, which reflected in the ideological sphere the realities of bourgeois economic and political power. Voting rights were introduced, gradually extending to wider and wider sections of the population, through such means as the British Reform Act of 1832. Constituent assemblies – such as the British House of Commons – were erected, and constitutional constraints on the abuse of political power put in place. The main concern of liberal democratic theory was thus 'to grant individuals civil liberties against the incursion of the state' (Bobbio, 1987, p.10).

For the bourgeoisie, rejecting the principle of divine ordination, the extension of citizenship rights was also a necessary stage in the legitimation of its own political power, as the dominant class of a new type of social formation. By 'formally requesting the consent of all citizens' (Ibid.) elected political leaders had the right to demand respect and loyalty even from those who had not voted for them. Equally, citizens had the right to dissent from the prevailing political wisdom, and to expect that they would be able to express their views at the ballot box at agreed intervals.

The citizen's right to choose presupposed the availability of alternatives from which a meaningful selection could be made, and a rational, knowledgeable electorate capable of exercising its rights. Democracy was real, in other words, only when it involved the participation of an informed, rational electorate. For Italian political sociologist Norberto Bobbio, liberal democracy assumes that citizens, 'once they are entrusted with the right to choose who governs them', are sufficiently well-informed 'to vote for the wisest, the most honest, the most enlightened of their fellow citizens' (Ibid., p.19).

Drawing these strands together, we can identify the defining characteristics of a democratic regime in the following terms: constitutionality, participation and rational choice.

## Constitutionality

Firstly, there must be an agreed set of procedures and rules governing the conduct of elections, the behaviour of those who win them, and the legitimate activities of dissenters. Such rules will typically take the form of a constitution (although some countries, like Britain, do not have a 'written' constitution) or a bill of rights.

## Participation

Secondly, those who participate in the democratic process must comprise what Bobbio terms a 'substantial' proportion of the people. In the early democratic period, as we have noted, citizenship rights were restricted to a small minority of the population – men with property and/or formal education. For John Stuart Mill, one of the great early theorists of liberal democracy, only this guaranteed the rational, informed electorate demanded by democracy.[1] In reality, of course, this restriction merely demonstrated the close relationship between democracy and the rise of the bourgeoisie.

Gradually, voting rights were extended to the lower classes and, by the early twentieth century, to women. In America, only in the 1950s were blacks given the vote. Conversely, societies which deprived the majority of their people of voting rights, such as South Africa until the elections of April 1994, have rightly been viewed as 'undemocratic'.

## Rational choice

A third condition of democracy, as already noted, is the availability of choice (Democrat versus Republican, Labour versus Conservative, Christian Democrat versus Social Democrat), while a fourth is the ability of citizens to exercise that choice rationally. This in turn presupposes a knowledgeable, educated citizenry.

## PUBLIC OPINION AND THE PUBLIC SPHERE

The importance of an informed, knowledgeable electorate dictates that democratic politics must be pursued in the public arena (as distinct from the secrecy characteristic of autocratic regimes). The knowledge and information on the basis of which citizens will make their political choices must circulate freely, and be available to all.

But democratic politics are public in another sense too. While democratic theory stresses the primacy of the individual, the political process nevertheless demands that individuals act *collectively* in making decisions about who will govern them. The private political opinions of the individual become the *public* opinion of the people as a whole, which may be reflected in voting patterns, and treated as advice by existing political leaders. Public opinion, in this sense, is formed in what German sociologist Jurgen Habermas has called 'the public sphere'.

> By the public sphere we mean first of all a realm of our social life in which something approaching public opinion can be formed . . . Citizens behave as a public body when they confer in an unrestricted fashion – that is, within the guarantee of freedom of assembly and association and the freedom to express and publish their opinions.
> (Quoted in Pusey, 1978, p.89)

Habermas locates the development of the public sphere in eighteenth-century Britain, where the first newspapers had already begun to perform their modern function of supplying not only information but also opinion, comment and criticism, facilitating debate amongst the emerging bourgeois and educated classes. Quoting Thomas McCarthy, Habermas shows how these new social forces gradually replaced a political system 'in which the [autocratic] ruler's power was merely represented *before* the people with a sphere in which state authority was publicly monitored through informed and critical discourse *by* the people' (quoted in Habermas, 1989, p.xi). In the coffee-house and salon cultures of Britain and France, debate and political critique became, for the first time, public property (meaning, of course, the bourgeois public, which excluded the mass of poor and illiterate underclasses). According to Habermas, the first use of the term 'public opinion' was documented in 1781, referring to 'the critical reflection of a [bourgeois] public competent to form its own judgments' (Ibid., p.90).

Gripsund notes that the public sphere thus emerged as 'a set of institutions representing a sort of "buffer zone" between the state/ king and private sphere, to protect them from arbitrary decisions that interfered with what they considered private activities in an irrational way' (1992, p.89). The press in particular 'was to function as an instrument or a forum for the enlightened, rational, critical, and unbiased public discussion of what the common interests were in matters of culture and politics' (Ibid.).

For Josef Ernst, the public sphere is that 'distinctive discursive space' within which 'individuals are combined so as to be able to assume the role of a politically powerful force' (1988, p.47). It is, in short, 'the bourgeois realm of politics' (Ibid.) which has gradually expanded from its elitist beginnings to include absolute majorities of the population in modern democratic societies.

The public sphere, as can be seen, comprises in essence the communicative institutions of a society, through which facts and opinions circulate, and by means of which a common stock of knowledge is built up as the basis for collective political action: in other words, the mass media, which since the eighteenth century have evolved into the main source and focus of a society's shared experience (see Figure 2.1). The modern concept of 'news' developed precisely as a means of furnishing citizens with the *most important* information, from the point of view of their political

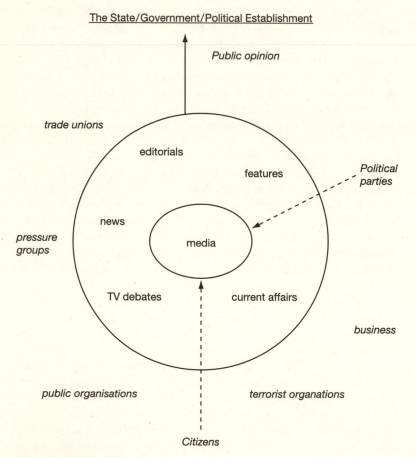

*Figure 2.1* The public sphere

activities, and of streamlining and guiding public discussion, functions which are taken for granted in contemporary print and broadcast journalism.

## THE MEDIA AND THE DEMOCRATIC PROCESS

From what has been stated thus far we may now suggest five functions of the communication media in 'ideal-type' democratic societies:

- Firstly, they must *inform* citizens of what is happening around them (what we may call the 'surveillance' or 'monitoring' functions of the media).
- Secondly, they must *educate* as to the meaning and significance of the 'facts' (the importance of this function explains the seriousness with which journalists protect their objectivity, since their value as educators presumes a professional detachment from the issues being analysed).
- Thirdly, the media must provide a *platform* for public political discourse, facilitating the formation of 'public opinion', and feeding that opinion back to the public from whence it came. This must include the provision of space for the expression of *dissent*, without which the notion of democratic consensus would be meaningless.
- The media's fourth function is to give *publicity* to governmental and political institutions – the 'watchdog' role of journalism, exemplified by the performance of the United States media during the Watergate episode and, more recently, the British *Guardian*'s coverage of the cash-for-questions scandal, in which investigative journalists exposed the practice of members of parliament accepting payment for the asking of parliamentary questions. 'Public opinion' can only matter – i.e., have an influence on 'objective' political reality – to the extent that 'the acts of whoever holds supreme power are made available for public scrutiny, meaning how far they are visible, ascertainable, accessible, and hence accountable' (Bobbio, 1987, p.83). There must be, to use Mikhail Gorbachov's famous formulation, a degree of 'openness' surrounding the activities of the political class if the 'public opinions' of the people are to have any bearing on decision-making.

21

- Finally, the media in democratic societies serve as a channel for the *advocacy* of political viewpoints. Parties, as noted in Chapter 1, require an outlet for the articulation of their policies and programmes to a mass audience, and thus the media must be open to them. Furthermore, some media, mainly in the print sector, will actively endorse one or other of the parties at sensitive times such as elections. In this latter sense, the media's advocacy function may also be viewed as one of *persuasion*.

For these functions to be performed adequately, and thus for a real 'public sphere' to exist (and, by extension, 'real' democracy), a number of conditions have to be met. For Habermas, the political discourse circulated by the media must be *comprehensible* to citizens. It must also be *truthful*, in so far as it reflects the genuine and sincere intentions of speakers (one may, for example, have disagreed with the politics of Margaret Thatcher, while acknowledging that she genuinely believed in the positive effects of an unrestrained free market). Hauser summarises Habermas's views thus:

> first, the [public sphere] must be accessible to all citizens . . . Second, there must be access to information . . . Third, specific means for transmitting information must be accessible to those who can be influenced by it . . . [and] there must be institutionalised guarantees for [the public sphere] to exist.
> (Quoted in Cooper, 1991, p.32)

In short, democracy presumes 'an open state in which people are allowed to participate in decision-making, and are given access to the media, and other information networks through which advocacy occurs' (Ibid., p.42). It also presumes, as we have stated, an audience sufficiently educated and knowledgeable to make rational and effective use of the information circulating in the public sphere.

## DEMOCRACY AND THE MEDIA: A CRITIQUE

Since the eighteenth century the media, and the functions listed above, have grown ever-more important to the smooth workings of the democratic political process. As we noted at the beginning of Chapter 1, the achievement of universal suffrage in most advanced capitalist societies during the twentieth century was paralleled by a technological revolution in the means of mass communication as print, then film, radio and television became available to mass audiences.

Since the 1950s especially, and the expansion of television into virtually every household in the developed capitalist world, inter-personal political communication has been relegated to the margins of the democratic process. Nowadays, as Colin Seymour-Ure puts it, television has become an 'integral part of the environment within which political life takes place' (1989, p.308). Surveys show that for the vast majority of people the media represent the main source of their information about politics.[2] How, then, does the reality of contemporary political discourse as communicated through and by the media correspond to the ideal described above? To what extent do the media perform the role allotted to them in liberal democratic theory?

Answering these questions requires a critical examination of both democratic structures and the media environment around them. It would, of course, be naive to expect that these two sets of institu-tions should function perfectly. It is important, however, to acknowledge the ways in which they fall short of the ideal, and the significance of these shortcomings.

## The failure of education

Firstly, it is argued by some observers that the normative assump-tion of a 'rational' citizenry is not realistic. For Bobbio, one of the great 'broken promises' of liberal democracy is the failure of the education system to produce rational voters, a failure which he sees reflected in the growing political apathy characteristic of such democratic exemplars as the United States. 'The most well-established democracies', he argues, 'are impotent before the phe-nomenon of increasing political apathy, which has overtaken about half of those with the right to vote' (1987, p.36). When those who have the right to vote decline to do so, democracy is clearly less than perfect. However, voter apathy is far from being a universal phe-nomenon of advanced capitalist societies. While the United States does bear out Bobbio's pessimism, the United Kingdom does not. Voter turnout in the 1997 British general election was just over 1 per cent less than that of 1945, at 71.3 per cent.

Looking at the phenomenon from another angle, it may be argued that political apathy is an entirely rational, if slightly cynical response to a political process in which it may appear to the individual citizen that his or her vote does not matter. While democratic procedures must include regular elections, it may be felt that voting once every four or five years for one of two or at most three rather similar parties is ineffective and pointless, particularly when, as was the case in Britain over four consecutive general elections, one party (the Conservatives) retained power with substantially less than 50 per cent of the eligible electorate's support. For Jean Baudrillard, the guru of post-modern nihilism, voter apathy is viewed as an intelligible strategy of resistance to bourgeois attempts to incorporate the masses into a 'game' which they can never really win. The 'silent passivity' of the masses is characterised by him as 'a defence . . . a mode of retaliation' (1983, p.23). If democracy is principally a set of rules intended to legitimise bourgeois power, voter (and particularly working-class) apathy (the denial of mass participation) may be interpreted as an assertion of the fundamental *illegitimacy* of bourgeois power.[3]

## Absence of choice

A further limitation on democracy is the absence of genuine choice, or pluralism. One could reasonably argue that there are more similarities in the policies and ideologies of the US Democratic and Republican parties than there are differences. Even in Britain, where the Labour and Conservative parties have traditionally been distinct ideologically, the late 1980s and early 1990s saw a coming together of agendas and policies on many social, economic, and foreign policy matters. In the 1997 general election, 'New Labour' unashamedly adopted many of what had previously been viewed (including by most members of the Labour Party itself) as right-wing Conservative policies, such as privatisation of the air traffic control system.[4] In doing so, New Labour proclaimed itself at the 'radical centre' of British politics, emulating the Clinton administration's 1996 re-election strategy of ideological 'triangulation' (Morris, 1997). Triangulation in the US, like Labour's radical centrism, meant taking what was popular and common sensical from the free market right (such as the reduction of 'big government'), while adhering to the core social democratic values of social justice and equality of opportunity.

Although, in the post-Cold War environment, there may be good reasons for the abandonment of long-standing ideological and political slogans which reflect an earlier phase of capitalist development, in such circumstances the voter may reasonably feel that a vote for one party or another will have little or no impact on the conditions and quality of life.

And what of the British Liberal Democrat, who sees his or her party permanently excluded from national political power despite gaining up to 25 per cent of the vote at general elections? Democratic procedures, in short, usually contain anomalies and biases which make them less than democratic.

## Capitalism and power

Socialist and Marxist critiques of liberal democracy are more fundamental, arguing that the real loci of power in capitalist societies are hidden behind formal political procedures: in the boardrooms of big business; in the higher reaches of the civil service and security apparatus; in a host of secretive, *non-elected* institutions. The people may elect a Labour government, the argument goes, but any attempt to implement a genuinely socialist programme (even if the government wanted to do so) inevitably meets with resistance in the form of bureaucratic obstruction, flights of capital abroad, the use of the Royal prerogative, and dirty tricks of the type described by Peter Wright in *Spycatcher* (1989). From this perspective, the democratic process as pursued in Britain and most other developed capitalist societies is merely a facade, behind which the real levers of political and economic power are wielded by those for whom the citizenry never has an opportunity to vote.

Many of these criticisms are accepted even by the most ardent defenders of liberal democracy. Let us assume, however, that the procedures of democratic politics *are* fundamentally sound; that election results are meaningful and effective in shaping governments and their behaviour; and that voters will respond rationally to the political information they receive from the media and elsewhere. Were all these assumptions justified, we may still identify a fundamental weakness of democratic theory as it relates to the media. According to the theory, the citizen is a rational subject who absorbs the information available and makes appropriate choices. He or she is, as it were, the repository of knowledge existing out there in the world, which is converted unproblematically into political behaviour. In reality, however, what the citizen experiences as political information is the product of several mediating processes which are more or less invisible to him or her.

## The manufacture of consent

These processes begin with the politicians. The legitimacy of liberal democratic government is founded, as we have noted, on the consent of the governed. But consent, as Walter Lippmann observed in the work cited above, can be 'manufactured'. 'The manufacture of consent' (1954, p.245), indeed, had as early as 1922 become a 'self-conscious art' in which politicians combined the techniques of social psychology with the immense reach of mass media. The detailed analysis of these techniques will be the subject of most of this book, but by acknowledging their existence at this point we recognise a major flaw in democratic theory: if the information on which political behaviour is based is, or can be, manufactured artifice rather than objective truth, the integrity of the public sphere is inevitably diminished. To the extent that citizens are subject to manipulation, rather than exposed to information, democracy loses its authenticity and becomes something rather more sinister.

The distinction between 'persuasion', which is a universally recognised function of political actors in a democracy, and manipulation, which carries with it the negative connotations of propaganda and deceit, is not always an easy one to draw. But only those with a touching and naive faith in the ethical purity of politicians would deny that the latter plays an increasingly important part in modern (or post-modern) democratic politics.

We shall return to the theme of manipulation later (see Chapter 7). Politicians, however, also seek to conceal information from citizens, sometimes for reasons of what is called 'national security', and sometimes to avoid political embarrassment. The public nature of politics identified as a prerequisite of liberal democracy by Bobbio often conflicts with the politicians' desire for survival, and may be sacrificed as a result. While secrecy, deception and cover-ups are hardly new features of politics, their continued use and occasional dramatic exposure (most notably in Italy's *tangentopoli* scandal) remind us that what the citizen receives as political information in the public sphere is often an incomplete and partial picture of reality. We may be conscious of that incompleteness when, for example, secrecy legislation is deployed on national security grounds. More commonly, the fact of concealment is itself concealed from the audience, unless a Bernstein, Woodward, or Campbell[5] succeeds in making it public.

Manipulation of opinion and concealment (or suppression) of inconvenient information are strategies emanating from political

26

actors themselves, pursued through media institutions. In some cases, journalists will attempt to publicise and expose what is hidden. As we shall see in Chapter 4, the media often have an interest in playing the watchdog role over the politicians. On the other hand, the media may be complicit in the politicians' concealment of sensitive information (if, for example, a newspaper is strongly committed to a government it may choose to ignore an otherwise newsworthy story).

More generally, there are many aspects of the process of media production which in themselves make media organisations vulnerable to strategies of political manipulation.

In 1962 Daniel Boorstin coined the term 'pseudo-event' in response to what he saw as the increasing tendency of news and journalistic media to cover 'unreal', unauthentic 'happenings'. This tendency, he argued, was associated with the rise from the nineteenth century onwards of the popular press and a correspondingly dramatic increase in the demand for news material. 'As the costs of printing and then broadcasting increased, it became financially necessary to keep the presses always at work and the TV screen always busy. Pressures towards the making of pseudo-events became ever stronger. Newsgathering turned into news making' (1962, p.14).

An important source of pseudo-events for the media has of course been the political process – interviews with government leaders, news leaks and press conferences all provide reportable material which is happily taken up by the media to fill newspaper column inches and broadcast airtime. Thus, argues Boorstin, the twentieth century has seen a relationship of mutual convenience and interdependence evolve between the politician and the media professional, as one strives to satisfy the other's hunger for news while at the same time maximising his or her favourable public exposure. For Boorstin in 1962, the trend was not welcome.

> In a democratic society . . . freedom of speech and of the press and of broadcasting includes freedom to create pseudo-events. Competing politicians, newsmen and news media contest in this creation. They vie with each other in offering attractive, 'informative' accounts and images of the world. They are free to speculate on the facts, to bring new facts into being, to demand answers to their own contrived questions. Our 'free market of ideas' is a place where people are confronted by competing pseudo-events and are

allowed to judge among them. When we speak of 'informing' the people this is what we really mean.

(Ibid., p.35)

For Boorstin there is something illusory and artificial about the
rationalist notion of public information and its contribution to
democracy. The political reportage received by the citizen has
become dominated by empty spectacle.

## The limitations of objectivity

A further criticism of the media's democratic role focusses on the
professional journalistic ethic of objectivity. This ethic developed
with the mass media in the late nineteenth and early twentieth centuries, and has been assailed ever since as fundamentally unattain-
able (McNair, 1999). For a variety of reasons, it is argued, the
media's political reportage is biased and flawed – subjective, as
opposed to objective; partisan, rather than impartial. As Lippmann
put it in 1922, 'every newspaper when it reaches the reader is the
result of a whole series of selections as to what items shall be
printed, in what position they shall be printed, how much space
each shall occupy, what emphasis each should have. There are no
objective standards here. There are conventions' (1954, p.354).

The nature of these conventions, and their implications for the
objectivity of the media, will be examined in Chapter 4.

# 3

# THE EFFECTS OF POLITICAL COMMUNICATION

As with all categories of media output there are a wide variety of approaches which one can take to the 'effects issue' in political communication, none of which produces easy answers to the question, 'does it work?' For the sake of clarity, this chapter approaches the effects issue from three broad perspectives.

Firstly, we shall consider the extent to which the purposeful communicative behaviour of political actors, such as political advertising and conference speeches, can influence the attitudes and behaviour of the intended audience. Effects of this type can be examined at the *micro-level* of the individual consumer of the message, or at the *macro-level*, when individual responses to political communication are aggregated together in the form of public opinion polls and other indices of collective political will.

Secondly, we shall examine how the political process of democratic societies – their procedures and practices – has been affected by the growing importance within them of mass communication.

And thirdly, we shall consider the systemic impact of the rise of political communication on advanced capitalist societies such as Britain.

Political communication, as already noted, is largely *mediated* communication, transmitted through the print and electronic media. The media alter the message, in their roles as reporters of and commentators on it. They are, therefore, as we noted in Chapter 1, political actors in their own right. Chapter 4 considers the effects of media coverage of politics, as discussed in the vast volume of research which has been conducted into the subject over many years.

Before considering any of these different types of effect, a few words on the difficulties associated with the 'effects issue' in general are appropriate.

## METHODOLOGICAL PROBLEMS IN
## POLITICAL EFFECTS RESEARCH

The student of the effects of political communication is confronted with fundamental epistemo-methodological problems familiar to all effects researchers.[1] Principally, how does one accurately trace the cause and effect relationship between a piece of communication and the behaviour of its audience? How can the effect of a particular message be identified and measured in isolation from the other environmental factors influencing an individual?

### The communication process

In an earlier age of communication studies such questions were rarely asked. The message was presumed to act on the individual rather like a hypodermic syringe or billiard ball, producing a direct effect which could be predicted and measured. The 'hypodermic model' of media effects was embraced by both European and American sociologists during the 1930s in response to, on the one hand, the rise of fascism in Europe and the Nazis' extensive and apparently successful use of propaganda techniques and, on the other, the power of advertising to sell commodities which was then becoming evident. Both phenomena encouraged support for a relatively simple, 'strong' effects model.

Unfortunately, extensive empirical research was unable to 'prove' specific media effects, prompting a recognition by the 1950s that effects were 'limited', or more precisely, 'mediated' by the range of social and cultural factors intervening between the message and its audience. The 'mediated-limited' effects model dominated the communication studies field throughout the 1960s, until it was developed and refined by the semiological school, in the work of Umberto Eco and others.

For this tradition, understanding the effects of media messages required an understanding of the *social semiotics* of a given communication situation, acknowledging the potential for differential decoding of the message which always exists; the plurality of meanings which it may acquire amongst the diversity of groups and individuals who make up its audience; and the variety of responses it may provoke.

These variations in meaning and response will be dependent firstly on the context of reception of the message, incorporating such factors as the political affiliation, age, ethnicity, and gender of the receiver, and, secondly, on the type of message transmitted. A party election broadcast on British television, for example, is clearly labelled as a motivated, partisan piece of political communication: if not 'propaganda' in the most negative sense of that term then undoubtedly a heavily skewed statement of a party's policies and values. The viewer knows this, and will interpret the message accordingly.

Using Stuart Hall's list of differential decoding positions (1980),[2] we might reasonably hypothesise that a Labour Party broadcast will prompt in a Labour supporter a *dominant* decoding, in which the receiver shares the world-view underlying the construction of the broadcast, its interpretation of the 'facts' behind current political and economic debates, and its preferred solutions. The 'floating voter', lacking in strong commitment to any particular party, might well adopt a *negotiated* decoding, agreeing with some aspects of the message and rejecting others. Such a response would include one in which the need for a more equitable distribution of income was accepted, but specific proposals for tax increases rejected as being too draconian. The Conservative supporter, on the other hand, will adopt an *oppositional* decoding position, rejecting both the values and the specific policy proposals contained in Labour's PPB.

The broadcasts of the other parties will meet with similar diversity of response. In short, one's knowledge that a piece of communication is partisan will to a large extent predetermine one's 'reading' of it. If, on the other hand, a political message is communicated through a news report, a chat show interview, or a live debate in a US presidential campaign (all contexts in which editorial control of the message is seen to reside beyond the politician him or herself), the audience may take the opportunity to judge abilities and policies from a more detached perspective. There will be less *interference* in the communication process, and the audience may be more open.

As a general rule, the effects of political communications of whatever kind are determined not by the content of the message alone, or even primarily, but by the historical context in which they appear, and especially the political environment prevailing at any given time. The 'quality' of a message, the skill and sophistication of its construction, count for nothing if the audience is not receptive. President Clinton's media adviser in the 1996 re-election campaign, Dick Morris, writes in his memoir that 'if the public won't buy your basic premise, it doesn't matter how much you spend or how well your ads are produced; they won't work' (1997, p.152) (see Chapter 6).

The aforementioned are *conceptual* difficulties, arising from the complexity of the communication process itself. They remind us that successful communication of a message (political or otherwise) cannot be taken for granted, but must be *worked* for by the sender.

## The evidence

A further problem for political communication research concerns the nature and quality of the evidence used to measure effects. There are, in the final analysis, only three ways to assess the effects of political communication on attitudes and behaviour. The first is to ask people how they have responded to specific messages, and then collate their responses into statistically significant aggregates, usually in the form of public opinion polls. Secondly, one may observe voting behaviour, relating this to the communication strategies of the contestants in a political campaign. Thirdly, one may conduct experiments intended to isolate the effects of particular elements of the communication process. Each of these data-gathering techniques has its methodological limitations.

## Surveys

Public opinion polling, for example, a technique which originated with commercially motivated survey sampling in the 1930s, depends for its accuracy on the application of sampling procedures which permit the survey to be 'representative'. The questions asked of those polled must be carefully formulated so as to avoid distortion, simplification, and exaggeration of response. The timing of polls must be taken into account, and results interpreted cautiously, with allowances made for a variety of potential sources of error. While the best-known and most frequently used polling organisations, such as Gallup, MORI, and NOP take considerable time and money to achieve the maximum degree of accuracy possible, many opinion polls, particularly those conducted independently by print and broadcast media, do not. As the 1992 British general election showed, even the established pollsters may get it substantially wrong when attempting to predict election outcomes.[3]

Public opinion polls are not only a measure (however imperfect) of political attitudes and intentions at a given point in time. Many observers agree that they can become a causal factor in voting behaviour. American news broadcasters have come under pressure in recent presidential elections to delay releasing the findings of their exit polls (taken after citizens have voted) conducted on the east coast of the country until polling booths on the west coast have closed (three hours later), or at least until the majority of west coasters have voted. In the view of some analysts, the results of these polls may affect those who have not yet voted. If, for example, exit polls conducted in New York indicate a landslide for one candidate, west coast supporters of the other candidate may decide not to bother voting, thus distorting the final result. One explanation for the unexpected Conservative victory in the British general election of 1992 is that opinion polls indicating a substantial Labour Party lead lulled both party members and supporters into what turned out to be a false sense of security, enabling the Conservatives to make decisive progress in the final few days of the campaign.[4]

It has also been argued that opinion polls may generate a demonstration effect, 'cueing' undecided voters on which party the majority is supporting, and thus becoming self-fulfilling prophecies. Robert Worcester cites evidence that about 3 per cent of British voters in general elections are influenced by opinion polls, and that in by-elections the impact is even greater. He suggests that at the Bermondsey by-election of 1983, when a controversial Labour Party candidate was contesting a safe Labour seat, opinion polls indicating a slight lead for the Liberal candidate generated an eventual Liberal landslide. In this case as in others, the poll alerted voters as to who they should vote for if they did not want the Labour candidate to win (Worcester, 1991, p.205).

Arguments of this type are highly speculative and – given the aforementioned difficulty of establishing cause and effect relationships – practically impossible to prove. It is beyond doubt, however, that public opinion polls become a *part* of the political environment they are designed to monitor. Just as a thermometer alters the temperature of the air around it, so a public opinion poll becomes part of the data upon which individuals calculate their future political moves.

## Voting behaviour

A second way in which the effects of political communication can be measured is to observe patterns in *actual* voting behaviour. Such evidence is clearly more tangible than opinion poll data, and frequently contradicts the former (as in the 1992 general election, when most opinion polls failed to predict a Conservative victory). It is no less difficult to interpret, however. The relationship between a party's campaign and its eventual vote may not be apparent. Despite the famous 'Kinnock – the Movie' party election broadcast (PEB)[5] shown during the 1987 campaign, and a communication strategy widely viewed as superior to that of the Conservatives, the latter's actual vote on polling day was virtually identical as a percentage of the national electorate to figures generated by opinion polls taken at the beginning of the campaign (43 per cent). Labour's support rose by only 3 per cent from the beginning to the end of the campaign, to give them a net gain of twenty seats on the 1983 result (Butler and Kavanagh, 1988).

This could be interpreted in several ways. Perhaps the campaign had no significant impact on the electorate (as opposed to the commentators who almost universally praised it). Perhaps Labour's vote would have been even worse without the softening impact of a good campaign. Perhaps voters recognised the quality of Labour's campaigning but regarded policies as more important than image, and preferred those of the Tories. Any or all of these assertions could be true, highlighting the deeper truth that even 'objective', empirically verifiable measures of voting behaviour (this is how people *actually* voted) are subject to wide variations of interpretation.

## Experimental research

The third method of assessing the effects of political communication shares with the first the fact that it relies on asking questions of people. Numerous experiments have been conducted in which a particular element of the political message is isolated before a subject group. Their responses are then noted, and conclusions drawn.

This laboratory-based approach is a much-used tool of behavioural effects research, frequently employed, for example, in the study of sexually explicit or violent material. The methodological objections to it are, once again, those of interpretation and contextualisation. Can a laboratory experiment, no matter how sensitively prepared, really reproduce the complex political environment in which individuals make their decisions? Can it compensate for the weight of cultural and social resonances that will accompany a political message in the real world?

To make these points is not to dispute the value of sensitively designed empirical audience research in the study of political or any other type of communication, but simply to highlight its limitations.

## DOES POLITICAL COMMUNICATION WORK?
## MICRO-EFFECTS

According to a MORI poll conducted during the British general election of June 1987, the determinants of voting behaviour, particularly for the crucial section of 'floating' or undecided voters who will ultimately decide the outcome, are threefold. They are, firstly (and still, apparently, most importantly), the image of party policy (44 per cent); secondly, the voters' image of the party leadership (35 per cent of choices in 1987 were attributed by respondents to this factor); and finally, the 'corporate' image of the party itself (21 per cent) (Worcester, 1991, p.111).

Each of these aspects of a party's identity have to be communicated, suggesting at the very least that the ability and skill to communicate *can be* important in influencing political behaviour and electoral outcomes.

Among the experiments conducted into the efficacy of political communication at this level is Rosenberg and McCafferty's study of the extent to which 'public relations experts [can] manipulate the public's impression of a political candidate' (1987, p.31). Their concern in this research was with non-verbal aspects of communication, or the candidate's 'image' defined in narrow, physical terms. As they put it, 'we are interested in exploring whether or not it is possible to manipulate an individual's appearance in a way that affects both voters' judgments of the candidate and the choice they make at the ballot box' (Ibid.).

To test the hypothesis that image *does* matter in shaping political behaviour, Rosenberg and McCafferty selected a group of American university students, whom they exposed to multiple photographs of a series of fictional election candidates. The pictures differed in ways intended to generate negative and positive responses, such as the inclusion or omission of a smile. It was found that such changes affected 'both the degree to which an individual is perceived to be fit for public office and the degree to which he is perceived to possess those qualities (competence, integrity, and likableness) that other research has shown to be relevant to voters' evaluations of political candidates' (Ibid., p.37). Furthermore, even when subjects were made aware of the respective candidates' policies on important issues, image as constructed by the photograph continued to exert an influence on voting intentions.

The researchers acknowledged the methodological limitations of their research, in so far as it was an artificial election with artificial candidates, lacking 'the social context and duration of a real campaign' (Ibid., p.45), but claim that they were able to repeat the experiment with similar results, thus strengthening their validity.

Research conducted in Germany by Kepplinger and Dombach indicated that certain camera angles, such as filming at eye level, produced a more favourable audience response to a politician than others. They concluded that 'camera angles influence perception, particularly among a politician's supporters' (1987, p.71).

Some research has been concerned with the specific effects of different media. Scott Keeter, for example, has found that of all voters, those who watched television were the most likely to be influenced by the candidate's 'image'. He accepted, however, that this may not be 'a reaction to the particular stimuli of televised politics – although such a direct effect is plausible – as a more general increase in the importance of candidate factors resulting from various political changes in which television has played a role' (1987, p.336).


## THE EFFECT OF POLITICAL ADVERTISING

We noted above the importance of distinguishing between types of political communication, such as election broadcasts and TV news interviews. If the candidate's image and personality (as perceived by the audience) is an important factor in shaping voting behaviour so too, arguably, is the party's political advertising. As we shall see in Chapter 6, advertising is a major component of modern political communication, consuming huge financial and creative resources during and between elections. The fact of parties' expenditure on advertising might be thought to point to evidence that it works in shaping behaviour. Such evidence is, however, conspicuously lacking.

Research cited by Diamond and Bates supports the 'uses and gratifications' thesis that the effects of political advertising (in which category we include British party political broadcasts) are heavily conditioned by the existing political attitudes of the audience. They note that 'some supporters of a particular candidate tend to project their views on to the candidate's advertising – they will hear what they want to hear, almost regardless of what the favoured candidate says. A number of studies have concluded that few people actually change votes due to political advertising' (1984, p.351). Advertising, these authors suggest, may reinforce existing political attitudes and behaviour patterns, but will rarely change them. Cundy discusses research suggesting that the effects of political advertising are in inverse proportion to the audience's knowledge of the party or candidate being advertised, and that 'once a candidate's image has been developed, new information is unlikely to generate any appreciable change' (1986, p.232).

This is true regardless of the aesthetic qualities of the advert. Advertising may receive praise from commentators and analysts, while failing to improve a party's votes. In the 1987 general election, the 'Kinnock – The Movie' PEB, as we have already noted, attracted numerous accolades for the skill of its construction, to the extent that it was shown twice on television during the campaign (a first for British political advertising). Labour's vote on polling day was not substantially affected, however, unless one believes that it would have been even lower without the positive image of Kinnock presented in director Hugh Hudson's film. In the 1988 US presidential election, on the other hand, the Republican's infamous 'Willie Horton' spot, accusing Democratic candidate Michael Dukakis of being dangerously liberal on crime, is widely believed to have contributed substantially to Bush's victory.

When all the empirical evidence is taken into account (and there is not so much of it as one might expect, given the extent to which image-management has become a central feature of political campaigning) we can conclude that there do appear to be ways in which a political message can be constructed so as to produce a favourable response in the audience. The cut of a suit, a hairstyle, a camera angle or the colour of a stage-set, are examples of formal aspects of the message which might, all other things being equal, positively influence audience perceptions of the communicator and his or her message. In other words, there are 'good' and 'bad' examples of political communication, as judged by aesthetic criteria. Political communication can be *directed*, and increasingly is, by the burgeoning political public relations industry (see Chapters 6 and 7). Like other types of communicator, the politician must work within conventions which are known and understood by the audience. These conventions may be poorly executed, competently realised or creatively subverted, in the manner of aesthetic innovation through the ages. The political communicator is a performer, and will be judged by the audience, at least partly, on the quality of performance.

It must not be forgotten, however, that an array of mediating factors intervene in the communicator–receiver relationship, affecting the meaning of the message and its likely impact on attitudes and behaviour. The status of the communicator is important (incumbent president or outlawed terrorist?), as is the form of the message (advertisement, conference speech, or terrorist act) and the social semiotics of its reception. One could have admired the communicative abilities of Ronald Reagan, for example, although one's position as an unemployed steelworker or environmentalist campaigner might have prevented acceptance of the Reagan 'message'. The politician can shape and work the message, but has relatively little control over the environment into which it is inserted and the uses to which it will be put.

## POLITICAL COMMUNICATION AND THE DEMOCRATIC PROCESS

An alternative to the empirical approach, with its emphasis on the effects of political communication on behaviour and attitudes, is to consider its impact on the democratic process itself. There is, undoubtedly, something qualitatively different about a political system in which the main means of communication are the mass media. Do these differences have negative or positive implications for the democratic ideal, as it was outlined in the previous chapter?[6] Butler and Kavanagh observe that

> more than ever, election campaigns are managed and orchestrated. Each party attempts to shape the agenda so that the media reflects its views on favourite issues. Public opinion is monitored through opinion polls. An election campaign is increasingly seen by those in charge as an exercise in marketing and many of the skills of selling goods and services to customers are now applied to the electorate. These developments have given greater scope to experts in opinion polling, advertising and public relations, and sometimes lead to tensions with the politicians and party offices.
>
> (1992, p.77)

For many observers the trends described by these authors are dangerous and damaging for the political process. If politicians have become more sensitive to public opinion as measured in polls they have also, it is frequently argued, become prisoners of that public opinion, allowing it to dominate the processes of policy-formulation and decision-making. Governments, and those who aspire to govern, allow their principles to be diluted on the recommendations of market researchers. Ideologies and value-systems are abandoned on the altar of popularity, and the activity of political persuasion becomes a cynical response to whatever this week's polls say. Not only policies, but leaders are selected and jettisoned according to the whims of public opinion, regardless of their intellectual qualities. The image of the leader, it is argued, counts for more than his or her abilities; the smoothness of delivery of a political message for more than its content.[7] The integrity of politics, in short, is undermined.

Undoubtedly, image is perceived to be more important than it once was. Ronald Reagan, it is universally accepted, was not a great American president because of his ability to govern, but because of how, with the assistance of his actor's training, he articulated his simple, homely messages. He was 'the great communicator' rather than the great thinker. Conversely, Michael Foot, the Labour Party's leader from 1980 until 1983, was acknowledged by supporters and opponents alike to have been a formidable intellectual and a skilful party manager. In the age of television, unfortunately, he did not look and sound 'right'. After Labour's 1983 defeat he was quickly shunted off into back-bench retirement, to be replaced by the more 'media-friendly' Neil Kinnock.

The examples of Reagan, Foot (and, to a lesser extent perhaps, the 1984 and 1988 US Democratic challengers for the presidency, Walter Mondale and Michael Dukakis) are regularly cited by those who bemoan the ascendancy of the image as a deciding factor in voting behaviour. The trend is alleged to represent a move away from the rationality of the democratic ideal to a more irrational, fickle political process in which the 'real' issues are marginalised by trivial considerations of appearance and personality.

An opposing argument asserts that the importance of image is overstated. How, such voices ask, did George Bush – Doonesbury's 'invisible man'[8] – win the 1988 presidential election? How did John Major, whose *Spitting Image*[9] puppet portrayed him with a deep grey pallor, defeat the more charismatic Kinnock in 1992? The suggestion here is that voters are in fact less vulnerable to manipulation by glossy images than has become the received wisdom, and that, in any case, one voter's attractive, homely leader is another's synthetic conman. John Major's success in the 1992 general election has been attributed by some to the fact that he was *not* packaged in the manner of a Reagan, Thatcher, or Kinnock, but stood for himself, warts and all. Some observers detected a backlash in the 1990s to the parties' focus on image (Bruce, 1992), and a return to 'authentic' campaigning tactics, although this predated the election of Tony Blair as the Labour leader in 1994, and his party's landslide victory in the subsequent election of 1997. Both events have been perceived, correctly, as triumphs of political marketing and image management (the re-branding of Labour as 'New', and of Tony Blair as the young, dynamic, family-loving good guy, in stark contrast to the left-wing bogey men of Labour's yesteryear).

Linked to the rise of 'the image', and exemplified by the story of New Labour, is the rise of the image-maker. Chapter 7 discusses this category of political actor in greater detail. Here, we note the view of many observers that politics should best be conducted by politicians, rather than by the growing ranks of professional pollsters, advertisers, marketing consultants, and public relations experts now routinely employed by organisations to design and organise their political communication strategies. If policies are increasingly determined by public opinion, then the design and presentation of policy has been delegated to those whose interests are not necessarily those of the public.

## THE RISING COSTS OF CAMPAIGNING

More tangibly, the cost of campaigning, as measured in pounds and pence, dollars and cents, is argued to have increased dramatically. As Herbert Schiller notes, 'the sums now spent on media advertising in elections begin to match the expenditure of the largest corporate advertisers for commercial products and services' (1984, p.117). Expenditure by British political parties on election communication has increased dramatically since the Second World War. In America, hundreds of millions of dollars are spent on elections for everything from presidents to local dog-catchers.

The damaging aspect of this trend, for those who are critical of it, is that it discriminates against individuals and organisations without access to the financial resources required for the pursuit of modern politics. Despite the legal restrictions which exist in many countries on how much funds may be raised for campaigning purposes, some parties have a great deal less money to spend than others. These will tend to be representatives of the already relatively disenfranchised, marginalised sectors of society, who are thus driven even further from the mainstream of the political process.

As money becomes more important to the pursuit of political communication, then, equality of opportunity and access to the political process declines. Even more threatening, political power becomes something which can be bought, in the manner of a Ross Perot, an Asil Nadir or a James Goldsmith. In the former case, a maverick billionaire used his money to create a significant political base for two assaults on the American presidency. In the latter, huge contributions to the British Conservative Party are alleged to have been linked to the expectation of legal and other favours. In the 1997 British general election campaign, the late industrialist and anti-European Union campaigner James Goldsmith used his substantial economic resources to organise a Referendum Party, calling for an immediate referendum on continued British membership of the EU. Although no Referendum Party candidates won a parliamentary seat, the approximately £20 million spent by Goldsmith on the campaign contributed significantly to Conservative defeats in a number of marginal constituencies, and demonstrated what many regarded as the inappropriate power of money to influence democratic politics. The fact that Goldsmith was not even resident in Britain made his financial usurping of the political process even more offensive.

On the other hand, having money does not necessarily buy good or effective political communication. As we have already observed, the Conservatives' relatively expensive 1987 campaign was widely viewed by observers as weak (although the party still won the election) in comparison to Labour's much cheaper one. Innovation and creativity in political communication, as in other forms of cultural activity, are not the monopoly of the wealthy.

Whether the producers of political communication are creative geniuses or not, however, money gives an advantage, all other things being equal. In 1992, for example, the Conservative Party was able to book 4,500 poster sites, at a cost of £1.5 million, as compared to Labour's 2,200 (cost, £0.5 million) and the Liberal Democrats' 500 (cost, £0.17 million) (Butler and Kavanagh, 1992, p.116). Campaign spending as a whole in 1992 was £10.1 million for the Tories, £7.1 million for Labour, and £2.1 million for the Liberal Democrats (Ibid., p.260).

Criticisms of the rising costs of campaigning are, as one would expect, more likely to be heard from those with less rather than more access to the financial and other resources discussed here. That does not invalidate them, but since power tends to attract money, it seems unlikely that in Britain, the US, or other big capitalist democracies, the powerless poor and less affluent will ever succeed in securing the kinds of electoral reforms which would remedy them. That being so, the poorer parties and organisations have had to accept the financial realities of modern politics and compete on those terms as best they can. As we shall see in Chapter 7, debates about how this should be done have driven the development of these organisations' communication strategies since the advent of mass television in the 1950s.

## THE COMMERCIALISATION OF POLITICS

The third level at which we can examine the impact of modern political communication is on the social system itself: the capitalist social formation, within which democracy usually comprises the defining political element. An important tradition within sociology has argued that the growing role of mass communication in politics represents the extension of capitalist social relations – in particular, the relations of consumption – to the political sphere. In the process, politics has become artificial and degenerate. Jurgen Habermas has argued that 'late capitalism brings with it the manipulation of public opinion through the mass media, the forced articulation of social needs through large organisations, and in short, the management of politics by the "system"' (quoted in Pusey, 1978, p.90). Using different language, but saying essentially the same thing, Herbert Schiller observes that in contemporary capitalism politicians 'are "sold" to the public, much like soap and automobiles . . . Issues of public policy, when considered at all, increasingly receive their expression and discussion in thirty second commercials' (1984, p.117). Robins and Webster suggest that the application of marketing and advertising techniques to the political process

> signifies something about the conduct of political life [in the advanced capitalist world]: Saatchi and Saatchi [the UK-based marketing and PR firm responsible for some of the most innovative political advertising of the 1980s] is an index of the way in which politics has been changing to become a matter of 'selling' ideas and 'delivering' up voters; a sign that 'scientific management' has entered into politics and market values have permeated deeper into social relations.
>
> (1985, p.53)

From this perspective, the notion that democracy has anything to do with rationality and 'public interest' is an illusion, since we choose our politics on the same grounds, and as a result of the application of the same techniques of persuasion as we choose our toothpaste. As Nicholas Garnham puts it in his discussion of the public sphere, the rise of political advertising and public relations expresses 'the direct control of private or state interests of the flow of public information in the interest, not of rational discourse, but of manipulation' (1986, p.41). The rational citizen of classic liberal theory has become 'a consumer of politics and policies . . . the competing political parties [present] electors with different policy options in broadly the same way as firms [offer] rival products to the consumers' (Greenaway *et al.*, 1992, p.51).

## POLITICS AND THE POST-MODERN

To this argument about the trivialisation of politics and the expulsion of rational discourse from the process may be added the 'post-modernist' variant, in which political communication is viewed as the one-way exchange of empty signifiers and meaningless messages across a barren media landscape. An early pioneer of this apocalyptic view was Daniel Boorstin who, as noted in Chapter 2, coined the term 'pseudo-event' in response to what he saw as the increasing tendency of the mass media to be preoccupied with unreal, unauthentic, manufactured 'happenings', or 'synthetic novelties'. His definition of a pseudo-event contained the following elements:

a) It is not spontaneous, but comes about because someone has planned, planted or incited it; b) It is planted primarily for the immediate purpose of being reported or reproduced. Therefore, its occurrence is arranged for the convenience of the media. Its success is measured by how widely it is reported. Time relations in it are more commonly fictitious than factitious; c) Its relation to the underlying reality of the situation is ambiguous; d) Usually it is intended to be a self-fulfilling prophecy.

(1962, p.11)

The phenomenon of the pseudo-event was, as already noted, directly associated with the rise of the mass media in the nineteenth century and their growing need to fill space (and later, broadcasting airtime). The media's demand for events to make into news was matched by the politicians' need to be reported, a mutual inter-dependence which still exists and which will be considered in great-er detail in Chapter 4. Here we note that it created a new species of event, 'created' by the politician, with the connivance of the journal-ist, which provided the latter with material and the former with coverage. The public, however, were not necessarily provided with anything of significance or value in helping them to formulate polit-ical choices (bearing in mind that this is one of the key functions of the media in liberal democracies).

Typical pseudo-events, in Boorstin's view, were interviews with politicians (the first with a US public figure was conducted by a newspaper in 1859); news releases (the first recorded example being in 1907); party rallies; press conferences, and 'leaks' – most of which, if not all, were of little value as rational political discourse.

The increasing prevalence of pseudo-events which he detected in the mass media of the 1960s was not, Boorstin believed, good for democracy, although probably inevitable in the electronic age.

Although Boorstin does not use the term, this is clearly recognis-able as a 'post-modernist' view of the world, and the political pro-cess, in which the rise of advertising and public relations in politics 'express[es] a world where the image, more interesting than the original, has itself become the original. The shadow has become the substance' (Ibid., p.204).

Chapter 2 noted Norberto Bobbio's criticism that liberal democracy has failed to encourage a sufficiently educated citizenry, resulting in political apathy amongst the public. For Jean Baudrillard, the proliferation of empty spectacle and image in contemporary political discourse is itself a cause of the phenom-enon of 'the silent majority' (1983). Through increased exposure to political marketing techniques, citizens have become *consumers* of politics, but not active producers of it. The political pseudo-event has become a 'hyperreality', leading to 'the forced silence of the masses' (1988, p.208).

The intrinsic pessimism of this perspective is rejected by others, often those with interests in the political marketing industries, who view it as elitist and patronising. Political communication consult-ants, note Denton and Woodward,

> believe that they are actually making the electoral process
> more democratic. They claim that they cannot control
> votes as the old political bosses did through the patronage

system. Also, consultants can't enforce voter discipline or the voting behaviour of elected officials. There is no empirical evidence of a direct causal relationship between watching a commercial or series of commercials and voting. Consultants further ague that they make elections more open and provide access for reporters to candidate strategy, views, and campaign information.

(1990, p.68)

The masses, it is argued, were hardly part of the political process before universal suffrage became a reality. Even after the majority of citizens gained the right to vote they were still relatively ignorant about political issues. The rise of the mass media, and television in particular, has brought the masses into the political process to an historically unprecedented degree. And the masses, such voices insist, are not so stupid as to be the passive victims of crude manipulation.

In any case, the argument continues, why *shouldn't* media performance be a legitimate criterion of political fitness, in a world where media are so fundamental to the political process? Critics of the media's expanded role, from this point of view, are simply expressing a modern variant of John Stuart Mill's argument against universal suffrage which, as we noted earlier, stated that the masses should be deprived of the vote because they were inferior educationally and intellectually.

## CONCLUSION

The debate introduced here will recur in subsequent chapters, as we examine the communication strategies and tactics of political actors in greater detail. Beyond argument, we may state at this point, is the notion that political communication is too important to be ignored by those with a concern for the workings of modern democracies. The precise nature of its effects – behavioural or attitudinal, short, medium, or long-term, direct or indirect, social or psychological – may still elude social scientists and observers of the political scene, but political actors themselves – those who are striving to influence society in directions consistent with the furthering of their interests – act on the assumption that there *are* effects sufficient to justify substantial expenditure of time and resources. As Doris Graber has noted, 'one cannot deny that people throughout the world of politics consider the media important and behave accordingly. This importance . . . is reflected in efforts by governments everywhere, in authoritarian as well as democratic regimes, to control the flow of information produced by the media lest it subvert the prevailing political system' (1984a, p.19). Arterton suggests of the United States that 'those who manage presidential campaigns uniformly believe that interpretations placed upon campaign events are frequently more important than the events themselves. In other words, the political content is shaped primarily by the perceptual environment within which campaigns operate' (1984, p.155). Molotch *et al.* agree that, without regard to the empirical measurability of effects, 'elected politicians, other political activists, and agency policy makers usually *"perceive"* that media are critical to both public attitude formation and to the policy process' (1987, p.27) [their emphasis]. Baudrillard, with typical mischievousness, put it well when he observed that 'we will never know if an advertisement or opinion poll has had a real influence on individual or collective will, but we will never know either what would have happened if there had been no opinion poll or advertisement' (1988, p.210).

# 4

# THE POLITICAL MEDIA

The media, or those who work in them, as was suggested in Chapter 1, should be viewed as important political actors in themselves. Not only do they transmit the messages of political organisations to the public, but they transform them through various processes of news-making and interpretation. What the politician wishes to say is not necessarily what the media report him or her as having said. In addition, the media make statements about politics in their own right, in the form of commentaries, editorials, and interview questions. These statements may have a significant impact on the wider political environment. The relationship between the media and the political process is a dialectical one, involving action and reaction. The media report on and analyse political activity, but they are also part of it, available as a resource for political actors and their advisers. The latter thus have a major interest in understanding how the media work, and how best to achieve their communication objectives through them.

This chapter and the next address each of these issues in turn, beginning with an analysis of the media environment confronted by contemporary political actors. This sets out the institutional and organisational frameworks within which the main mass media in Britain are organised, and the relationships which they have to political institutions. We then analyse the media production process, focussing on those aspects of it – journalism in particular – in which the politicians are most interested, and the various approaches taken to understanding the media's impact on individual citizens, political organisations, and the wider political environment. In Chapter 5, we examine the ways in which media play a direct role in politics.

## THE MEDIA ENVIRONMENT

When Edmund Burke described the embryonic media of the late eighteenth century as the 'Fourth Estate' (the first three being the executive, legislative and judiciary arms of the state), he was acknowledging their importance to the health of liberal democracy. The media represented an independent source of knowledge, not only informing the people about politics, but protecting them from abuses of power.

To realise this role the media had to be free from the threat of political interference. As Scannell and Cardiff put it, 'the struggle to establish an independent press, both as a source of information about the activities of the state, and as a forum for the formation and expression of public opinion, was . . . an important aspect of the long battle for a fully representative system of democratic government' (1991, p.10).

For the first media – the press – 'freedom' was founded on the principle of independent economic organisation. The early news-papers were private, commercial institutions, which existed to make profits for their owners. They were sold as commodities in a marketplace, initially (because of their high cost) only to wealthy elites. But as literacy advanced throughout the capitalist world in the nineteenth century, and as the technology of print production was developed, newspapers fell in price and became available to wider and wider sections of the population. Print became a genuine 'mass' medium. By the beginning of the twentieth century titles like the *News of the World* and the *Daily Mail* were selling millions of copies. Excluding the former organ of the British Communist Party – the *Morning Star* – by 1999 in Britain eleven daily and ten Sunday newspapers were being published nationally (throughout the United Kingdom of England, Scotland, Wales and Northern Ireland), by nine companies. There were in addition several hundred local newspapers, serving communities varying in size from the countries of Scotland and Wales to small towns and villages. There had also come into being by the 1990s a substantial 'free sheet' sector of newspapers distributed without charge to relatively small, precisely drawn communities.[1]

As private institutions the British press have traditionally been relatively free from interference in their activities by either of the other three 'estates'. Having emerged from the oppression and cen-sorship of the absolutist feudal state, the freedom of the press to pursue its operations has always been viewed as central to the democratic process. Governments, while frequently falling out with elements of the press, have been constrained from imposing legal regulation that could be interpreted as 'political censorship'.

Restrictions on the freedom of the press have been limited to issues of 'national security', such as the reportage of official secrets, and certain ethical infringements, such as libel. The areas of reportage subject to constraints are the subject of ongoing debate, and as this book went to press, the introduction of new restrictions designed to protect individual privacy was still very much on the agenda in Britain. The new Labour government was committed to the adoption of European human rights legislation, as well as, for the first time in Britain, freedom of information legislation.

## THE BROADCASTING ENVIRONMENT

While the press has from the beginning functioned essentially as a set of capitalist businesses, broadcasting has taken a variety of organisational forms. In the United States radio and later television – like the press – were developed commercially, funded by advertising revenue. In Soviet Russia and the fascist states of the 1930s and 1940s, broadcasting was co-opted as a propaganda tool of authoritarian government. In Britain, however, broadcasting was conceived and born as a 'utility to be developed as a national service in the public interest' (Scannell and Cardiff, 1991, p.8).

Development in this form was preferred for one main reason; the perception, amongst politicians, social scientists and intellectuals, that broadcasting was a uniquely powerful medium. Too powerful, in fact, to be placed in the hands of untrammelled commercial interests. Too powerful, also, to be vulnerable to political abuse. None of the parties in Britain's multi-party democracy wished to permit the possibility of any of its rivals gaining control of broadcasting for the pursuit of its own interests. Thus, the British Broadcasting Corporation came into being as a publicly-funded (from taxation, in the form of a licence fee) but politically independent institution, protected from interference in its activities by the government of the day. Even when commercial principles were allowed to enter the British broadcasting arena with the establishment of the Independent Television network in 1954, legislation was passed to prohibit its output from being subjected to political or economic pressure.

The public service duopoly, comprising by 1982 four channels

(BBC1, BBC2, ITV and Channel 4) lasted until the late 1980s, when the flowering of cable and satellite technologies, reinforced by the Conservative government's policy of broadcasting deregulation, began to erode it. By 1999 British viewers already had access to dozens of television channels, most of them financed by subscription revenues and advertising. With the introduction of digital TV in 1998, Britain was well on the way to becoming what America had already been for many years: a multi-channel broadcasting environment.

Unlike the press, British broadcasting has always been subject to close regulation, both by legal means and through regulatory bodies such as the Independent Television Commission, the Broadcasting Standards Commission, and the Broadcasting Complaints Commission. These monitor the performance of the broadcasters to ensure that it is consistent with public service criteria such as good taste, diversity and, of particular relevance to the present discussion, political impartiality.

The 1990 Broadcasting Act requires broadcasters to observe 'due impartiality' in their coverage of political issues, ensuring 'adequate or appropriate' balance during and between election campaigns, for party and non-party political actors (McNair, 1999). This requirement does not extend to political organisations which, like the Provisional IRA and loyalist paramilitaries in Northern Ireland before the conclusion of the 1998 Good Friday peace agreement, adopt unconstitutional campaigning methods.


## DEMOCRACY AND THE MEDIA

We have already referred in general terms to the important role assigned the media by liberal democratic theory. As Nimmo and Combs put it, 'historically, the mass media were heralded as the ultimate instruments of democracy ... [They] were destined to unite, educate, and, as a result, improve the actions and decisions of the polity' (1992, p.xv). Of broadcasting, Scannell and Cardiff observe that the BBC's role, from its very earliest years, was to create 'an informed and reasoning public opinion as an essential part of the political process in a mass democratic society' (1991, p.8).

The media's democratic role would be fulfilled, on the one hand, by journalists' adherence to the professional ethic of objectivity in reporting the facts of public affairs. Objectivity implied a clear journalistic distancing from the opinions expressed in political debates, and a determination not to confuse the expression of opinion with the reporting of fact. The broadcasters' guiding principle of impartiality went further in seeking to ensure, from as early as 1923, 'that on every occasion when political issues were touched on the three parties should be given as nearly as possible equal attention' (Ibid., p.26).

The fact that airtime has been a scarce resource (at least until the advent of cable, satellite and digital television) determined that the impartiality principle be retained by British broadcasters throughout the twentieth century, with some exceptions (such as coverage of Northern Ireland). Opportunities for the expression of political opinion by broadcasting journalists were thus extremely limited. The press, by contrast, with its particular role in the free exchange, or 'marketplace' of ideas, were permitted, and indeed expected, to take up political positions. They were 'partial', as opposed to the studied impartiality of the broadcasters. This meant that even after the British press abandoned their organisational links with political parties in the nineteenth century (Negrine, 1993), individual newspapers continued to have views and expressed them in their content. The democratic principle was preserved in so far as newspapers and periodicals expressed a *plurality* of opinions, corresponding to the variety of opinions circulating in the public sphere. The diversity of the party system was paralleled in the pluralism of the press.

In adhering to these principles, therefore – objectivity and impartiality for broadcasting, partisanship and advocacy for the press – the media performed, in their different ways, their democratic role. And indeed, as audience research and public opinion surveys have consistently shown, the media have in the course of the twentieth century come to represent for most people, most of the time, their primary source of political information. The press and broadcasting have become 'the principal means of *"mediating"*, that is, standing between people and the world and reporting to them what they could not see or experience themselves' (Nimmo and Combs, 1983, p.12) [their emphasis]. As Jay Blumler puts it, 'at a time when the public's confidence in many social and political institutions has steeply declined . . . voters have become more dependent on media resources . . . for impressions of what is at stake, as previous suppliers of guiding frameworks have lost their credibility' (1987, p.170). The media not only provide *cognitive* knowledge, informing us about what is happening, but they also order and structure political reality, allotting events greater or lesser significance according to their presence or absence on the media agenda.

Indeed, the agenda-setting function of the media is argued by many observers to be their main contribution to the political process (McCombs, 1981). As citizens, we are unable to grasp or assimilate anything like the totality of events in the real world, and thus we rely on the media to search and sift reality for the most important happenings. During election campaigns, for example, David Weaver points to 'considerable support for the conclusion that the news media are crucial in determining the public importance of issues . . . at least those issues generally outside the experience of most of the public' (1987, p.186).

Chapter 2 noted that a key objective of political communication is to set the public agenda in ways favourable to an organisation's achievement of its goals. Politicians, as we shall see in Chapters 6 and 7, thus direct considerable energies to having their preferred agendas accepted and endorsed by the media. The media, however, are agenda-setters in their own capacity as providers of information, highlighting some issues and neglecting others, for reasons which are often beyond the capacity of politicians to influence significantly. When the British media pursued Tory Cabinet Minister David Mellor to resignation in 1992 over his affair with an actress, we can be sure that this was not an issue placed on the news agenda by Conservative media managers. Rather, the story was driven by commercial and other criteria (the need to sell newspapers, and the British fascination with sex scandals). These same pressures, reinforced by some proprietors', editors' and journalists' determination to expose what they perceived as a tired and corrupt ruling elite, drove the 'sleaze agenda' which dogged the Conservative government throughout most of its 1992–7 term, and contributed substantially to the party's defeat in the May 1997 general election. The 1997 electoral agenda was, in this respect at least, set by the media, rather than the politicians.

By contrast, the general election campaign of 1992 witnessed careful and largely successful efforts by all the major parties to set the news agenda from day to day, with Labour's emphasis on the future of the National Health Service countered by the Tories' stress on taxation and the Liberal Democrats' focus on proportional representation. Often, it is difficult to distinguish the agenda-setting activities of the media from those of the politicians in this way, but the distinction is important analytically.

A variation on the agenda-setting theme, and one which views the media institutions as working closely with political actors, is advanced by Greenaway *et al.*, in their analysis of the factors involved in governmental policy-making and implementation (1992). In the case of the HIV/AIDS epidemic, they note that the issue was largely absent from the political agenda until 1986 or thereabouts, at which point it began to receive extensive media coverage. As a result of this coverage, argue Miller *et al.*, the Thatcher government began for the first time to use the media as an anti-HIV/ AIDS educational tool (Miller *et al.*, 1998). The media, in this sense, put HIV/AIDS on the public agenda, and permitted a response to the epidemic at the official level. Before 1986 moral considerations prevented the Conservative government (with its espousal of 'Victorian' moral values) from acknowledging the scale of the HIV/AIDS problem, addressing its causes, or applying preventive public health measures with the requisite degree of sexual explicitness. When the media took the issue on – albeit in a sensationalistic and often inaccurate and homophobic manner – these constraints were removed. Thereafter, the media became an important channel through which anti-HIV public health messages and policies could be transmitted to the population. 'The media could be seen to legitimate government action, and then to provide the channels through which policy was implemented. The net effect of press and TV attention was to establish a climate of opinion which required governmental action, or gestures of action' (Greenaway *et al.*, 1992, p.87).

Greg Philo's study of the '1984' Ethiopian famine notes that although the scale of the disaster was evident as early as 1982, it became an international news story only in July 1984, when the BBC and ITN produced harrowing filmed reports from the scene. Only then did the international community of policy-makers formulate a response. The media played a key role in putting the famine on to the international agenda. Philo concludes, 'although it is government and relief agencies which provide aid, the media are central in galvanising an international response and in pressing governments to provide more adequate levels of aid' (1993a, p.105). Journalist Martin Woolacott, in an article pointing to the negative impact of the media's agenda-setting role in foreign news, observes wryly of the world's disaster spots that 'if you are visible on television and in the papers, you are attended to. If you are invisible you are dead, sometimes literally so'.[2]

Molotch *et al.* describe the connection between media coverage and political decision-making in terms of an 'ecological' model, based on 'a need for working models which include, not only ways of understanding how public and policy actors form *their* agendas and perspectives, but how journalistic agendas are shaped as well, and how these two sectors of reality-making are interlinked'(1987, p.28) [their emphasis]. They add that 'media effects are embedded in the actions of the policy actor, just as the policy actors' own behaviour comes to be reflected in journalists' formulations. Media and policy are part of a single ecology in which cultural materials cumulate and dissipate, often imperceptibly, throughout a media-policy web' (Ibid.).

## SOME CRITICISMS OF THE MEDIA

To say that the media have important cognitive and agenda-setting effects in modern democracies is perhaps, by this stage in our history, a statement of the obvious. More contentious, however, is the benign view of the media's role described in the previous section. Many observers have challenged the liberal democratic notion of the 'public sphere' and the media's contribution to it (Entman, 1989). For some, the very form of media output militates against understanding on the part of the audience, while others perceive the media as ideological institutions in societies where political power is not distributed equitably or rationally but on the basis of class and economic status.

The former criticism is voiced by Colin Sparks who notes the importance for media culture, in Britain and in other capitalist societies, of 'popular', 'tabloid' journalism, with its focus on issues 'not normally associated with the public sphere, such as sex scandals, human interest, and bizarre crime stories' (1992, p.22).

'Quality' journalism, in the words of one observer, produces information 'required for the smooth operation of the public sphere and of governmental party politics. It is a generalised knowledge of policy – of broad social events and movements that is distanced from the materiality of everyday life' (Fiske, 1992, p.49). By contrast, argues Sparks, the popular press 'offers an immediate explanatory framework [of social and political reality] in terms of individual and personal causes and responses' (1992, p.22). This fragmentation and trivialisation of complex social reality is argued to undermine the audience's ability to make sense of events, and hence to think and act rationally.

Until recently, tabloid journalism was associated with the press.

Now, of course, it occupies an increasing proportion of British television output, in the form of such programmes as *Lights, Camera, Action* and *True Crimes* (in America, 'tabloid TV' is already well-established). Even 'serious' current affairs programmes, such as *Panorama* and *World in Action*, have been accused of simplifying and sensationalising complex events, concentrating overwhelmingly on the dramatic consequences of the social processes investigated, rather than on their causes and possible resolutions. Such journalism, it is argued by critics, is fundamentally *apolitical*. For Josef Gripsund, it encourages 'alienation, silence and non-participation' in the political process (1992, p.94), and is 'part of a tendency to distract the public from matters of principle by offering voyeuristic pseudo-insights into individual matters'. *Panorama* interviews with the late Princess of Wales in 1996, and convicted child-killer Louise Woodward in 1998, exemplify this alleged voyeurism. In the first case, the whole world watched as Diana revealed her marital unhappiness and (as she eloquently claimed in the interview) her mistreatment at the hands of the Windsors. In the Louise Woodward interview, investigative journalism into the rights and wrongs of her conviction in an American court was avoided in favour of giving her the opportunity to declare her innocence and victimhood. In both cases, the critics would maintain, personalities were elevated over issues, and the audience encouraged to peep into other's private torments, to the overall detriment of public debate.

This rather pessimistic account of the media's role in degrading and undermining democratic political culture is rejected by others, such as John Fiske, who argue that popular journalism is frequently subversive, even if it does not intend to be. We will examine the political bias of the tabloids shortly. Here we note Fiske's argument that even conservative (whether with a capital 'C' or not) media have, as a result of their commercial position, a deep interest in maximising audiences. To do so often involves drawing them in with stories which are by no means pro-establishment, such as the aforementioned exposure of David Mellor's extra-marital affair. More recent and equally 'threatening' stories, from the point of view of the British ruling elite, included the wave of sex scandals, 'sleaze', which engulfed the Conservative Party at the beginning of 1994; the revelations of the Matrix-Churchill and cash-for-questions affairs, and the intense, ongoing media speculation around John Major's qualities (or lack of them) as Conservative prime minister which preceded his electoral defeat.

For Fiske, such journalism is to be welcomed in so far as it produces a 'disbelieving' citizen, exposing suppressed official information and discrediting establishment shibolleths. 'The tabloid press [and increasingly, as noted above, tabloid television] constantly attempts to incorporate popular tones of voice and popular stances towards official knowledge . . . this informed popular scepticism can be, if all too rarely, turned towards events in the public, political sphere' (1992, p.61).

Fiske goes further, asserting that popular journalism is more honest, less reactionary and more relevant to the world in which most citizens live than the 'quality' journalism regarded as superior by the majority of liberal commentators. For Fiske, the collision between commercial necessity and popular rhetoric creates a space where significant political criticism and dissent can surface. The existence of this space is independent of the 'official' political complexion of a media organisation. A good example of this phenomenon was the monarchy debate referred to in Chapter 1. Presented by Trevor McDonald, one of ITN's most conservative and reverential broadcasters, and broadcast at peak-time on the main commercial channel, the programme was at times fiercely anti-royal, as the following angry statement by one member of the participating audience shows:

> The Queen is . . . the richest woman in the world. She is the head of a rotten, class-ridden, corrupt political and social establishment which is directly responsible for this nation's terrible decline.

Carlton TV, which produced the debate, was no hotbed of political subversion, but in giving space to popular feelings about the monarchy (and there were pro-monarchy statements too), in what was undoubtedly a commercially-driven search for high audience ratings, a kind of subversion was the result.

For other observers, however, the fact that the popular media, and newspapers in particular, *do* have political allegiances, is more important to an understanding of their democratic function than any acknowledgement, no matter how generous, of their anti-establishment content. We have already seen that in a capitalist society such as Britain, the press are permitted to have opinions and are expected to express them. In a pluralist democracy, ideally, those opinions should reflect the structure of partisanship in the society as a whole, serving diversity and promoting rational debate, in the public interest, between distinct viewpoints. Historically, of course, the great majority of British newspapers support one party – the Conservatives, a pattern of bias which culminated in the early 1990s. Table 4.1 shows the party political affiliations of each national newspaper at the 1992 general election. Of twenty daily and Sunday titles, six supported the Labour Party, two declined to declare a preference, and *twelve* supported the Conservatives. The Tory-supporting press accounted for 70 per cent of national newspaper circulation in total, as compared to Labour's 27 per cent. This pro-Conservative bias, consistent with the pattern of press partisanship throughout the twentieth century, was in sharp contrast both to the spread of votes in the election (the Tories took 41 per cent of the total votes, compared to Labour's 37 per cent and the Liberal Democrats' 20 per cent) and, in some cases, such as that of the *Daily Star*, to the declared party preferences of the readers.[3] Thus the *Star*, whose readers are predominantly Labour supporters, took an aggressively anti-Labour editorial stance. For this reason, the press have been viewed by many as instruments of ideological indoctrination, in the service of the wealthiest and most powerful of Britain's political parties. Chinks in the armour, such as the *Financial Times*' tentative endorsement of the Labour Party in 1992, were viewed as the exceptions which proved the rule. Events since 1992 have challenged that perception, however. For reasons which I discuss in more detail elsewhere (McNair, 1999), the 'Tory press', as it was once quite justifiably described, began to shift its editorial allegiances after 1994. Sleaze (moral and political – the cash-for-questions scandal mainly concerned Tory MPs) surrounding the governing party; the emergence of a remodelled Labour Party with the election of Tony Blair as leader in 1994; and Labour's sustained courting of the press in the run-up to the 1997 poll, all contributed to a structure of editorial bias which was almost the exact reverse of that prevailing in 1992 (see Table 4.2). This time, only seven daily and Sunday titles urged their readers to vote for the Conservatives, while eleven backed Labour. The *Sun* and the *Star* in particular, both traditionally Tory 'cheerleaders', came out for Labour.

That the overwhelming majority of the British press have consistently supported the party of big business is not seriously in dispute. What has changed since 1992 is the readiness of the still conservative (with a small 'c') British press to view Labour as a party it can do business with. Still in dispute, however, is the impact which media coverage has on political behaviour. Harrop and Scammell state that 'the Conservative tabloids generally, and the *Sun* in particular, did a good propaganda job for the party in the last

Table 4.1 Party political affiliations of the British press, April 1992

| | Conservative | circ. (mlns) | % circ. | Labour | circ. (mlns) | % circ. | Non-aligned | circ. (mlns) | % circ. |
|---|---|---|---|---|---|---|---|---|---|
| Daily | Sun | 3.571 | 26.4 | Mirror | 2.903 | 21.4 | Independent | 0.39 | 2.9 |
| | Star | 0.806 | 6.0 | Guardian | 0.429 | 3.2 | | | |
| | Today | 0.533 | 4.0 | Fin. Times | 0.29 | 2.0 | | | |
| | Express | 1.525 | 11.0 | | | | | | |
| | Telegraph | 1.038 | 7.6 | | | | | | |
| | Times | 0.386 | 2.8 | | | | | | |
| | Mail | 1.675 | 12.4 | | | | | | |
| Total | | | 70.2 | | | 26.6 | | | 2.9 |
| Sunday | News of the World | 4.768 | 27.1 | Sunday Mirror | 2.774 | 15.8 | Ind. on Sunday | 0.402 | 2.3 |
| | Sunday Express | 1.666 | 9.5 | Sunday People | 2.165 | 12.3 | | | |
| | Sunday Telegraph | 1.734 | 9.9 | Observer | 0.541 | 3.1 | | | |
| | Mail on Sunday | 1.941 | 11.0 | | | | | | |
| | Sunday Times | 1.568 | 8.9 | | | | | | |
| Total | | | 66.4 | | | 31.2 | | | 2.3 |

Source: Audit Bureau of Circulation.

Table 4.2 Party political affiliations of the British press, May 1997

| | | Conservative | Labour | Lib Dem | None | Circulation* | Share |
|---|---|---|---|---|---|---|---|
| Daily | Sun | | * | | | 3,819,908 | 27.5 |
| | Mirror** | | * | | | 3,052,362 | 22.0 |
| | Star | | * | | | 740,568 | 5.3 |
| | Mail | * | | | | 2,153,868 | 15.5 |
| | Express | * | | | | 1,220,439 | 8.8 |
| | Telegraph | * | | | | 1,132,789 | 8.2 |
| | Times | | | | * | 756,535 | 5.4 |
| | Guardian | | * | | | 429,101 | 3.1 |
| | Independent | | * | | | 263,707 | 1.9 |
| | FT | | * | | | 319,400 | 2.3 |
| Total | | | | | | 13,888,677 | |
| Sunday | News of the World | | * | | | 4,429,387 | 30.0 |
| | Sunday Mirror | | * | | | 2,211,527 | 15.0 |
| | People | | * | | | 1,908,363 | 13.0 |
| | Mail on Sunday | * | | | | 2,129,376 | 14.3 |
| | Sunday Express | * | | | | 1,153,873 | 7.8 |
| | Sunday Times | * | | | | 1,331,656 | 9.0 |
| | Sunday Telegraph | * | | | | 910,803 | 6.1 |
| | Observer | | * | | | 480,426 | 3.2 |
| | Ind. on Sunday | | * | | | 278,465 | 1.9 |
| Total | | | | | | 14,833,876 | |

Source: Audit Bureau of Circulation.

Note
* Average figures for May 1997.
** Incorporates figures for Daily Record in Scotland.

crucial week of the [1992] campaign' (1992, p.180). They point out, however, that the pro-Tory bias in 1992 was no less extreme than in 1987 or 1983, when the Labour Party did considerably worse at the polls. These observers doubt that the press had a decisive impact on the campaign, which was won by the Conservatives on an unexpected (and largely undetected by opinion polls) 'late swing'. On the other hand, the tabloids' relentless and vicious campaign of personal and political abuse against Labour leaders and their policies, exemplified by the *Sun*'s 'Nightmare on Kinnock Street' headline, was accredited with the Conservatives' victory by leading member Lord McAlpine.[4] The *Sun*, indeed, congratulated itself and its readers after polling day on a job well done.

Political analyst Bill Miller has suggested that late swings to the Tories in 1987 were most apparent amongst working class *Sun* readers of the type who reside in marginal seats such as Basildon. Here in 1992, where *Sun* readers are said to be found in their greatest numbers, the swing to the Tories was the largest in the country. Miller notes of the 1987 election that working class readers of the Tory-supporting tabloids shifted in larger numbers to the Conservatives than other groups of voters (1991). As this edition went to press convincing evidence of the impact of the newly pro-Labour press on voting behaviour was not available. It is not clear, for example, if Labour's strong vote on May 1, 1997 was a consequence of press support and the impact of that on voters' intentions, or if press support for Labour was a consequence of proprietors' perceptions that the political environment in Britain had changed – that the Tory era was over, at least for the present, and that readers wanted their newspapers to reflect this shift in their editorial allegiances. In short, did the press follow the people, or the people follow the press in 1997?

If this question cannot be conclusively answered, the outcome of the 1997 campaign did lend support to former journalist, and now Labour MP, Martin Linton's claim that it is impossible for any party to win a British general election without a majority of the press (as measured in share of circulation) behind it.[5] In 1992, with only 27 per cent of circulation in its support, Labour lost. In 1997, with considerably more than 50 per cent, it won. This fact does not resolve the 'chicken and egg' problem, of course – which came first, press support or electoral popularity? But it does mean that British political parties will pay even more attention to wooing the press in the future than they have tended to do in the past. The days (not long gone) when the Labour Party, angered by the 1986 Wapping industrial dispute and generally hostile to News International, could 'boycott' journalists on the Murdoch titles, are over for good.

Opponents of the 'it's the *Sun* wot won it' effects model in political communication argue that, like other categories of media output, as was noted in Chapter 3, information about politics can only have effects in specific contexts, which structure and shape the audience's response. As noted by Ericson *et al.*, 'the effects of [news] content vary substantially . . . according to whether the consumer is directly involved in the story . . . [or] whether the events are local or distant. There is substantial variation in how people attend to particular news communications, and what they recall' (1991, p.19).

A further objection to the 'hypodermic' effect of tabloid political journalism would be the fact that if, as has been indicated, the Labour Party in 1997 enjoyed the support of around 70 per cent of national press circulation, why did that output not secure for it 70 per cent of the popular vote? Why do so many Tory-tabloid readers insist on voting for other parties?

This is a long-standing debate which has thus far evaded reso- lution, and will probably continue to do so. The evidence assembled by Miller and others suggesting a link between readership of the press and voting behaviour is ambiguous and difficult to interpret, as it is in all aspects of media effects research. To reach firm con- clusions, researchers would have to establish with much greater certainty the extent to which working-class readers are attracted to the political content of their newspapers, as opposed to the football and racing results, and the extent to which they believe the often ridiculous propaganda of some tabloids, or read it with tongue firmly in cheek.


## THE MEDIA AND HEGEMONY

The 'political effects' of the media may be viewed in broader terms than simply short- or medium-term behavioural or attitudinal change. As we noted in Chapter 2, democratic politics are founded on the existence of agreed rules and procedures for running the political process. There must be *consent* from the governed, and political power must have authority in the eyes of those over whom it is wielded. An influential strand in twentieth-century political sociology, originating with Italian Marxist intellectual Antonio Gramsci in the 1920s, has been concerned with how this consent and authority can be mobilised, in the conditions of social inequality and imperfect democracy typical of even the most advanced capitalist societies. When society is stratified along class, gender, ethnic and age lines (to name but four status criteria); when, as Bobbio notes, levels of education and rates of democratic participation are substantially lower than the theory of liberal democracy would seem to demand; and when, as many argue, political pluralism is limited to deciding how best to administer free markets, popular consent is perpetually at risk of being withdrawn. Thus, it has to be constantly worked for by those who currently constitute the ruling elite of a society.

When elites were successful in mobilising consent, Gramsci referred to their *hegemonic* position, by which he meant that there was no need to protect the social structure by coercion and force of arms, but that citizens consented to the system, and their place within it. The maintenance of hegemony was, he argued, a *cultural* process, in which the media played a great role. For Daniel Hallin, to whose work on US media coverage of the Vietnam War we will return in Chapter 8, 'to say the media play a "hegemonic" role is to say that they contribute to the maintenance of consent for a system of power' (1987, p.18).

The emphasis here is not on the media's support for a particular political party (bias or partisanship in the narrow sense) but the part they play in reinforcing and reproducing a generalised popular consensus about the inherent viability of the system as a whole. Gwynn Williams defines hegemony as

> an order in which a certain way of life and thought is dominant, in which one concept of reality is diffused throughout society in all its institutional and private manifestations, informing with its spirit all taste, morality, customs, religious and political, and all social relations, particularly in their intellectual and moral connotations.
> (Quoted in Miliband, 1973, p.162)

Ericson *et al.* suggest that 'hegemony addresses how superordinates manufacture and sustain support for their dominance over subordinates through dissemination and reproduction of knowledge that favours their interests, and how subordinates alternatively accept or contest their knowledge' (1991, p.12). For these writers, 'journalists and their news organisations are key players in hegemonic processes. They do not simply report events, but participate in them and act as protagonists' (Ibid., p.16).

The media's 'hegemonic' role, as defined here, may of course be viewed as wholly benign, if one chooses to accept the self-legitimating ideology of capitalist societies. From such a perspective (what some would call the *dominant ideological* perspective) the media provide the social structure with an outlet for the expression of shared values (as well as the political functions of rational information discussed earlier). If, however, one objects to the system, or parts of it, the hegemonic role of cultural institutions such as the media is viewed negatively. For the late Ralph Miliband the media 'in all capitalist societies have been consistently and predominantly agencies of conservative indoctrination' (1973, p.200).

How is this agency realised? The broadcasters' concept of *impartiality*, for example, works to contain political debate within a more or less tightly drawn consensus, which admits only an established political class, and marginalises or excludes others. In coverage of politics, as was noted above, impartiality in practice means giving equal representation (representation proportionate to an organisation's electoral support) to the main political parties, particularly during election campaigns. It does not mean the reporting of all significant participants in a political debate. In Northern Ireland, 'impartiality' was explicitly withheld from the para-military organisations and their political wings, because they operated outside the established democratic procedures of the United Kingdom's constitutional system. The broadcasting ban introduced by the Conservative government in 1989, and removed only in 1994, prevented television and radio from airing the voices of some elected Northern Ireland politicians because they were deemed to support those who challenged the legitimacy of the British state.

In this case, from the viewpoint of the hegemonic school, the media were erecting a barrier between legitimate and illegitimate political discourse, excluding the latter from the public sphere.

The media also contribute to the maintenance of consent, it is argued, by reporting problematic events and processes in ways favourable to the established order. Major industrial disputes, overseas military expeditions (we exclude here wars of national survival, such as the Second World War) and domestic opposition to key military policies, are examples of issues which tend to be reported from an establishment perspective, thus arguably influencing the political environment in a particular direction. Chomsky and Herman's *Manufacturing Consent* makes explicit reference to this process in its title, analysing how the American media, over many decades, have presented their audiences with a view of the world and its conflicts which corresponds closely to the interests of the US military-industrial complex (1988). Third World liberation struggles were reported as 'communist aggression'; attempts to restrain economic exploitation of the Third World by US companies as 'threats to US interests'; and vicious repression in East Timor, Chile and elsewhere as legitimate anti-subversive activity, if not ignored entirely. The wealth of data and illustrative material presented in Chomsky and Herman's work comprises no less than a post-Second World War history of the US media's hegemonic role.

No comparable volume of analysis is available for the British case, but a number of studies claim to have found similar patterns of coverage (Glasgow University Media Group, 1985; McNair, 1988). The British media, like those of other capitalist democracies, have frequently functioned to police the parameters of legitimate dissent, presenting citizens with a view of the world consistent with the maintenance of the *status quo*. They do so for a variety of reasons. In some cases, the political demands of proprietors are important (as is apparent with the Murdoch newspapers). In broadcasting and the press, structural dependence on official sources frequently allows an official view of events to prevail. British broadcasting is part of an established culture of shared values and ideological assumptions, which inform the construction of news. All these factors have been advanced as reasons for the deep pro-systemic bias of the media.

The hegemonic model has itself been criticised, however, for its overly simplistic reading of how the media reports politics. Daniel Hallin's study of the Vietnam War showed, on the one hand, that coverage in the initial phase of the conflict was consistent with a 'hegemonic' role for the media, but that as consensus around US policy in the conflict fragmented in the late 1960s and early 1970s, coverage changed to reflect this (1986). Kevin Williams agrees that 'for most of the war the media shared the same framework for understanding events in South East Asia as the [US] government', but that 'after public opinion had moved decisively against the war the media [began] to regularly challenge the official explanation' (1993, p.306). This, for Williams, reflects the fact that 'elite sources are not always successful in their attempts to dictate the agenda. The political elite is not homogeneous and the divisions are reflected in the media's reporting' (Ibid., p.326).

David Murphy's analysis of how the media reported the John Stalker affair[6] is similarly sceptical of the hegemonic model, arguing that the media in this case actively promoted an anti-establishment

conspiracy theory to explain Stalker's treatment in Northern Ireland. Referring specifically to the press (but in terms which apply
equally to broadcasting) he notes that their account of the Stalker
affair 'conflicts utterly with the conventional academic picture of a
right-wing dominated press, producing an ideological justification
for the status quo and the forces of control' (1991, p.8). In this case
the media 'largely arrived at a consensus which challenged the legitimacy of the state in its handling of the affair'. Coverage of the
Stalker affair revealed a willingness on the part of journalists 'to call
into question not simply the wisdom of government policies or
the good faith of individual politicians, but a questioning of the
good faith and legitimacy of the state and its agents, and of the
establishment which is seen as lying behind them' (Ibid., p.262).

It has been argued, on the other hand, that in reporting objectively manifestly corrupt or unethical behaviour by the political
class, which may be causing fragmentation and disunity amongst
the establishment (such as the Watergate scandal in America, or
cash-for-questions in Britain) the media are contributing to a wider
popular belief in the self-rectifying properties of the system. They
may be doing this, but they are also carrying out what journalists
regard as their professional duty, independently of the political
class. Liberal journalism has evolved over three centuries or more as
an autonomous cultural and political force, the power and prestige
of which is measured at least in part by the readiness of journalists
to act as a 'fourth estate', looking out for and exposing the abuse
of political power. Much of the critical political coverage which
emerges from the application of this professional ethic may be
viewed as tokenistic and superficial, posing no real threat to the
centres of power in capitalist societies. 'Monicagate', for example,
in which the US media were filled with full and explicit coverage of
a president's sexual habits, did not threaten American capitalism,
although allegations of cover-up and lying under oath did evoke
memories of Watergate and the possibility of presidential impeach-
ment. What it *did* do, unquestionably, like Watergate twenty-five
years before, was to demystify and undermine the institutional
power of the American presidency.

However we choose to interpret the significance of media criticism of the establishment, it is clear that assertions of a 'hegemonic
role' for the media must be able to accommodate those frequent
examples of the 'breakdown of consensus' and the splitting of elite
groups. To that end we may usefully distinguish between the work
of Chomsky and others, who stress the 'propagandistic' nature (if

not necessarily always intent) of the media, and others such as Hallin, who prefer to emphasise the media's flexibility and adaptability in the context of a fluid, dynamic political system, governed not by a single ruling class but by rotating elites drawn from different parties and factions within parties. In the latter perspective, the adaptability of the media to shifting lines of debate is esential to the retention of their legitimacy as facilitators of political discourse in the public sphere and hence, ultimately, to their 'hegemonic' role.

## POLITICS AND MEDIA PRODUCTION

Many of the features of media output discussed in the previous section can be better understood by an analysis of the media production process: the conventions, practices, and constraints which shape the output of political journalism, in ways which sometimes favour the politician, and at other times subvert him or her. These can be grouped into three categories: 'commercial', 'organisational', and 'professional'.

### Commercialisation

On *commercial* constraints Greg Philo notes that 'a simple truth underpins the everyday practices of the media institutions and the journalists who work within them – that they are all at some level in competition with each other to sell stories and maximise audiences . . . They must do this at a given cost and at a set level of resources' (1993a, p.111).

As was noted at the beginning of this chapter the main purpose of the press, since its emergence as a mass medium in the nineteenth century, has been to produce information in the commodity form, and to maximise advertising revenue by selling that information to the largest possible number of readers. Broadcasting, on the other hand, for most of its relatively brief existence, has been sheltered in most countries from naked commercialism. In Britain, the BBC, as we have noted, was defined from the outset as a 'public service' and given lofty goals of cultural enlightenment and education. ITV, too, while a commercial organisation in so far as its revenues derived from advertising, was required under law to broadcast a substantial proportion of news and current affairs programming, and to make those programmes within the same rules of impartiality which guided the BBC.

Since the development of cable and satellite television, however, all of the established terrestrial broadcasting organisations in Britain, public or private, have had imposed upon them a much stronger commercial remit. The government's White Paper on broadcasting, published on July 5, 1994,[7] confirmed that the BBC will survive for the foreseeable future as a public service body, funded predominantly by taxation in the form of the licence fee, and the Labour government has endorsed that policy. The BBC's senior managers are well aware however that in the longer term the case for continuation of the licence fee system will depend on the corporation's retaining its popularity with an audience which now has access to dozens of new TV and radio channels, and can be relied upon to exercise that choice. At the same time, the commercial channels ITV and C4 have, since the passing of the 1990 Broadcasting Act, been forced to pay much more attention to the maximisation of their ratings than had previously been the case.

Fortunately, journalism has proved to be popular and profitable, and there is no evidence that the commercialising of British broadcasting will, as some observers feared in the late 1980s, be accompanied by its gradual exclusion from the airwaves (McNair, 1999). On the contrary, with 24-hour news channels on Sky and BBC, and the explosion of breakfast news on television since the 1980s, there is now more broadcasting journalism available to the British viewer than ever before. But the need to maximise ratings has been argued to be driving a shift in content away from the in-depth, often critical investigative journalism for which British public service broadcasting has been internationally renowned, towards the racier style characteristic of the tabloids. Peak-time factual programming is increasingly concerned with real-life crime shows (such as *Crimewatch UK*), exposés of sharp practice in the economy (*The Cook Report*), 'docu-soaps' and 'shock horror' reportage of various types. Even *Panorama*, once renowned (and occasionally mocked) for the seriousness and depth of its analyses of official policy, party politics and the like, now frequently addresses such issues as drug abuse and juvenile crime. These are, of course, the legitimate stuff of journalistic inquiry, but their growing prevalence in the British media reflects a commercially driven shift in newsvalues.

The previous section examined the views of those who see these trends as fundamentally damaging to the democratic process, further relegating serious 'quality' journalism to the margins of late night BBC2, Channel 4, or Radio 5. More often than not, it is argued, this type of journalism is crucially lacking in substance, dealing only with the spectacular, epiphenomenal aspects of social and political problems, while avoiding the discussion of solutions. The viewer is shocked, or entertained, or outraged, but not necessarily any wiser about the underlying causes of the problem being covered. The entertainment value of events begins to take precedence over their political importance. Others welcome the confrontational, subversive style of much of this material, stressing that much of it is not only more watchable, but more politically useful than long, detailed and, for many, boring analyses of health or education policy.

Arguments about tabloidisation aside, commercialisation has also enhanced the media's long-standing tendency to pursue 'pack' journalism, whereby individual organisations pursue a shared agenda. When a story is deemed to have become 'news' by one organisation, the others feel compelled to follow suit. This is not necessarily because the story has 'objective' importance, but will often be the product of editorial assumptions that to be left behind by the pack is dangerous for an organisation's commercial position and legitimacy as a news provider.

In an intensifying commercial environment, therefore, the political process comes to be seen by journalists as the raw material of a commodity – news or current affairs – which must eventually be sold to the maximum number of consumers. Inevitably, those aspects of the process which are the most sellable are those with the most spectacular and dramatic features, and which can be told in those terms. In some cases, such as the cash-for-questions affair, or the bizarre death of Conservative MP Stephen Milligan in early 1994, it might be thought that the commercial interests of the media in pursuing a 'sexy' news agenda, and the public interest of citizens in finding out the truth about their political representatives, coincides. The Stalker affair, as David Murphy asserts, is another example of the media uncovering uncomfortable truths which any political establishment would rather leave hidden. This case, and many others arising from the conflict in Northern Ireland, demonstrates that 'the process of media production is an arena of contest and negotiation in which official sources cannot always take it for granted that they will be able to set the agenda' (Miller and Williams, 1993, p.129).

The important (politically speaking) and the entertaining are not mutually exclusive. In many instances, however, when commercial considerations drive both print and broadcast media, pack-like, after philandering ministers and bishops, sexually deviant MPs, and princesses with eating disorders, it is not always clear what public interest is being served. We may in such cases be enthralled at how the mighty are fallen, while remaining ignorant as to the less glamorous, but more important details of how political power really works and is exercised.

The commercialisation of the media may with some reason be viewed by politicians as a threat to traditional loyalties and alliances. When in 1992 the *Sun*, having been widely criticised for yet another intrusion into someone's privacy, let rumours circulate that it had 'dirt' on a number of senior politicians which only discretion and political allegiance prevented it from revealing, a palpable wave of unease swept through the professional political community. And after the series of sex scandals which bedevilled the Conservative Party after 1992, no one can doubt that, pro-Tory or not, the British press will not hesitate, out of loyalty alone, to embarrass or force out of office any government minister guilty of sleaze if there are papers to be sold. For many politicians, this cannot be a comforting thought.

## THE ORGANISATIONAL NEED FOR NEWS

While the commercialisation of the media may have some unwelcome conseqences for the political class, another related trend promises considerable benefits. Part of the increased competitive pressure under which the established broadcasters have been placed is the consequence of the expansion of media outlets made possible by cable, satellite and digital technologies. The expansion has included journalism, in the form of *Sky News*, with its 24-hour 'rolling' service, and CNN, which is slowly increasing its reach in Europe and the UK (although it may be too US-focussed in its news agenda ever to be a mass news provider in the British market). Partly in response to these new providers of journalism, the BBC has expanded *its* journalistic output, both on television and radio, including a 24-hour rolling news service on Radio 5, BBC24 on television, and a rapidly developing global television news service. All of this means that there is an increasing demand for news material, which politicians are exceptionally well-placed to serve.

For a news-hungry media, the political arena is the potential source of an unending flow of stories, some of them unwelcome to the politicians, as we have seen, but others attractive in so far as they provide publicity and promotion for a party, government, or leader. This source becomes more important as the demand for news increases. Thus develops a relationship of mutual inter-dependence between politicians and journalists, in which each can benefit the other (Blumler and Gurevitch, 1981). Rodney Tiffen observes that 'news is a parasitic institution. It is dependent on the information-generating activities of other institutions' (1989, p.51). One researcher writes of coverage of political affairs in Germany that

> approximately two out of every three [news] items are, on the basis of their respective primary sources . . . the out-come of press releases and conferences, whereas the rest may be traced back to public events, journalistic investiga-tions, or non-public events to which journalists were invited . . . hence, the shaping of reality as presented by the news media may thus, on the basis of empirical evidence, be attributed primarily to this sector, and not the autonomous activities of journalists.
>
> (Baerns, 1987, p.101)

While some observers complain about what they see as the media's uncritical, non-discriminating use of public relations material (Bagdikian, 1984; Michie, 1998), for the political actor in such cir-cumstances there is much to be gained by learning how the media work – their newsvalues, professional practices and routines – and using this knowledge to present journalists with information in a way most likely to be accepted and turned into news. As Tiffen notes, news production 'generates patterns of [journalistic] responsiveness which political leaders [and political actors in general] can exploit' (1989, p.74).

Skilled politicians have been manipulating the media in this fash-ion for decades, as Daniel Boorstin's 1962 discussion of the 'pseudo-event' makes clear, but there are undoubtedly greater opportunities to do so in an era when the news space to be filled has expanded so dramatically. The astute politician will know, for example, that in a situation where media organisations have finite resources of time and money, where deadlines are tight and exclusives increasingly important, there is much to be gained by ensuring the journalists' ease of supply, providing, as Schlesinger and Tumber put it, an 'information subsidy' (1994).

A media event which is timed to meet the deadlines for first edi-tions or primetime news bulletins will have more likelihood of being

reported than one which is not. An event which provides opportunities for interesting pictures and, in the case of broadcasting, sounds
('soundbites'),[8] will be more attractive to the news organisation
under pressure than one which does not. Issues which can be neatly
packaged and told in relatively simple, dramatic terms will receive
more coverage than those which are complex and intractable.

The process of media production is, then, one which can be studied, understood, and manipulated by those who wish to gain access
– on favourable terms, of course. It so happens that those political
actors with the greatest resource base from which to pursue such a
strategy are those located in established institutions of power, such
as governmental and state organisations. They have the most
money with which to employ the best news managers, organise the
grandest events, and produce the slickest press releases.

## THE PROFESSION OF JOURNALISM

Another element of the media production process which can be seen
to favour the establishment is the professional ethic of objectivity
itself (and its close relation, impartiality) to which the majority of
political journalists subscribe. Objectivity, as we noted above, is
important to the democratic process because it permits the media to
report political events accurately, fairly, and independently. In con-
crete terms, the objectivity ethic has gradually evolved into a set of
signifying practices and conventions which, when present in a piece
of journalism, are intended to secure the audience's endorsement of
its 'truthfulness'.

These practices include the explicit separation of fact from opinion; the inclusion in coverage of all opposing sides in a debate
(excluding, usually, terrorists and other non-constitutional actors);
and the validation of journalistic narratives by the quotation of
reliable, authoritative sources. It is fair to say that for most journalists, the most reliable and authoritative sources when constructing a
political story are the established politicians, their senior civil servants and secretaries, and other leading figures in state and public
organs. If, moreover, these sources have embraced the lessons of the
previous paragraphs – that they should actively seek to supply the
media with material – then not only are they the most reliable and
authoritative (a culturo-political factor) but also the most convenient and accessible from the journalists' perspective (an organisational reality). The professional requirements of objectivity are thus

reinforced by the technical constraints imposed by the news-gathering process.

Conversely, those political actors which lack sophisticated public relations machinery, and which are not a part of the established institutions of mainstream political discourse, will tend to be neither especially credible to the journalists nor particularly convenient as news sources. In Chapter 8 we will discuss how many non-establishment (and indeed anti-establishment) organisations have learnt to combat these 'biasing' features of media production with a variety of alternative public relations strategies. Although the resources required for media manipulation (if I may use that term without implying disapproval) are unequally distributed throughout society, it is possible, as we shall see, for the PR 'poor' to compensate to some extent with skill and entrepreneurship.

# 5

# THE MEDIA AS POLITICAL ACTORS

Chapter 1 included, in its list of political actors, media institutions and those who work in them. This draws our attention to the fact that in contemporary liberal democracies media institutions perform not only cognitive functions of information dissemination but also interpretative functions of analysis, assessment, and comment. Not only do the media *report* politics, they are a crucial part of the environment in which politics is pursued. They contribute to policy discussion and resolution, not only in so far as they set public agendas, or provide platforms for politicians to make their views known to the public, but also in judging and critiquing the variety of political viewpoints in circulation. In this chapter we examine the many formats in which the overtly interpretative work of the political media is done.

## DEFINING POLITICAL REALITY

We begin at the most general level, noting that the media are active in defining political 'reality'. Through the processes of newsgathering and production described in the previous chapter, the audience is finally presented with a 'finished' articulation of what 'really' matters in political affairs at any given time. Journalists communicate to us the 'meaning' of politics (Gerstle *et al.*, 1991). They insert the events of political life into *narrative frameworks* which allow them to be told as news stories. These frameworks do not spring fully formed from the journalistic pen, of course, but develop over time in the interaction and competition between different news media, and between the various actors in, or sources of, a story. Over time, competing frameworks are narrowed down and eliminated until one, *dominant* framework remains. Although always subject to challenge and revision, the dominant framework, once established, provides the structure within which subsequent events are allocated news value, reported, and made sense of.

For example, the dominant narrative framework for making sense of events within the British Conservative Party, following the 1992 election, can be expressed in terms of a 'leadership crisis'. Political journalists – encouraged by Thatcherite elements in the Conservative Party, resentful of their leader's abrupt dismissal from office – told a continuing story of John Major's buffeting by the harsh winds of political misfortune. The 'story' of the Labour Party over the same period, on the other hand, was the relatively positive one of modernisation and renewal. When Labour leader John Smith died suddenly on May 12, 1994, media coverage of his success in transforming the party's image and improving its 'electability' was uniformly positive. Tony Blair's election as Labour leader on July 21 that year took place in an atmosphere of euphoric endorsement of his abilities, shared even by such formerly right-wing organs as the London *Evening Standard*. Journalists also appreciated New Labour's skill in public relations and news management, and the invincibility of Labour's 'spin doctors' (see Chapter 7) became a powerful narrative framework in the media's making sense of Labour's transition to an electable government. The Conservatives, meanwhile, were dogged from 1994 onwards not only by having all that they said and did interpreted as part of the ongoing leadership crisis, but by the developing narrative of sleaze, which added corruption and moral hypocrisy to the party's perceived problems. From 'leadership crisis' the dominant framework for making sense of the Conservatives developed into one of decay, decline and imminent defeat. So powerful did this framework become as a journalistic structuring device that nothing the party leadership could do to highlight the strengths of the economy (and when the Tories left office in 1997 the economy was performing exceptionally well by British standards) could undermine it.

## THE PRESS

The press and broadcast media, by the nature of their functioning and role, employ different modes of intervention in politics. The former, as we have seen, have always been more overtly partisan in their approach to political affairs, perceiving their role as very much that of opinion-articulation. At election time the views expressed are in terms of party preference. Individual newspapers actively campaign on behalf of their preferred party and denigrate or criticise the others. The popular tabloid press will do so in an openly propagandistic, 'populist' manner, accompanied by various levels of distortion, untruth, and sensationalism, while the broadsheet newspapers will outline their views in more reasoned terms. Both will select news stories with an eye to constructing a particular image (positive or negative) of a party. James Curran's analysis of 1980s press coverage of the London Labour Party – the 'loony left', as it became known – shows clearly how some local and national newspapers attempted to smear Labour councillors in the capital by associating them with extreme or bizarre political crusades (1987). In many of the cases examined, stories reported as 'fact' were manufactured or exaggerated until they had only a tenuous connection with reality.[1]

The so-called 'quality' newspapers are also capable of such coverage. In 1991, not long before the 1992 general election, Rupert Murdoch's *Sunday Times* produced a long report on the Labour leader Neil Kinnock's 'links' with the Soviet Communist Party.[2] Although the connections were, on close examination of the story, no more substantial than would be expected between a potential British prime minister (as Mr Kinnock then was) and the government of another major power, the construction of the story and the headlines used implied an altogether more sinister relationship.

'Straight' news can, then, be viewed as a form of political intervention, intended to smear political organisations and influence voters. In certain situations, such as the conflict in Northern Ireland, or the Gulf War, news often becomes a blatant form of propaganda, intended to demonise and dehumanise 'the enemy'. The *Sun*'s reference to Sinn Fein president Gerry Adams (in the period before the Good Friday peace agreement and the setting up of the Northern Ireland assembly turned him into a statesman of sorts) as 'the worst two words in the English language'[3] can only be viewed in this light.

In the case of Northern Ireland, and on a wide range of current political issues – racism, sexual harassment and assault, the future of the British welfare state – newspapers use their power as information disseminators to influence the policy-making environment; to move their readers in certain directions if they can; and to put pressure on decision-makers in government. Hall *et al.*'s still valuable study, *Policing the Crisis*, showed how, on the issue of law and order, British newspapers in the 1970s intervened in and contributed to a debate about the crime of mugging (1978). In a 'spiral of deviance' the press first highlighted the 'problem' – which, these authors showed, emerged primarily as a consequence of changes in policing policy in London – gave it a meaning in terms of the UK's 'copying' of American crime waves (a pattern repeated in more recent discussions of 'crack', 'yardies', and the rise in illegally held firearms); articulated 'public outrage' about this crime wave, and encouraged the judiciary to come down hard on convicted 'muggers'. The press were major contributors, in short, to the creation of a moral and political climate of enhanced police repression, which had very real consequences for young blacks in Britain. Following the massacre of schoolchildren and their teacher by a gunman at Dunblane in 1996, the press actively campaigned for the introduction of draconian restrictions on firearms – even those used by competitors in Olympic shooting competition. Like the case of 'devil dogs' in the early 1990s, when a wave of savaging incidents by pit bull terriers and Rottweilers resulted in ill-thought out and ineffective legislation to clamp down on 'dangerous dogs', the anger and revulsion caused by the Dunblane incident was seized on by the press to push politicians into what many observers regarded as hasty, vote-catching legislation, of little practical relevance to the circumstances which caused the killings in Dunblane to occur.

## THE PUBLIC VOICE OF THE PRESS

While news can be and frequently is used in the manner described here, there are more 'authored' forms of political intervention available to the press. The most important 'voice' of a newspaper is its editorial, which embodies its political identity. It also, as Hall *et al.* noted in *Policing the Crisis*, seeks to articulate what the newspaper's editors believe to be the collective voice of its readers. Hence, editorials in the *Sun* and the *Sunday Times*, although expressing fundamentally similar political viewpoints, determined largely by the opinions of proprietor Rupert Murdoch, will address the issues of the day in completely different terms. The *Sun* claims to 'speak' for the working classes, voicing their frequently racist, sexist and xenophobic prejudices, while at the same time irreverential and critical of the establishment, whether it be in the form of Royal 'scroungers', gay judges, or two-timing Tory politicians. The *Sunday Times*, also basically supportive of the Conservative Party (in the 1997 election, the *Sunday Times* reluctantly endorsed John

Major, 'warts and all', in its eve-of-poll editorial, and since May 1997 has led the way in trying to embarrass the Labour government), seeks to hold on to and expand its relatively young, affluent readership with a new right-of-centre iconoclasm which, like the *Sun*, is by no means averse to putting the editorial boot into the establishment.

At the other end of the political spectrum, the *Guardian*'s editorials reflect the kinder, gentler views of that paper's liberal, left-of-centre readers. The *Financial Times* speaks with the detached, business-like voice of hard-headed British capital, and so on.

There is of course no necessary connection between the public voice of a newspaper's editorial and the actual beliefs of its readers. We have already noted the distinction between the *Daily Star*'s pre-1997 editorial support for the Conservative Party and the Labour-supporting views of most of its readers. The *Sun*'s thundering endorsement of Tony Blair in the 1997 election neglected the fact that a substantial proportion of its readers still supported the Conservatives. But there is a clear commercial motive for a newspaper to 'speak the language' of its readers, or at least to speak in a language which does not offend them unduly.

It has been argued by some that the commercial status of newspapers over-rides any political objectives which they may have, and as I suggested above, the shift in so many British newspapers' editorial allegiances from Conservative to Labour in 1997 was largely due to harsh commercial calculations of where the readers were going. But as James Curran and others have convincingly argued (Curran and Seaton, 1997), and as the actions and declarations of the media barons, past and present, make abundantly clear, the benefits of newspaper ownership, for those few multi-millionaires in a position to be able to afford it, are not just those of short-term profit. Corporate giants such as News International and United Newspapers have an obvious interest in shaping the political environment of the markets in which they operate. If they can do so effectively, as Rupert Murdoch and Silvio Berlusconi have shown, the longer-term financial (and in the latter case, political) rewards can be enormous.

## THE JOURNALIST AS PUNDIT

Newspaper editorials, while they are unmistakably subjective expressions of opinion, are rarely signed by a particular editor or journalist. *Authored* political journalism, on the other hand, will be contained in columns, feature articles, and a variety of shorter formats such as diaries and cartoons, some of which have a satirical function. We are now moving into the realm of the political 'pundit', a term derived from Sanskrit which dates to the early nineteenth century and survives in modern India to refer to a 'learned person or teacher who is not only an authority but also a renowned political figure' (Nimmo and Combs, 1992, p.6).

Since Walter Lippmann legitimised the profession of journalism in the early twentieth century, what Nimmo and Combs refer to as a 'priestly establishment' has evolved. This establishment of pundits they define as 'a loose collectivity of journalists, analysts, policy experts, and other specialists who voice their special knowledge in public forums' (Ibid., p.24). The journalist-pundit is someone who is accepted by a newspaper reader as an authority on political affairs. They become 'a source of opinion-formation and opinion-articulation, agenda-setting and agenda-evaluation' (Ibid., p.8). The journalist-pundit is a wise, knowing observer of and commentator on the political scene, making sense of its complexities for the rest of us.

To achieve such status, the pundit must also be accepted by the political class, so that he or she can move among them, gather information – often in confidence – and make reliable judgments. Thus, the journalist-pundit is part of the political world, moving in it with ease, but distanced from the political fray. It remains the case that political journalists will usually reflect the partisanship of the newspapers which employ them. Indeed, a pundit's access to the prime minister for a private briefing may be granted only on condition of editorial support from the journalist's newspaper, or on the understanding that favourable coverage will result. The important thing for a political journalist of the press is not partisanship, however, but credibility. The *Daily Telegraph* reader will expect Boris Johnson to review politics from a right-wing perspective, but also that he should do so knowledgeably and authoritatively.

## THE COLUMN

The highest form of political punditry in press journalism is the column (known in the United States as the 'op-ed' column) situated on or close to the editorial page. Here, such writers as Hugo Young of the *Guardian* or Michael Jones of the *Sunday Times* select the issue of the moment, as they see it, and attempt to present readers with an informed assessment. Typically, the form includes an appeal for action at its conclusion. As Nimmo and Combs put it, the 'column is a stylistic dramatisation not only of the subject or issue at hand but also of the pundit's rightful status to speak on it authoritatively' (Nimmo and Combs, 1992, p.12)

The issue selected for such treatment need not be 'objectively' the most important, as judged by the media as a whole at any given time. Hugo Young's column may, for example, reflect the left-of-centre character of the *Guardian*'s editorial and readership by focussing on what might, to a *Telegraph* reader, seem a rather obscure point about the Labour Party's leadership election rules. The political columnist, having authority, also has licence to go against the 'pack' referred to in the previous chapter.

Columns are not devoted only to politics, as defined in the narrow sense of party political affairs, but to political issues in general. Quality newspapers will have economics columnists, social affairs columnists and columnists dealing with 'women's issues'. While these categories of journalist may not move in the same high circles of political power as Hugo Young, Alan Watkins, and the like, their role as political actors is the same: to make sense of complex reality for a lay-audience; to identify important issues, assess the arguments involved in them, and relay advice to the politicians with responsibility for taking decisions. These columnists, too, will use politicians as sources, confidential or otherwise, for what is written.

Some columnists are themselves former politicians, or individuals who have been closely involved in the political process, such as Margaret Thatcher's press secretary in the 1980s, Bernard Ingham, who went on to work for the *Daily Express*. The *Guardian* has employed the services of Roy Hattersley, although he writes less frequently on politics than he does on a variety of idiosyncratic 'little England' themes. Ken Livingstone has written for the *Sun* (one of the rare examples, as is Martin Jacques's employment by the *Sunday Times*) of a columnist not reflecting the newspaper's broad editorial stance.[4]

Livingstone's column for the *Sun* was a reflection of his popularity, founded on the controversial image of 'loony leftism' which the *Sun* itself played a major role in constructing. It illustrates an important feature of the press column: it can be a very popular journalistic form. In the tabloids particularly, to quote Nimmo and Combs, 'punditry has become a form of entertainment, both shaping and adjusting to popular expectations regarding how to keep up with and understand "what's happening"' (Ibid., p.41). The credibility of such politician-columnists as Ken Livingstone, Bernard Ingham or Norman Tebbit, is founded on their status as political 'insiders'. They, as opposed to other politicians, are employed as columnists because their names have audience pulling power, and because their plain-speaking, extremist viewpoints are assumed to help circulation figures.

## THE FEATURE

Another important form of political journalism is the *feature* article. While not, of course, restricted to coverage of politics, the feature article is the arena for a more detailed exploration of political affairs than straight news allows. Features frequently accompany news stories, expanding on issues and events which a news story can only report in a summary fashion. Like the columnist, the feature writer will enlist if possible the aid of political insiders to obtain reliable material, although the feature must stick closely to the conventions of objectivity described above. When addressing a political theme, the feature writer must convince the reader of his or her 'objectivity' as a journalist, while at the same time pressing a personal agenda. Alternatively, the research for a feature (the data upon which its objectivity will be founded) can be gained by on-the-spot interviews with participants in the events underlying a current political issue. When, for example, a journalist wishes to draw attention to the failings of government foreign policy towards a particular region, he or she may travel there, record the scene and the views of its inhabitants, and fashion a piece which condemns the government, if not always explicitly. Among the most notable political feature writers working in the British press are Paul Foot, formerly of the *Daily Mirror*, now of the *Guardian* and *Private Eye*, and John Pilger.

Features straddle the line in political journalism between the hard news which is the staple of a newspaper, and the column, where its 'priestly pundits' wax eloquent (or indignant) about the events of the day. The best feature writers function, like Foot and Pilger, as pundits *and* reporters, combining the research skills of good journalism with the analytical and intellectual prowess of the top pundits.

## THE BARDS

Rather different in their function are what Nimmo and Combs call the 'bards' of political journalism (as distinct from the 'priests'). The bardic journalist or pundit plays the role of 'a court jester, that ruling elites can tolerate' (1992, p.67). The bard employs humour, satire, and irony to comment on political affairs, although frequently with serious intent. Political cartoonists attempt to make their readers laugh while highlighting important political issues. Andrew Rawnsley, formerly of the *Guardian*, made his reputation as a wickedly funny diarist of the House of Commons' daily business, giving the routine grind of debate a gently subversive satirical twist. The magazine *Private Eye* may also be regarded as 'bardic', in its constant investigative exposure and parodying of the absurdities and injustices of British political life.

Magazines such as *Private Eye*, and the more conventionally journalistic *New Statesman*, are examples of a press which exists for the purpose of reporting and reflecting on politics from what we can call a 'dissenting', anti-establishment perspective. These periodicals (there are no British newspapers of this type, unless one counts the *Morning Star*) are often engaged in extremely tough critiques of aspects of the system, as witnessed by the number of banning orders taken out against them over the years. They are, in a very real sense, 'watchdogs' over the political establishment.

## BROADCASTING

Several of the forms of political journalism deployed by the press are also used in broadcasting, which has also produced its own class of pundits. Paralleling the bardic role of *Private Eye* on television was the now-defunct *Spitting Image*, a puppet show which satirised current political figures in rather unforgiving terms. One should also include in this category output which, although clearly not to be confused with journalism, strives to represent the people against their leaders – impressionists with a strong political content in their materials, such as Rory Bremner and Chris Barrie, and comedians like Ben Elton who specialise in heavily politicised stand-up routines. Moving closer to journalism are those interviewers, such as Clive Anderson, who employ a chat-show format, but lace it with an element of satirical mockery of the powerful. Anderson's show frequently sends up politicians – notably Jeffrey Archer, who was

accused of plagiarism on air – and consciously sets out to undermine their status and credibility. All these 'bards', while distinct
from the conventions of journalism, make an important contribution to the public discourse of politics, exploring current issues and
concerns in a populist style which 'straight' broadcast news must
avoid.

British broadcasting, as has been described, is bound by strict
rules of impartiality, which inevitably constrain the extent to which
journalists can match the strongly opinionated pundits of the press.
They must be seen and heard to be scrupulously fair, balanced, and
neutral, at least with regard to constitutional politicians of the
mainstream party system. We have already noted the oft-made criticism of broadcast news for its deviations from the ideal of 'impartiality', and the suggestion that in reality it contains a deep structural
bias towards the *status quo*. Our concern here, however, is with the
broadcasters' tendency, and legally imposed responsibility in the
interests of a strong and healthy democracy, not to take sides in
political disputes.

One expression of this impartiality is the broadcasters' role as
transmitters of political discourse. The press can report what a politician says, but the broadcasters can transmit it live, in colour.
Despite the controversy which accompanied the first live broadcasts
of Parliament, on radio and then television, it has now become an
accepted component of the British political process (Hetherington
*et al.*, 1990; Franklin, 1992). Live transmission remains, for essentially commercial reasons, restricted to Prime Minister's Question
Time and special occasions, but has gradually expanded (helped by
*Sky News*) into a range of 'review' programmes which give the
interested viewer and listener a more substantial overview of
parliamentary business.

In 1992 a consortium of British cable operators set up the Parliamentary Channel, a non-profit service transmitting live coverage of
debates in the houses of Commons and Lords, the proceedings of
select committees, and sessions of the European parliament. The
service was taken over by the BBC in August 1998, and renamed
BBC Parliament. Although as yet watched only by a small number of
cable subscribers, it can be expected to expand its reach in the digital
era ahead.[5] Through this output the citizen encounters, in a uniquely
raw and unedited fashion, the *process* of political debate, and may
judge the performances of participants accordingly. Of course, many
of the truly important debates remain hidden from public view, but
when a government has only a small majority, as did the post-1992

Conservative government, House of Commons debates can become a significant factor in political life, and thus their availability through radio and television can only be seen as a democratic asset.

## Debates and talk-shows

Another format in which the broadcaster can provide a platform for the exchange of political views is the structured debate programme, exemplified by the BBC's *Question Time* on television and *Any Questions* on radio. On these programmes an impartial chairperson presides over a debate between four participants, usually grouped into, broadly-speaking, right, left, and centre (though non-politicians are also included). The 'public' makes their contribution by asking questions which the panellists must answer, prodded and shepherded when necessary by the presenter. Here, one might argue, the liberal democratic role of broadcasting is found in its purest form, *mediating* between the public and its politicians, providing the former with access to raw political discourse, and providing the politicians with a channel of direct access to the people.

Of course, these formats have always been strictly controlled, with panels, audiences and questions carefully selected so as to minimise the chance of extreme positions getting on air, or of excessive confrontation between participants breaking the mood of polite, parliamentary style debate. But as social deference has declined in recent years, and citizens grow used to treating their politicians like equals, traditional debate show formats have come to be seen as rather tame and excessively rule-governed. In America, meanwhile, the rise of the 'confessional' talk-show has shown a new approach. In response, the British schedules have seen a growth in the number of more lively, unpredictable talk-shows, as well as the reform of established programmes like *Question Time*. In the latter case, audience members are now invited to speak more freely than they once did, and to 'vote' at the end of debates. The chairman (at the time of writing, David Dimbleby) intervenes on behalf of the audience more aggressively than was traditionally the case, embarrassing the sometimes reluctant panellists into going beyond political 'waffle' and answering a question with some degree of clarity and directness. New programmes like *You Decide* and the *People's Parliament* seek new ways of organising public debate on television so that it is both informative, educational and entertaining. Although they have had varying degrees of success, all such experiments are valuable attempts, as Livingstone and Lunt put it, to establish 'new forms of relationship between experts and laity' (1994, p.131).

> In the audience discussion programme, experts [politicians in particular] and lay people are put together, setting an agenda of social issues and offering both established elites and ordinary people the opportunity at least to discuss the lived experience of current affairs issues in relation to expert solutions.
>
> (Ibid.)

### Broadcast punditry

Notwithstanding the requirements of impartiality imposed on the broadcasters in these and other contexts there are some formats in which broadcasting journalists, like their press counterparts, can go beyond the mere reporting of politics and move into the role of active participants. At the most general level, broadcasting works as part of the wider media system to define agendas and 'political realities' at any given time. Television and radio to a large extent follow the news agenda set by the press, one set of media feeding and reinforcing another's perceptions of what is important.

Straight news programmes do not, for the reasons already mentioned, stray far beyond the narrow reportage function. Mainstream bulletins on BBC1 and ITV, as one would expect, move quickly through the day's events, dealing only briefly with each. Moments of definition *are* included, however, in the form, firstly, of special correspondents. Like the political columnists of the press, the correspondents are in a sense pundits although, unlike the latter, their subjectivity and interpretative work must be confined to analysing the situation, as opposed to instructing, and appealing to, the audience. *Channel 4 News'* Elinor Goodman, for example, will frequently be asked by the programme's presenters to assess or make sense of a political event, be it a party leadership crisis or a crucial debate in the House of Commons. She will do so from a position of authority, based on her track record as an 'expert' in broadcasting terms, and on the fact that she clearly has access to reliable elite sources. In this respect she, and her colleagues like the BBC's Robin Oakley or John Sargent, trade on the same privileged access to elites enjoyed by the senior press columnists, and build their status as pundits upon that access. Where Hugo Young can say what he thinks about the Conservative or Labour parties, however, and even presume to advise them on a suitable course of action, Goodman, Oakley and their collegues on other channels must be satisfied with giving their audiences an insiders' view of 'what is really going on'. Their opinions and partialities on the substance of the issues must remain private. There are subtleties of language and tone which can be used by a correspondent to signify suspicion or distrust towards a politician, but such perceptions cannot be made explicit.

In general, then, the presenters of main news programmes maintain a clear distance from the events they are introducing to their audiences. They announce the news, and the special correspondent or political editor defines its meaning and significance. Some viewers of TV news may detect in a presenter's facial expression or voice tone an *attitude* towards the events being represented, but this is a deviation from the self- proclaimed norm.

### The political interview

The main context in which presenters may openly play a more active role in the political process is when they have the opportunity to interview political actors. The increased awareness of the importance of public relations by political actors means, as we shall see in Chapter 7, that they routinely make themselves available to the electronic media for interview whenever there is a news story which concerns them or on which they are particularly competent to speak. In the early days of broadcast journalism such interviews were rare, and pursued with a tooth-grinding deference on the part of the journalist, who would function essentially as a cue for the politician to make a series of pre-prepared, uncontested points. ITN, when it came on air in the 1950s, was the first British news organisation to seriously challenge this style, with Robin Day in the vanguard. His aggressive interviewing style became commonplace, and is now pursued even by presenters on peak-time news programmes, much to the chagrin of some politicians. Presenters such as Nicholas Witchell and Trevor McDonald, once rightly perceived as rather meek when confronted by a senior politician, now routinely engage in quite aggressive questioning. Interviewing styles which used to be reserved for left-wing anti-heroes like Arthur Scargill and Ken Livingstone are now directed towards government ministers, senior opposition figures, and other respected members of the political establishment.

That peak-time presenters with mass audiences should pursue such a confrontational relationship with political actors is not to be confused with 'subjective bias' (although many politicians who are victims of the style may prefer to think otherwise) but as an extension and development of the media's 'watchdog' role. One might also view it as a conscious effort to more effectively represent 'the people' who watch these bulletins in their millions, against the political elite.

The less popular broadcast news slots (Radio 4's *Today*, BBC2's *Newsnight*, *Channel 4 News*) have also developed the art of confrontation, partly because it makes for good viewing and listening, but also in recognition of the fact that *not* to confront a politician, not to play the role of 'devil's advocate', is now perceived as deferential and old-fashioned. The late Brian Redhead on Radio 4, Jon Snow and Zeinab Bidawi on Channel 4, and most famously of all in this respect, BBC2 *Newsnight* presenter Jeremy Paxman, have all adopted this approach to the politicians who agree to enter their studios. Jeremy Paxman's style itself became satirised, alongside the political caricatures, in *Spitting Image*. Paxman's approach is one of permanent, knowing scepticism of all that a politician says, an attitude which is communicated both to the audience and the interviewee in a variety of facial and linguistic gestures. While he and the other presenters who adopt a similar approach are unable to say out loud what they think of the responses received to their questions, audiences are hardly likely to miss the sarcasm and contempt which frequently emerges from the phrasing of a question or the tone of a voice. We may view these presenters, returning to Nimmo and Combs's categorisation, as 'bardic' pundits, not only in their advocacy of the popular against the elite, but in the dry humour which often accompanies the interview.

In broadcast news programmes the political interview is one element in a mix of reportage, commentary, and analyses. Some journalists, however, have elevated it to the status of a programme genre in itself. Robin Day's election interviews with party leaders, Brian Walden's and David Frost's Sunday interviews, Jonathan Dimbleby's lengthy interviews on the BBC's *On the Record*, and John Humphrys's *Today* interviews have been important agenda-setting moments in the political cycle. The politicians' motives and interests in subjecting themselves to interview have been discussed already. Here, we note again the combative, sometimes accusatory style of the Humphrys or Paxman interviews, and the now commonplace assumption that such an approach is both legitimate and necessary. These interview-celebrities, who with rare exceptions are very much the 'stars' of their shows, confront the politician with 'what the public wants to know'. Some, like Paxman, hang on to their victim like a pit-bull terrier, until the politicians' refusal or inability to answer is transparently revealed. Robin Day too, in his prime, had sufficient status as a pundit to discard the conventions of etiquette and deference which politicians could once expect to be observed in broadcasting studios. Such status is acquired, like that of the press columnist, by the interviewer's history of access to the inside track of politics, and the audience's knowledge that he (they are, as yet, mainly men, although Zeinab Badawi, Kirsty Wark and Sheena McDonald have emerged as future contenders) move in the same circles as those being interviewed. Indeed, both Robin Day and Brian Walden had backgrounds in professional politics.

The phenomenon of the 'star' interviewer, and the increasingly combative, adversarial style of broadcast political interview in the 1990s, has been a cause of considerable tension between the politicians and the broadcasters, especially the BBC. First the Tories, and then Labour in office, have attacked the BBC's most aggressive (some would say most effective) interviewers, like John Humphrys, Jeremy Paxman, Anna Ford, and Sue MacGregor, on the grounds that they are usurping the right of the elected politician to present his or her arguments on air. BBC managers have been regularly leaned on by both Labour and Conservative media 'minders' anxious to protect their clients, and to create a less adversarial interviewing environment. The interviewers have responded by saying that they are merely doing what their fourth estate role requires of them – standing up for the public, and representing its interests against a political class whose members now come to the broadcast studio armed to the teeth with sophisticated public relations and news management techniques, designed to maximise the free flow of nice-sounding but politically empty rhetoric. The adversarial interview, say its advocates, is a necessary tool to cut through this rhetorical gloss and expose the hard core of policy beneath.

In a notorious case of this technique in action, Jeremy Paxman once asked a Conservative minister exactly the same question *fourteen* consecutive times, and still failed to get the straight answer he wanted, thereby communicating a powerful message about the politician's prognostication and evasiveness. At other times interviewers have crossed the line from legitimate questioning into the realm of rudeness and self-importance, elevating the demonstration of their own inquisitorial cleverness over the carrying out of the journalistic tasks at hand. On balance, however, and in the face of such intensively deployed public relations techniques as are explored in

Chapter 7, the adversarial interview is best viewed as an important, if sometimes flawed means of broadcast analysis and interpretation of political rhetoric.

In all of the above-mentioned formats, the political journalist is balancing the role of advocacy with the requirements of impartiality set down by law and convention. There is now one type of programme, however, in which the pundits can 'come out', as it were, and say what they think – the political talk-show. The best example of such a show on British television has seen Channel 4's *A Week In Politics*, which contains most of the elements listed above – reportage, interviews, etc. – but also features the relatively new (for British broadcasting) device of bringing together two pundits – Andrew Rawnsley and the late Vincent Hanna – to chat in informal, relaxed tones about the events of the week. The comments made are rarely controversial, but they *are* subjective, and presented as such to the viewer. The continuing proliferation of TV channels and journalistic outlets, and the resulting decline in importance of any single channel, is likely to mean greater efforts by the broadcasters to 'subvert' the conventions of impartiality, and allow TV to approximate more closely to the more overtly authored, opinionated forms of coverage long established in the press.


## THE EXPERTS

We note, finally, the participation in political journalism of non-journalists: the politicians, of course, but also those who, by virtue of scholastic achievement, or some other legitimating mechanism, are defined as 'experts' on a particular political issue. These specialist pundits are 'qualified' to speak on the issues, making sense of them for the layperson. Like the educated elites of the early public sphere (Habermas, 1989) they are called upon to share with us, the people, their wisdom and learning. Their views are taken seriously precisely because they have been defined as expert. I have written elsewhere about patterns of access to television news on the subject of East–West relations (McNair, 1988), noting there that these experts – or 'primary definers', as Stuart Hall has called them (Hall *et al.*, 1978) – are not necessarily especially knowledgeable. The point, from the journalists' perspective, is that they are *seen* to be expert, and can thus help to confirm the authority and credibility of the news or current affairs programmes to which they contribute.

Expert pundits are used with particular frequency in coverage of economic policy (usually recruited from City finance and banking houses), obscure or faraway places (note *Channel 4 News*'s reliance on Professor Peter Franks of Essex University to make sense of events in Russia), and military policy, where retired generals and admirals are regular contributors.

Retired politicians, for the same reasons as academics and other experts, are employed as pundits to give an insider's view on current issues. Nimmo and Combs write of the 'pundit-sage' (1992, p.67), referring to those elder statesmen (and occasionally women) who pontificate with the authority of village elders on the current generation of leaders. In America, such a sage is Henry Kissinger. In Britain, Denis Healey and Edward Heath play the role, as do Margaret Thatcher and John Major.

We should also note here the role of the opinion pollster, usually called upon in person only during election campaigns, although opinion polls are a constant element of press and broadcast coverage of politics. The opinion pollsters are authorised to tell us what the public thinks, and give their views on how to interpret those thoughts.

## CONCLUSION

At the end of this chapter, and of Part I, we have done five things. Firstly, the normative role of the media in liberal democratic politics was defined. Secondly, the media environment within which contemporary politics, and political journalism in particular, must be pursued, has been described. Thirdly, we have outlined the effects debate, as it relates to political communication. We then looked at those determinants of the media production process which shape the extent to which politics is covered, and how it is covered. And finally, a description was given of the many forms in which media professionals talk about politics, or provide platforms and spaces for others to do so.

Throughout these chapters, we have stressed the importance for those involved in politics of knowing and understanding how the media works. Part II will consider how and with what degree of success political actors of various kinds have applied this knowledge to the construction and presentation of effective political communication.

# Part II

# COMMUNICATING POLITICS

# 6

# PARTY POLITICAL
# COMMUNICATION I
## Advertising

Robert Denton argues that in America, thanks to the growth in the role of television in political campaigning, the pre-eminent form of political oratory has become the advertisement. The political ad, he writes, is 'now the major means by which candidates for the presidency communicate their messages to voters' (1988, p.5). Nimmo and Felsberg suggest that 'paid political advertising via television now constitutes the mainstream of modern electoral politics' (1986, p.248). In Britain and other comparable countries too, although regulatory and stylistic conventions differ from those of the United States, political advertising is central to political communication.

Advertising's power – if power it has (a by no means uncontentious assertion, as Chapter 3 suggested) – is exercised on two levels. Firstly, the political advertisement disseminates information about the candidate's or party's programme to a degree of detail which television journalists can rarely match. As Chapter 4 argued, television news has developed generic conventions and narrative practices which inhibit in-depth analysis of political parties' policies. Instead, the broadcasters fasten pack-like on to the day's soundbites (often deliberately planted by the politicians' public relations staff) which are repeated endlessly. Hart's analysis of TV coverage of US presidential speeches shows just how few, on average, of a speechmaker's words are reported in the news (1987), and how much amounts to mere repetition of a few key words and phrases. In this context, to the extent that television is the major source of political information for most people, the advertisement is the format in which a political actor has the greatest opportunity to impart 'the issues' as he or she sees them.

Of course, as in the world of commerce, the advertisement does not merely inform individuals in society about the choices available to them as political consumers. They are also designed to *persuade*.

And in persuasion, as well as information dissemination, the advertisement has clear advantages for the politician. Most obviously, editorial control resides with the politician, and not the media. Within legal constraints of truth and taste, which vary from one country to another, the producers of political advertisements have the freedom to say what they like; to replace the journalists' agenda with their own; to play to their clients' strengths and highlight the opponents' weaknesses. The advertisement, in short, is the only mass media form over the construction of which the politician has complete control.

At the same time, the viewer is aware of this control and may, as Chapter 3 suggested, reject the message contained in an advertisement. The political actor controls the *encoding* of an advertisement, but not its *decoding*. That said, a *New York Times*/CBS poll conducted during the 1988 US presidential election found that 25 per cent of the voters claimed that political ads had influenced their choice of candidate (Denton and Woodward, 1990, p.56).

Notwithstanding the uncertainty inherent in transmitting political messages through the format of advertising, it has steadily grown as a proportion of campaign resources. In 1988, George Bush and Michael Dukakis spent between them some $85 million on television advertising (Ibid., p.56). During the 1992 presidential campaign George Bush's team spent upwards of $60 million on television advertising alone. In 1996 the Clinton campaign spent more than $50 million. In the 1997 British general election campaign, more than ever before was spent by the three main parties. Whether advertisements work or not, therefore, no discussion of political communication would be complete without consideration of them.


## POLITICAL ADVERTISING: A DEFINITION

Bolland defines advertising as the 'paid placement of organisational messages in the media' (1989, p.10).[1] Political advertising therefore, in the strict sense, refers to the purchase and use of advertising space, paid for at commercial rates, in order to transmit political messages to a mass audience. The media used for this purpose may include cinema, billboards, the press, radio, and television.

In the United States, television ads are known as 'spots', and their cost in the world's richest media market largely accounts for the extraordinary expense of US political campaigning. In some countries, however, paid political advertising on television and radio is restricted by law. In Britain, while paid advertising can be bought in newspapers, cinemas, and billboards, parties are pro-hibited from buying broadcast airtime. Instead, they are allocated free airtime in which to transmit party political broadcasts (PPBs) and party election broadcasts (PEBs). The allocation of airtime is based on the number of candidates which a party stands at a general election.

While PPBs and PEBs (and their equivalents in other countries) are not 'paid for' advertisements in the American sense, they are produced by companies like Saatchi using the same techniques and with the same budgets as commercial advertisers. For our purposes, therefore, PPBs are included alongside American 'spots' in this chapter's discussion of political advertising, both forms having in common the fact that the politicians (or the creative staff to whom they delegate the work) have complete artistic and editorial control over them.

## HOW ADVERTISEMENTS WORK

Advertising, as was noted above, has two functions in the process of exchange between a producer (of goods, services, or political programmes) and the consumer. Firstly, it *informs*. The political process, as we observed in Chapter 1, is supposed to involve *rational* choices by voters, which must be based on information. Journalism represents one important source of such information, advertising another. So, just as early product advertisements were little more than simple messages about the availability of a brand, its price and function (use), so contemporary political advertising can be seen as an important means of informing citizens about *who* is standing, and what they are offering the citizenry in policy terms.

But advertising, as already noted, also seeks to persuade. In the 1950s, writing of the role of advertising in American consumer capitalism, Pierre Martineau observed that

> in our competitive system, few products are able to main-tain any technical superiority for long. They must be invested with overtones to individualise them; they must be endowed with richness of association and imagery; they must have many levels of meanings, if we expect them to be

top sellers, if we hope that they will achieve the emotional attachment which shows up as brand loyalty.

(1957, p.50)

In a marketplace where there are twenty brands of soap powder, all performing essentially the same function (or thirty automobiles, or fifty types of margarine), each brand must take on a unique identity in the minds of the consumer. To use the language of Marx: the manufacturer creates a commodity by endowing raw materials with 'use-value' (or utility). The advertiser gives it 'exchange-value', which will be based partly on utility, but also on its meaning as a distinctive entity in a status-conscious world. Baudrillard writes of products having 'sign-value', in so far as they 'are at once use-value and exchange-value. The social hierarchies, the invidious differences, the privileges of caste and culture which they support, are encountered as profit, as personal satisfaction, and lived as "need"' (1988, p.59). Commodities come to *signify* meanings other than those of their utility. A Porsche is more than a vehicle for transporting people from one point to another. Levi 501s are more than hard-wearing work garments. Flora margarine is more than an oily spread. And in so far as commodities take on these meanings, advertising is the most important means available to producers for bringing them to the market.

Advertisements function, therefore, by making commodities *mean* something to their prospective purchasers; by distinguishing one product from another, functionally similar one; and by doing this in a manner which connects with the desires of the consumer. As Leiss *et al.* put it, 'in advertising, the creators of messages try to turn signifiers [commodities] with which audiences may have little or no familiarity, into meaningful signs that, they hope, will prompt consumers to respond with appropriate behaviour' (1986, p.153).

A variety of strategies are available to advertisers in pursuing this goal. All have in common that they import *familiar* (to the audience) meanings and signifiers from outside the narrow world of the product itself, and load them on. The products being advertised appropriate meanings from other signifiers existing in the culture (Williamson [1978] calls them 'meaning systems'). For example, the advertising of soap powder is frequently organised around the meaning system of 'science'. In advanced capitalist societies, 'science' carries with it many positive connotations – objectivity, authority, reliability, 'modernness', and so on. Thus, in a soap powder ad we frequently find a white-coated 'scientist' 'proving' the effectiveness of the product as against others in the market. The high cultural status of the scientist, and the scientific procedure which he (it is, usually, a 'he') demonstrates, legitimises the product.

Another frequently used meaning system is that of nostalgia. In the classic British example of this technique – the 1985 advertisement for Hovis bread[2] — the product was placed in a mythical past where 'natural', 'wholesome' techniques of manufacturing bread were used, and in which people were honest and hard-working. These attributes – 'naturalness', 'wholesomeness', 'honesty' – were implied by the structure of the ad to be in the bread. Such a strategy could only work in a culture which values nostalgia, and associates it with the attributes mentioned. In Britain in the 1980s, such a culture was clearly thought to exist by the advertiser concerned.

Advertisements may be constructed so as to associate their product-signifiers with well-known icons from the wider culture. Perfumes, for example, are often 'sold' by associating them with former models and film stars. Each 'star'-signifier has a distinctive meaning for the audience (Vanessa Paradis is not Elizabeth Taylor, who is different from Kate Moss, who is not Catherine Deneuve, etc.). The perfume manufacturer aspires to borrow this meaning, and thus give the product an analogous distinctiveness. This strategy is perhaps the most commonly used, in the advertising of everything from training shoes to banking services (Pirelli's Sharon Stone ad, and Michelin's use of the Velvet Underground song 'Femme Fatale' reveal the subtleties of selling tyres in modern capitalism), and may be applied not just to human icons, but also to famous movies (such as *Close Encounters of the Third Kind* and *Star Wars*), songs, paintings, and other signifiers with broad cultural resonance. In this manner 'advertising affects a "transfer of value" through communicative connections between what a culture conceives as desirable states of being and products' (Leiss *et al.*, 1986, p.222).

## ADVERTISING AND POLITICS

The perceived success of advertising in post-war consumer capitalism (made possible by the advent of mass television) led directly to the hypothesis that such strategies of persuasion could be applied to the political process. By the 1950s there were in the United States some 19 million television sets. Advertising executive Rosser Reeves, inventor of the marketing concept of the 'Unique Selling

Proposition' (USP) and responsible, among other famous slogans, for the 'M&Ms melt in your mouth, not in your hand' campaign, pioneered the view that if commercial 'spots' could sell products, they could sell politicians too.

There are, of course, significant ways in which political advertising, by the nature of what it is selling, differs from commercial advertising. However, the strategies of association described above are, as Rosser Reeves suggested that they could be, frequently applied to politicians. As was noted in Chapter 2 politics *has* become, for better or worse, a process in which 'consumers' are presented, through the mass media, with a range of policies from which they must select. As Nimmo and Felsberg put it, 'political candidates must frequently offer themselves as differing brands of the same product' (1986, p.252).[3]

These choices are 'manufactured', moreover, to contain not merely a 'use-value' (political party A will run the country efficiently) but an exchange or sign-value (political party A *means* this, as opposed to political party B, which means something else entirely). In the process of endowing political actors with meaning, advertisers have deployed all the techniques of their commercial colleagues, while also producing a few of their own.

## A BRIEF HISTORY OF POLITICAL ADVERTISING: THE UNITED STATES

A history of political advertising should begin with the United States because it is here that the techniques of the form were pioneered and where they have reached their highest level of sophistication. America, having become the twentieth century's most successful capitalist power, has gone faster, and further, in commodifying the political process by the use of advertising than any other country. Moreover, the techniques developed in the United States have been exported to Britain and other countries, as we shall see in the next section.

Political advertising is sometimes viewed as a distinctively modern, not entirely welcome product of the electronic media age. While this is obviously true for television advertising, the use of media to sell politicians is by no means a recent phenomenon. Kathleen Jamieson points out that long before the era of mass electronic media US political campaigning was still very much about motivating citizens to exercise their democratic prerogative by voting. By means of pamphlets, posters, and public events such as parades and rallies, nineteenth-century Americans were persuaded to support particular candidates and reject others. Candidates and parties wrote campaign songs, which functioned like modern ads, summarising policy themes and promises. As Jamieson notes:

> those who pine for presidential campaigns as they were in Jefferson, Jackson, or Lincoln's times and who see our nation's political decline and fall mirrored in the rise of political spot advertising remember a halcyon past that never was. The transparencies, bandanas, banners, songs and cartoons that pervaded nineteenth century campaigning telegraphed conclusions, not evidence ... Their messages were briefer ... than those of any sixty second spot ad. The air then was filled not with substantive disputes but with simplification, sloganeering and slander.
>
> (1986, p.12)

If such features of political campaigning preceded the electronic age, however, they were invested with a qualitatively different significance by the invention of radio and TV. Political advertising ceased to be a form of interpersonal communication experienced simultaneously by a few hundreds or thousands of people at most, and became mass communication about politics, with audiences of many millions.

By the early 1950s, as already noted, television had become a truly mass medium in the United States, supported financially by advertising revenue. In the 1952 presidential campaign General Eisenhower became the first candidate to employ a professional advertising company to design television advertisements, on which $1 million were eventually spent. The agency of Batten, Barton, Dustine, and Osbourne was selected to design the campaign, while Rosser Reeves assisted in formulating Eisenhower's 'unique selling proposition'. This was based around the idea of 'spontaneity', in the sense that Eisenhower's television campaign would focus on his ability to be spontaneous when meeting citizens, answering their questions and presenting his policies with ease and accessibility.

This was indeed a 'unique selling proposition' in the context of the times, and in some contrast to the approach of his opponent, Adlai Stevenson, who conveyed an impression of serious bookishness which, as with British Labour leader Michael Foot some thirty years later, was perhaps better suited to the pre-television age.

Eisenhower's spontaneity was articulated in a series of 'Eisenhower Answers America' spots, showing him answering questions from the American public. The setting up of the questions and answers was far from being spontaneous, of course, and to a 1990s audience the results look stilted and clumsy. Eisenhower, nevertheless, won the election, reinforcing a growing belief in political advertising's effectiveness as a campaigning instrument.

The 'Eisenhower Answers America' spots were primitive, but nevertheless established political advertising as an essential element of any self-respecting candidate's armoury. From the 1952 campaign onwards, 'spot' political advertising increased in sophistication and production values, acquiring what Diamond and Bates describe as 'distinctive rhetorical modes and visual styles' (1992, p.x), with several trends clearly apparent.

## The shrinking spot

Firstly, US political ads have tended to become shorter in duration. Although the Eisenhower spots were relatively brief (around 30 seconds), the 1956 campaign saw the introduction of five-minute advertisements, sandwiched between popular entertainment programmes in an effort to benefit from the latter's large audience share. Candidates also bought airtime in 30-minute chunks, which were then used to elaborate at length on their policy positions. Research found, however, that audiences quickly grew bored with advertisements of such length, and switched off (literally or figuratively). In response, political advertisers moved towards shorter spots after 1956. With some exceptions (such as Ross Perot's 1992 presidential campaign) the preference of campaign organisers ever since has been for 30- or 60-second spots. This format is clearly not one in which campaign issues and candidate's policies can be discussed at any length, giving rise to the aforementioned criticism of advertising's negative impact on the political process. The *form* of the 30/60-second spots, it is argued, determines a content which is inevitably grounded in image rather than substantive issues.

## The rise of image

The second general trend in US political advertising, then, is towards greater emphasis on the construction of a candidate's image (or the destruction of an opponent's), and away from the communication of an issue or policy position. Richard Joslyn observes that of 506 'spots' shown on American television between 1960 and 1984, only 15 per cent contained information about specific policies, while 57 per cent addressed the personal and professional qualities of the candidate – his or her 'image' (1986).

In 1992, successful candidate Bill Clinton's image was constructed around notions of youth, vigour, and radicalism, contrasting vividly (as it was surely meant to) with the advanced age and conservatism of his opponent George Bush. Ronald Reagan's image was that of a 'nice guy' – handsome and congenial, while firm and unbending against the enemies of freedom. Jimmy Carter's image, which helped him to be elected in 1976, was of a self-made small businessman (peanut farmer), independent of the Washington establishment which had produced the corruption of Richard Nixon and the complacency of Gerald Ford.

For Joslyn, the prominence of image in advertising is 'a troubling discovery' (Ibid., p.180), confirming the widely-held view that advertising-dominated election campaigns are far removed from the normative ideal of the liberal democratic process, in which citizens learn and choose rationally on the basis of policy. As he puts it, 'we are forced to ponder the possibility that our electoral process does not enhance the type of information-holding and political choice that are the most clearly and directly associated with democratic theory' (Ibid., p.183).

## Myth and symbol

If it is a matter of empirical fact that American political advertisements have become steadily more image-oriented, rather than issue-oriented, in terms of what they say about the candidates they are selling, it is also true that ads have become more symbolic, or mythological (in the Barthian sense). In the 1960s US 'spots' began to apply the socio-psychological theories of motivation and consumer behaviour then prevailing in the commercial advertising world. In the 1964 presidential campaign Tony Schwarz prepared spots for the Democrats which reflected his belief that 'the best political commercials are similar to Rorsbach patterns. They do not tell the viewer anything. They surface his feelings and provide a context for him to express those feelings. Commercials that attempt to tell the listener something are inherently not as effective as those that attach to something that is already in him' (quoted in Diamond and Bates, 1984, p.133). From this perspective, the political advertiser should not seek to win a presidential vote by packing a spot with rational information about policy. Rather, the fears, anxieties, and deep-rooted desires of a culture should be uncovered and tapped into, and then associated with a particular candidate.

In 1964 Schwarz pioneered this method with the 'Daisy' advertisement, made for Lyndon Johnson's presidential campaign against right-wing republican Barry Goldwater. The advertisement began with the image of a little all-American girl, sitting in a field and plucking the petals from a daisy. As she does so, she counts 'one, two, three', etc. Then, this idyllic image of American childhood is shattered by the rude intervention of another, male voice, counting down 'ten, nine, eight' to zero, at which point the screen is filled with the dramatic image of a thermonuclear explosion. A voiceover then tells the viewer that to avoid this scenario he or she should vote for Johnson and not Goldwater.

The advertisement works by surfacing the widespread anxiety of the American people (at the height of the Cold War), about the dangers of nuclear annihilation in conflict with the Soviet Union, and linking that danger with the policies of the Republican candidate. Goldwater was vulnerable in this respect because of his openly hawkish attitude to the Soviets, and a tendency to make jokes about 'dropping atom bombs in the men's room at the Kremlin'. Schwarz's spot exploited Goldwater's reputation and made it work on behalf of the Democratic candidate.

The manifest emotionality of the ad's construction generated controversy at the time, and indeed such was the feeling of outrage at the use of such manipulative tactics that it was shown only once during the campaign (and once in the context of a news item). Subsequently, however, the emotional appeal has become a routinely deployed tactic, if not always in such dramatic fashion. In 1984 the Reagan re-election campaign produced a 'Morning for America' spot, depicting in glossy rustic tints an America of hard-working, God-fearing pioneers. The advertisement tapped into what the campaign's researchers had established was a deep longing amongst many Americans for a past and a country like the one depicted in the film. The 'American dream', or myth, was then attached to the concept of the Reagan presidency.

The same strategy was applied by the Reagan campaign team to foreign policy. In one spot a deep, soothing voice warned viewers that 'there's a bear in the woods'. Here, the Reagan campaign was manipulating the fear of communism and the 'Russian bear'. Demonising the Soviets was of course a central feature of Reagan's presidency, and this ad sought to identify him with the defence against it. Although the name of Reagan's opponent in 1984, Walter Mondale, was not mentioned in the ad, the film attempted to secure the audience's assent to the notion that another Reagan term was the best defence America had against communism.

To manipulate mythology and deep-rooted cultural values in this way implies a degree of sophistication in the market research carried out by campaigners. Ronald Reagan's electoral success has been ascribed in large part to the market research efforts of key media advisers like Dick Wirthlin and Roger Ailes, who successfully identified the motivations and values underlying the voting behaviour of key sectors of the American electorate. As former Conservative media adviser Brendan Bruce puts it, Wirthlin's *value* research for the Reagan campaigns 'represents the most important advance in political communication of the last two decades. It provides the image makers with the best possible guide to the effective presentation of policy, by creating a clear understanding of how voters make their choice of party. It also supplied them with a rich and subtle vocabulary of persuasive language and motivating symbols' (1992, p.87). As we shall shortly see, such techniques are now also applied to the British campaigning process.

### Signifying power

Before leaving the subject of values, emotions and symbolism, we should note the importance in political advertising of symbols of power and status, and the advantages which these give to an incumbent candidate or party. A candidate in office, such as Nixon in 1972 and Reagan in 1984, inevitably acquires a stock of experience and credibility which can be represented in advertisements by the use of archive footage of press conferences, foreign tours, meetings with international leaders, and so on. These visuals, with appropriate verbal accompaniments, become powerful signifiers of authority against a challenger whose administrative experience may be limited to the governorship of a small state.

In 1988 George Bush made effective use of this device. Although not himself an incumbent president, he deployed his considerable experience as vice-president, and former head of the CIA and Congress, to market himself as practically a president already. One spot showed him in a protective embrace with Ronald Reagan (signifying the trust and endorsement of the still-popular president), meeting Gorbachov and Thatcher, and signing treaties – all images of 'presidentness' to which Michael Dukakis had no response. Bush tried to appropriate to himself the symbolic power of the presidency, a tactic which may have contributed to his win in 1988, although it failed to prevent his defeat four years later.

## Negatives

Another controversial or 'attack' trend in US political advertising has been towards the 'negative' spot, i.e., advertisements which focus on the alleged weaknesses of an opponent rather than on the positive attributes of the candidate him or herself. In the context of American television, negative advertising has played a part in campaigning from the outset, taking on a more important role from the 1964 presidential election onwards. Tony Schwarz's 'Daisy' spot was a negative, highlighting Goldwater's alleged propensity to be confrontational towards the USSR. The spot was structured around Goldwater's 'negative', rather than Johnson's positive characteristics (other than, of course, the fact that Johnson was not Goldwater). While, as Kathleen Jamieson noted earlier, 'simplification, sloganeering, and slander' (all usually important elements in a negative spot) were not invented by televisual political advertising, the perception of most observers has been that negatives have become more prevalent with the growing centrality of television in campaigning. Kaid and Johnston argue that the 1980s in particular were a decade in which negative campaigns and 'mudslinging' came to predominate. In the presidential election campaign of 1988, they calculate, between 60 and 70 per cent of all political advertising consisted of negatives (1991).

Indeed, 1988 was the year of the best known negative of all – the 'Willie Horton' spot produced by supporters of George Bush in his presidential contest against Michael Dukakis (Diamond and Bates, 1992; Jamieson, 1992). The spot accused Dukakis of being 'soft' on crime during his tenure as governor of Massachusetts, citing the release on weekend leave of convicted murderer Willie Horton. Horton, the ad informed viewers, took the opportunity of his break from jail to sexually assault someone else. Dukakis's liberal approach to law and order in Massachusetts became a negative, used against him with what most observers of the 1988 campaign considered to be devastating effect.

Another negative spot by the Bush side contrasted Dukakis's declared 'green' policy with his record as governor in Boston, where it was alleged he had allowed the harbour to become polluted. Successful in 1988 (in so far as he won), Bush's negatives in the

1992 campaign against Bill Clinton did not prevent the latter from winning. One ad, for example, highlighted Clinton's avoidance of the draft in the 1960s, asking viewers if this was the kind of man they would wish to see as US Commander-in-Chief. Other ads referred to well-known Clinton lapses, such as smoking (but not inhaling) marijuana and having extra-marital affairs. Clinton won nevertheless, the voters apparently regarding such peccadilloes as irrelevant to his presidential potential, or at the very least out-weighed by what they perceived as Bush's poor record. This failure suggests that the fears of some observers as to the impact of negative political advertising on the democratic process are overstated. Ansolabehere and Iyengar, for example, state that negative ads 'sup-press voter turnout', are responsible for 'record lows in political participation, and record highs in public cynicism and alienation' and 'thus pose a serious anti-democratic threat' (1995, p.9). We might just as reasonably argue, however, not least on the evidence of two Clinton election victories, won against ferocious negative advertising from his opponents, that the effects of such messages are heavily qualified by other features of the political environment, and by the voters' readiness to discount them if they do not resonate.

## A typology of political advertising

As political advertising evolved in the United States political scien-tists attempted to identify the main stylistic conventions of the genre. Based on an analysis of more than 30 years of political spots, one observer has listed eight types (Devlin, 1986).

In the beginning, as already noted in our discussion of 'Eisen-hower Answers America', ads were *primitive*, in so far as their rehearsed, constructed quality was obvious to the viewer.

Then came *talking head* spots, designed 'to focus on an issue and allow the candidate to convey an image impression that he can handle the issues, and most importantly, that he can handle the job' (Ibid., p.26). An early example of this type was Richard Nixon's 1956 'Checkers' speech delivered to the nation on paid-for televi-sion time, and in which, as Eisenhower's vice-presidential running mate, he sought to counter allegations of corruption. During the 1992 campaign the format was used by Ross Perot to address the American people on economic issues.

The aforementioned *negative* type of political ad is generally accepted to have fully emerged in the 1960s, becoming more visible ever since, as has the *production* (or *concept*) ad, designed to convey important ideas about candidates' (Ibid., p.27). Concept ads avoid overly personalising a campaign (Jamieson, 1986), seeking instead to project 'the big idea' about a candidate. The Reagan 'concept', for example, was frequently expressed in terms of 'getting government off the backs of the people', or 'being tough with the commies'. George Bush's was 'experience' and 'reliability', while Bill Clinton's successful 1992 concept was 'a time for change' – the need for it, and the suggestion that he embodied it.

*Cinéma-vérité* spots are those which depict the candidates in 'real life settings interacting with people' (Devlin, 1986, p.29). We referred above to the tactic often used by incumbents of using archive news footage to show a candidate being 'presidential', 'governorial', etc. The *cinéma-vérité* technique may also be used in more informal settings such as meet-the-people walkabouts, or in depicting scenes from a candidate's home or work life (one of Jimmy Carter's 1976 spots showed him at work on his Georgia peanut farm).

It goes without saying that such footage will often be scripted and rehearsed, even if the intention is to give the impression of spontaneity and informality.

Devlin also identifies two forms of what Jamieson calls 'personal witness' ads (1986), in which the views of non-candidates are enlisted for the purposes of endorsement. Those interviewed may be the *man-in-the-street* [sic], using vox pop techniques to demonstrate the 'ordinary voters' support for a candidate. More commonly, personal witness ads are *testimonials*, in which the endorsing is done by famous and respected personalities from the worlds of politics, entertainment, the arts and sport. This is the political advertisers' variant of the association strategy used by commercial advertisers described above. In testimonials, the authority and status of the witness is (the advertiser hopes) transferred to the candidate/ product.

To this list Jamieson adds the *neutral reporter* format, in which the viewer is presented with a series of apparently factual statements about a candidate (or the opponent) and then invited to make a judgment. While 'neutrality' is obviously absent from such an advertisement (the tactic is used frequently in the most cynically negative of spots) the speaker adopts the narrative conventions which signify neutrality and objectivity to impart the message. The intended *impression* is one of neutrality.

From the professional perspective of the advertiser, each of these types of ad will present different problems and objectives. Sometimes (though relatively rarely, as we have seen) the goal of an ad will be to articulate policy. Elsewhere, particularly in relation to an incumbent's campaign for re-election, it will be necessary to claim credit for real or alleged successes. The challenger's advertising, on the other hand, will aim to prioritise the real or alleged failures of the incumbent. In other cases still, the aim of the ad will be problem-identification. A key element of Ross Perot's 1992 television campaign, for example, was to identify for voters a problem – the economy and how to improve it – which he felt was being neglected. Problem-identification of this type may also be thought of as agenda-setting.

Diamond and Bates (1992) identify four phases of a typical US political advertising campaign:

- Firstly, the basic identity of the candidate must be established as a foundation on which to build subsequent information. In this phase, positive biographical details are highlighted, such as a distinguished war record (a tactic used by John F. Kennedy and George Bush in their presidential campaigns), or outstanding business success.
- Secondly, the candidate's policies are established in broad terms with the minimum of extraneous detail, and with emotional charge (as in Bush's 'Read my lips! No new taxes!' slogan, or Bill Clinton's 'It's the economy, stupid', also of 1992).
- Thirdly, the opponent should be attacked, using negatives.
- And finally, the candidate must be endowed with positive meaning in the context of the values and aspirations of the electorate (as these have been identified by market researchers). In this phase the campaign will seek to synthesise and integrate the candidate's positive features, allowing him or her to acquire resonance in the minds of the voters. Thus, Ronald Reagan comes to stand for the reassertion of traditional American values; Bill Clinton for 'change' in 1992, and 'continuity' in 1996. Dick Morris's account of the Clinton re-election campaign shows how the president, with the help of sophisticated political marketing, shrewdly positioned himself between left and right, adopting a strategy of 'triangulation' (1997). This meant, as already noted, taking the most popular themes and policies from the Democrats on the one hand (a strong welfare programme, for example), and the Republicans on the other (strong on law and order, welfare to work).

## POLITICAL ADVERTISING IN THE UNITED KINGDOM

Political advertising, as noted at the beginning of this chapter, was pioneered in the United States, and has reached its highest level of sophistication there. But the techniques, styles, and formats described above have been exported to other liberal democracies in which the media play an equally central cultural role. In Britain, as already noted, paid political advertising on television is prohibited (though not advertising in the press, the cinema, or on billboards). As the Independent Television Commission's Code of Practice puts it, 'no commercial made by a body of a political nature is allowed, or an ad directed at a political end, or one related to an industrial dispute, or one which shows partiality in political or industrial controversy, or which relates to current public policy'.

But 'party political broadcasts' can easily be viewed as advertising, given that, in them, 'the source controls the message' (Johnson and Elebash, 1986, p.303) and that, increasingly, professional advertising and marketing agencies are employed by the parties to make them.

As was the case in America, British political advertising predates broadcasting, with parties utilising print and other media to disseminate campaign messages from the nineteenth century. As in the USA, it emerged as a major element of the political process only with the spread of television as a mass medium in the 1950s. Unsurprisingly, perhaps, professional advertising and marketing techniques were first adopted in Britain by the party of capitalism, the Conservatives. For reasons which we shall examine later (see pp. 114–21), the Labour Party, though initially enthusiastic about the use of television as a political marketing tool, spent most of the period between the mid-1950s and the mid-1980s resisting the appeal of professional image-makers, a factor which may well have contributed to their gradual decline as a party during this period.

The Tories, on the other hand, began to employ television advertising as early as 1955, having noted the success of Eisenhower's 1952 campaign and the role of advertising in it. Early Conservative broadcasts were, according to the typology introduced in the previous section, 'primitive', depicting the government of Harold Macmillan in obviously staged 'spontaneous discussion' about the successes of their term in office. Like the 'Eisenhower Answers America' spots, these were pioneering but essentially flawed advertisements, the understandable product of unfamiliarity with a new medium.

In Michael Cockerell's view, the first 'television election' was that of 1955, when the Tories hired Roland Gillard as their media adviser, ushering in a period of professionalism in their political advertising which the Labour Party completely failed to match (1988). The 1955 campaign included a powerful broadcast starring Harold Macmillan articulating Britain's continuing role as a force for peace and progress in the world. In 1959 the Conservatives became the first British party to hire a commercial advertising company to run its campaign. Colman, Prentice and Varley were paid £250,000 for a campaign which directly targeted the young, affluent, working-class electorate on whom the Tories then depended for the retention of political power. For the first time, argues Cockerell, advertising was used 'to promote the Party and its leaders like a commercial product' (Ibid., p.66).

The Conservatives won the 1959 election, but lost the 1964 campaign, despite the best efforts of Colman, Prentice and Varley, against the background of a party deeply divided and demoralised by the Profumo affair and other scandals. In 1969, as another election loomed, the agency of Davidson, Pearce, Barry, and Tuck, Inc., introduced *target marketing* for the Tories, and the subsequent general election of 1970 witnessed the most media-conscious campaign ever in Britain. As Cockerell puts it, 'the Tories attempted to use the techniques and idioms of television with which viewers were most familiar. They . . . employed all the most sophisticated modern means of persuasion and marketing that the advertising industry had devised . . . [as a result] the Tories succeeded in increasing the marginal propensity to buy among the voters' (Ibid., p.169) and won the election. One advertisement used the visual and narrative style associated with ITV's popular and authoritative *News at Ten* programme. Another played with the conventions of commercial advertising, depicting a housewife 'fed up' with the old brand – Labour – and willing to try the new, Conservative, product.

Despite its successful use of political advertising in 1970 the Conservative government led by Edward Heath became publicly associated with severe economic and industrial problems, such as the miners' strike and the three-day week, leading to its defeat in the general election of 1974. In 1976 Heath was replaced as leader by Margaret Thatcher, who continued the Tories' pioneering approach to political advertising with the appointment of Saatchi and Saatchi to run the 1979 election campaign.

By 1983 the Conservatives had employed a full-time Director of Marketing, Chris Lawson, who worked with Saatchi and Saatchi to design a campaign which relied to a greater extent than ever before on US-style value research and 'psychographics' of the kind described above in connection with Ronald Reagan's campaigns. Johnson and Elebash note that 'during the pre-election months, the Conservatives were conducting focus groups on political words and phraseology' (1986, p.301). Cockerell writes that throughout the previous year 'Saatchi and Saatchi had been engaged in "qualitative" research about voters' attitudes. Their surveys revealed a powerful nostalgia for imperialism, thrift, duty and hard work which chimed in with the Prime Minister's own beliefs' (1988, p.278). On her return from a post-Falklands War public relations tour Margaret Thatcher 'endorsed "Victorian values" ', the need for a return to which underpinned much of the Tories' advertising. As Ivan Fallon has described it in his biography of the Saatchis, their 1983 campaign was to be based on what account executive Tim Bell called:

'the emotional attitudes which emerge when ordinary people discuss politics'. There were hours of discussion about finding the right tone, which had to be 'warm, confident, non-divisive, and exciting', and analysis of what all these objectives actually meant. There was quantitative and qualitative research, much talk about 'directional research', 'target areas', how to attract women voters, skilled workers, and much else.

(1988, p.157)

In the general election campaign of 1987 the same approach was adopted, with Saatchi and Saatchi again producing the PEBs. This time, qualitative market research showed a popular desire for a more 'caring' image on the part of Margaret Thatcher and her government. By 1987, moreover, as the next section describes, the Labour Party had joined in the professional marketing game, providing the Conservatives, for the first time, with serious competition in the advertising elements of the campaign. Amongst the broadcasts prepared by Saatchi and Saatchi was one depicting the prime minister in 'elder stateswoman' mode, travelling to the Soviet Union (as it still was), meeting and 'doing business' with Gorbachov, being fêted and adored on the streets of Moscow, and ending (by implication) the Cold War.

In the five years between the Tories' landslide victory of 1987 and the general election of 1992, much changed within the party. Most importantly, Margaret Thatcher had been deposed as prime minister by dissidents within her own party, to be replaced by John Major, a political figure of distinctly different image and personality. The change of leadership thus required a change in communication strategy, such that a government which had been in office for 13 years could claim to be offering something new. In 1991 party chairman Chris Patten re-appointed Saatchi and Saatchi to handle the upcoming campaign, in an attempt to 'rebuild the creative atmosphere of 1978 and 1979' (Butler and Kavanagh, 1992, p.35). The company utilised the qualitative research methods and results of Richard Wirthlin, who had been consulted extensively after the perceived failures of the 1987 campaign. Wirthlin

> claimed that, although voters' preferences on personalities and policies fluctuated, values were more stable; if the Party could understand and, to some extent, shape those values, then it would be much better placed to develop an effective communication strategy. The research required time-consuming and expensive in-depth interviews ... [and] suggested that the most important values which the electorate sought in parties were, in order: 1. Hope; 2. Security; 3. Peace of Mind.
>
> (Ibid., p.36)

On the basis of these findings Saatchi and Saatchi developed for the Conservatives an advertising campaign which emphasised the party's reputation for being strong in economic management, while avoiding Labour's chosen ground of social issues. Labour's alleged 'tax and spend' plans became the subject of the successful 'Tax Bombshell' poster of January 1992 (see Figure 6.1), a theme returned to in posters and advertisements during the election campaign itself.

The most memorable Conservative advertisement of the 1992 campaign was directed by John Schlesinger, and presented a personal profile of John Major. The profile fits into the *cinéma-vérité* category of political advertising discussed above, in that it took Major back to his 'roots' in Brixton, London, showing him visiting and talking with 'ordinary people' on the streets and at the market. In one scene, he wonders 'spontaneously' if his old house will still be standing. 'It is!', he says poignantly, as the prime ministerial car

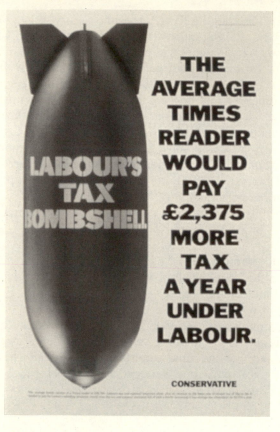

*Figure 6.1* Labour's 'Tax Bombshell'
*Source:* Reproduced courtesy of Conservative Central Office.

drives up. 'It is!'. It was later revealed that the scene had been rehearsed and the area secured well in advance of Major's arrival, but the broadcast succeeded for many in conveying Major's lower-middle-class social origins to an audience widely perceived to be fed up with 13 years of Margaret Thatcher's haughty grandeur. The Conservatives' advertising in the run-up to, and during, the 1997 campaign was less successful. As was noted in Chapter 3 above, the effects of political advertising are determined not by content alone, but by the environmental context within which a political message is sent and received. Between 1992 and 1997, much had changed in British politics. The Labour Party had renewed itself under the leadership of Tony Blair, while the Tories had been damaged by media-fuelled perceptions (reasonably accurate) of moral and financial sleaze on the one hand, and internal division over policy on European union on the other. As a result, when they attempted to reprise the 'Labour's tax bombshell' theme which had played so well in 1992 (with different specifics, of course, but essentially the same message – that a Labour government would tax voters until the pips squeaked) it failed utterly. Indeed, Labour's counter-propaganda successfully conveyed the notion that it was the Tories who were the high-tax party.

The Conservative campaign managers also attempted to make a negative of New Labour's widely regarded skills in political marketing and public relations (see below and Chapter 7). In August 1996, while the journalistic 'silly season' was underway in Britain, leading left-wing MP Clare Short had given an interview to the *New Statesman* magazine, in which she referred to her own party's communications specialists as 'the people who live in the dark'[4]. In doing so she was articulating the dislike amongst many of her colleagues of Labour's new communications professionalism; a traditional left-wing hostility (see next section) towards the packaging of politics. In the interview she declared that 'we could throw away victory . . . I think the obsession with the media and the focus groups is making us look as if we want power at any price and we don't stand for anything. I think they [the people who live in the dark] are making the wrong judgment and they endanger our victory'.

Conservative campaign managers seized on this dissent, and the dramatic, menacing imagery which Short used to express it, to design a series of ads highlighting the allegedly sinister, manipulative nature of New Labour. The infamous 'demon eyes' poster, depicting Tony Blair literally as the devil, was the most spectacular example of a campaign which tried to convince the electorate that professional political communication was only marginally more acceptable in a democratic society than devil worship. It failed, however, in so far as it had no discernible impact on public opinion and voting intentions, and did not prevent the landslide Labour victory of May 1997.

The Tories also tried to exploit Labour's relatively pro-European policy with a poster ad depicting Tony Blair sitting, puppet-like, on the knee of the then German chancellor Helmut Kohl (Figure 6.2). This too failed to resonate with the British people, and merely succeeded in generating negative publicity for the Conservatives, who stood accused of xenophobia and political immaturity. Both the 'demon eyes' and 'Blair as Kohl's puppet' campaigns showed that the political environment was no longer one in which crude

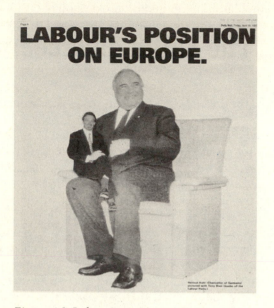

*Figure 6.2* Labour's position on Europe
*Source:* Saatchi.

Labour-bashing messages could find a receptive audience (although such tactics had worked well in previous campaigns). The British people (or enough of them, at any rate) had grown tired of the Tories, and sceptical of their messages, and were prepared to give Labour a chance. Evidently, they were not to be put off by attack ads of the type almost wholly relied on by the Tories in 1996–7.

## POLITICAL ADVERTISING IN THE UNITED KINGDOM: LABOUR

In stark contrast to the Conservatives' unashamedly commercial approach to the selling of politics the Labour Party was, for most of the period under discussion here, resistant to the charms of the professional advertisers. In the 30 years up to the election campaign of 1987, only in one of the earliest campaigns – 1959 – did Labour successfully use the medium of television as a marketing tool. Iron-ically enough, the two figures most associated with this use were Woodrow Wyatt, who later became a prominent member of the British right, and Anthony Wedgwood Benn, better known as Tony

Benn, the left-wing bogeyman of British politics in the 1980s. Together, these two presented a series of party political broadcasts which, like the Tories' 1970 ads discussed earlier, used already familiar conventions of British television to connote authority to their audience. In the manner of broadcast current affairs presenters, they introduced the issues, Labour's policies, and criticisms of the Tories, in a style widely viewed at the time as highly effective.

Benn's role in this campaign was particularly ironic because it was the British left – of which he subsequently became the leading figure – which after 1959 came to view the conscious application of professional marketing techniques to the political process as a kind of betrayal. As Johnson and Elebash put it, Labour – with the singular exception of 1959 – approached campaigning as if it believed that 'amateurism equalled sincerity in politics' (1986, p.299). The party 'distrusted advertising as a capitalist business'. Amongst the left in general, argues Kathy Myers, advertising was seen as 'part of capitalism's self-justification system, its ideology' (1986, p.85), and thus rejected as a vote-winning device.

In this sense the British left was subscribing to what was described in Chapter 2 as the normative ideal of liberal democratic political discourse. Political persuasion, the Labour left believed, should be based on objective information and rational debate, rather than on manipulation and hard sell. To pursue the latter was to devalue the political process and patronise the people, who could be relied upon to distinguish right from wrong if given the opportunity to do so by their political parties. The pursuit of this ideal, and the consequent wholesale rejection of professional, persuasive communication methods, deprived Labour and the left in general, throughout the 1960s, 1970s and into the 1980s, of an important weapon with which to combat the Conservative opposition. The pragmatic, and entirely rational goal of achieving political power was sacrificed in the cause of a romanticised ideological purity of discourse which television was rapidly making redundant.

As late as 1983, in the midst of another disastrous general election campaign, the party's then general secretary Jim Mortimer stated defiantly: 'I can assure you that the Labour Party will never follow such a line of presentation in politics [i.e., the use of professional advertising], for very serious reasons: the welfare of human beings, the care of people and the fact that we want to overcome unemployment. These are the real tasks before us, not presenting people as if they were breakfast food or baked beans' (quoted in Myers, 1986, p.122).

An illustration of the British left's deep-rooted unease with the concept of advertising – even if one was advertising a 'good thing' – was the launch in 1987 of the left-of-centre Sunday tabloid, *News on Sunday*. Following the results of expensive market research conducted by Research Surveys of Great Britain – at a cost of £1.5 million 'the most comprehensive research ever carried out for a new paper' (Chippindale and Horrie, 1988, p.99) – plans were made to produce a paper with a potential market (according to the research) of three million people. A collective was formed to manage the new paper, and a £1.3 million advertising budget raised from various sponsors and investors in the labour movement, local government, and the business community. The advertising agency Barth, Bogle and Hegarty used this money to design a humorous, irreverent campaign which exploited such positives as *News on Sunday*'s lack of page three girls and its anti-establishment editorial line. As Chippindale and Horrie put it, 'the overall brief [as the advertisers understood it] was quite simple. *News on Sunday* was to be a popular newspaper. Therefore the advertising had to get as many people as possible to sample the product' (Ibid., p.99).

In doing so, however, B,B&H overstepped the line between sending up sexism, racism, etc., and seeming to pander to it. This at least was how the management of *News on Sunday* saw it. The result, as Chippindale and Horrie describe it, was a tragic failure of marketing and promotion, leading ultimately to the closure of the paper and the loss of several million pounds. In rejecting the professionals' advice the management of *News on Sunday* were following a long tradition amongst the left which viewed the use of commercial advertising as, at best, an evil to be reluctantly and grudgingly endorsed only when absolutely necessary and, at worst, 'supping with the devil' of capitalist propaganda techniques.

Equally illustrative of this attitude was the Labour Party's experience with the agency of Wright and Partners in 1983. Having been convinced that some concessions to professional marketing were essential if Labour was to compete electorally with the Tories, the party hired Wright and Partners to run its 1983 campaign. Having done so, it refused to let agency representatives sit in on strategy meetings, and party leaders generally kept their distance from the professional communicators. As Johnson and Elebash put it, 'an intolerable client/agency relationship developed' (1986, p.302). The 1983 campaign – which ended with the Labour Party's lowest popular vote since the 1930s – comprised a series of ads on the traditional social democratic themes of unemployment, the

National Health Service, and homelessness. Aesthetically, they were unsuccessful, being described by one author as 'dark, depressing montages' (Myers, 1986, p.122).

On a television discussion of political advertising produced in 1989, presenter Michael Ignatieff and then Labour Director of Communications Peter Mandelson looked back at the amateurishness and clumsiness of the campaign with barely suppressed disbelief and mockery,[5] but the party leadership's approach to the agency, and the management of its own campaign (see next chapter) were equally lacking in skill.

The transformation in the Labour Party's approach to advertising, which by the 1987 election saw them being widely praised for having the best campaign, was provoked firstly and most obviously by the uniquely poor result of the 1983 election. The party in Parliament was reduced to 209 MPs, with even that number reflecting a significant over-representation of its voting performance, thanks to the British first-past-the-post electoral system.

There can be little doubt that after the 1983 election Labour was facing the loss of its post-war status as the junior partner in a two-party system, and along with it any realistic hope of access to government. Clearly, something had to be done to halt the decline. A change in approach was further encouraged by the experience of the Labour-controlled Greater London Council in its struggle with the Thatcher government.

In 1983 the abolition of the GLC was announced by a government which detested the thought of this nest of 'reds under the beds' running the capital city. Led by Ken Livingstone, the GLC was unmistakably 'hard left', promoting and implementing a wide range of progressive, socialist-inspired programmes, such as cheap fares on public transport, anti-sexism and anti-racism in schools, and public services for gay, ethnic and other minorities.[6] While in these terms 'left', the GLC administration differed from the traditionalists in the Labour Party in understanding the role which advertising could play in their campaign against abolition.

London was essentially a Conservative heartland, and the GLC the archetypal 'loony left'. Livingstone and his colleagues appreciated that the battle with the government could not be won by the left's preferred tactics of public demonstrations and rallies. Consequently, the GLC hired the agency Boas, Massimi and Pollitt (BMP), who had worked for unions and local governments but were primarily a commercial organisation. For BMP, in the words of its accounts director Peter Herd, 'developing advertising in a

117

political context is just the same as developing it in a commercial context. You find out what it is you can reasonably achieve, who you will have to persuade in order to do that, and then research to find out what is most likely to affect them. That is the process we went through with the GLC, as we would with Cadbury's, Courage or the *Guardian* [all of whom BMP had worked for]. It's the same process' (quoted in Myers, 1986, p.111).

BMP's market research established that Londoners were not especially concerned with the survival of the GLC as an institution *in itself*, but *were* concerned about losing their right to vote for local government, which was one obvious consequence of the GLC's abolition. In the light of their findings, and to maximise support amongst predominantly pro-Tory voters for an organisation run by the Labour left, BMP developed a dual strategy of, firstly, informing Londoners about the basic public service (and largely apolitical) activities of the GLC, such as running a cheap and efficient mass transport network. Secondly, they sought to combat the Tory government's (and its supporters in the press) demonisation of the GLC and Ken Livingstone in particular. The resulting advertisements were of two basic types: those dealing with the issue of the GLC were in black and white, connoting 'seriousness'; those tackling the demonisation of the left were humorous and mocking of the government.

Although the GLC campaign was unable to prevent the powerful Tory government from proceeding with its abolition legislation, opinion polls indicated that, by its end, a majority of Londoners – including those who would declare themselves to be Conservative voters – favoured the continuation of the GLC, and opposed government policy on this issue. The campaign consequently 'won plaudits for BMP throughout the advertising world, and grudging admiration from Livingstone's opponents in the political world' (Hughes and Wintour, 1990, p.55). It also showed, in the view of Labour's media adviser Philip Gould, that 'sophisticated communication techniques, and in particular advertising, can be used by a radical organisation without compromising either the message, or the policies underlying [it]' (Ibid.).

So successful was the campaign perceived to be, by friends and enemies of the Livingstone-led GLC alike, that the government later introduced measures to prevent a repetition of it in future struggles with local government, of which, in the era of the poll tax and rate-capping, there were to be many, and not just with Labour-controlled authorities. The Local Government Act of 1986 declared that henceforth 'a local authority shall not publish any material which in whole or in part, appears to be designed to effect, or can reasonably be regarded as likely to effect, public support for a) a political party, or b) a body, cause or campaign identified with, or likely to be regarded as identified with, a political party'.[7]

The example of the GLC was a major factor in breaking down Labour's long-standing resistance to the use of advertising techniques, although the process had begun with the trauma of the 1983 defeat and the election of Neil Kinnock as leader to replace Michael Foot. Nick Grant, one of Labour's media advisers reflected the 'new realism' when he accepted that the party was now in the business of 'selling a set of social values. What you have to do is substitute the offending aspiration for one you've researched. One that is harmonious with your socialist principles' (quoted in Myers, 1986, p.122). The party still had reservations, however. 'Selling a philosophy, because it is intangible, is much more complex than selling a product. All we are endorsing about advertising is the narrow, highly methodological technique. We are not endorsing the style, the form, or any particular way of advertising a product. We're trying to extract benefits from the scientific technique of marketing and apply it to a different world' (Ibid.).

In October 1985 the new leader, Neil Kinnock, appointed a current affairs television producer, Peter Mandelson, to the post of Campaign and Communications Director which he had just created. Mandelson in turn appointed advertising executive Philip Gould to undertake a review of Labour's campaign techniques. In 1990 Peter Mandelson himself became a Labour parliamentary candidate, and his post was taken over by John Underwood, a former television journalist and producer. Underwood's tenure was very short, due to conflicts of approach, and he resigned in June 1991 to be replaced by Dave Hill, who co-ordinated campaign planning for the 1992 election.

The theme of the 1992 campaign was 'It's Time for Labour' and again, as in 1987, the advertisements elaborating on the theme were well-produced and widely-praised. One broadcast backfired, however, producing what Butler and Kavanagh call 'the only real confrontation of the campaign . . . the war of Jennifer's Ear' (1992, p.122). 'Jennifer's Ear' was the subject of Labour's PEB on health. It presented, in glossy and emotional terms, the sad tale of a young girl unable to get treatment for a painful ear condition because of long National Health Service waiting lists. Although the characters were portrayed by actors, the film was based on a 'true' story, passed on to the party by an angry parent, who also happened to be a Labour supporter. Unfortunately, 'Jennifer's' other parent, her mother, was a Conservative supporter, as was 'Jennifer's' grandfather. Hearing of the use to be made of 'Jennifer's' condition, they contacted the Conservative Party, and thus began a 'war', conducted amidst huge media attention, between rival claims as to the truth of 'Jennifer's' ear: was it the cynical manipulation of a child's illness by unscrupulous (Labour) politicians, presented without context and understanding of the real situation, or was it a legitimate exposure of Tory health policy in action?

As the 'war' progressed, giving the media their most extensively covered story of the campaign, it moved away from the debate on health to one of ethics, in which both parties' campaign teams were implicated. The advertisement became a story in itself, over which the parties had little control. Labour's 'A Time for Change' message was premature in 1992, and the Conservatives won a fourth consecutive general election, though with a much reduced majority. Although Labour's communication apparatus was much more professional and 'scientific' than ever before, the political environment remained unsympathetic to its core message, and presentational errors on tax and other issues were enough to maintain majority support for the Tories. By the time of the 1997 campaign, however, with Tony Blair installed as leader, and Conservative sleaze and in-fighting dominating the news agenda, electoral success and political power were within Labour's reach for the first time in eighteen years. With further improvement of the communications machinery, and wholesale adoption of Clinton-style political advertising and marketing techniques, Labour's advertising strategy in 1996–7 was simply to hold on to the huge lead in the opinion polls which it had established. Adapting the Clinton strategy of 'triangulation' to the British context, new Labour set out to steal the best Tory clothes, while retaining left-of-centre social democratic values, repositioning itself as the 'radical centre' in British politics. The results of the strategy were seen in such ads as those depicting a British bulldog (a traditionally Tory symbol of a rather unpleasant and aggressive British nationalism), remaking it as a symbol of Labour's ease with patriotism (albeit a humane, ethical patriotism compatible with socialist philosophy) (Figure 6.3). In this way, Labour developed a 'brand' capable of appealing to the large numbers of 'soft' Tory, affluent working- and middle-class voters who had kept the Conservatives in power for eighteen years, as well as their traditional supporters.

*Figure 6.3* Labour's British bulldog

## POLITICAL ADVERTISING: THE FUTURE

The role and place of advertising in political communication continues to generate debate, with each new election campaign providing material for further controversy, though rarely resolution of the issues which have occupied political and communication scientists ever since the first 'I like Ike' spots. In America, criticism of the sheer cost of political advertising remains at the forefront of debate, though the allegedly negative effects of 'attack' ads also worry many (Jamieson, 1992). The third edition of Diamond and Bates' classic study of American political advertising takes a pragmatic tone, pointing out, as was noted above, that political campaigns have always been negative and 'dirty' (1992). Kathleen Jamieson, while complaining of a general deterioration in the quality of mediated political discourse, to which political advertising has contributed, accepts that 'simplistic dualities' have always been at the centre of campaigning (1992, p.44). There is, in America as well as other countries, growing acceptance that there is nothing intrinsically wrong with negative campaigning, if the claims made are fair and reasonable. Lies and deception are not acceptable, of course, but they are hardly unique to our political culture. Modern media give attack ads more reach and visibility, but did not invent them, or the principles of political competition underpinning them. Attack is as much part of the political process as defence, and if modern advertisers do it with ever-increasing slickness and sophistication, it seems pointless, indeed futile, to spend too much intellectual energy on condemning them. As Diamond and Bates put it, in the history of political advertising, as in so many other forms of political communication, 'the political golden age of the past, upon close inspection, turns out to be made of brass' (1992, p.384).

In Britain, with its distinctive traditions and conventions, the issues are rather different. The controversy which Conservative government advertising for its 1980s privatisation campaigns provoked, fuelled by legislation (quoted on p.119) prohibiting local governments from using public revenues for political advertising purposes, has long called into question the logic of a system which prevents political advertising on television and radio, while allowing the government to spend hundreds of millions of pounds promoting ideologically based policies. Advocates of reform have argued, reasonably enough, that since the privatisation campaigns were clearly 'political' and paid for by the tax-payer, other organisations with political objectives, such as environmental groups, trade unions, and even political parties, should be permitted to purchase broadcast advertising time at commercial rates, as is the case in the United States. There, pressure groups and political organisations of all kinds can buy up television time to protest, nationally or locally, about the environment, or factory closures, or any of the issues around which political campaigns regularly develop. Why not in Britain, therefore?

The future of political advertising has taken on greater urgency as the British broadcasting system becomes more commercialised and the financial pressures on broadcasters increase. Can the political parties take it for granted that they will always have access to free airtime in the form of PPBs and PEBs? When ratings are everything in a broadcasting system increasingly run as a profit-making industry, will media managers be content to provide prime-time slots free of charge to pontificating politicians? Quite possibly not, argued a confidential internal Labour Party document in the late 1980s, warning that 'parties may be forced to find ways of entering this hostile broadcasting environment directly, either through paid political advertising . . . or by the production of programmes or by sponsorship of programmes. Naturally such developments would be costly and the richest party – or the party with the richest friends – would be best able to take any advantages there might be'.

And here, precisely, is the great danger, as opponents of paid political advertising on British broadcasting perceive it. As was noted in Chapter 3, the growing importance in political campaigning of *paid-for* media inevitably favours those who *can* pay, and discriminates against those who cannot. In an unequal society, in which political and economic resources are already closely linked, the concentration of power and the disenfranchisement of the economically deprived would be even greater than it currently is. In Britain, to put it simply, the political party with the richest friends and supporters would have much greater access to paid-for broadcast advertising than their opponents.

To some extent the debate about political advertising parallels that on the future of broadcast news and current affairs (McNair, 1999). In a media environment where wavelength scarcity is no longer a determining factor, and in which there is a multitude of channels beaming to increasingly fragmented, 'targeted' groups, why not allow some overt political advertising, as is permitted in the United States and other countries? We have it in our print media, so why not on television and radio?

Opposition to this viewpoint is based not only on financial

grounds, but also on resistance to the 'trivialisation' of the political process and the degradation of the public sphere discussed in Chapter 3. This returns us once again to a debate that continues to defy neat resolution. As this edition went to press, there were no government plans to permit paid political advertising on British television or radio, and it seems unlikely that such a form of political communication will ever be permitted on the main 'terrestrial' channels. A consultation paper released by the main British broadcasters (BBC, ITV, Channels 4 and 5, Independent Radio) after the 1997 election, with a view to reforming the system of party political broadcasting in the UK, stressed that 'there is little enthusiasm amongst either broadcasters or the political parties to move to a system of paid political advertising'.[8] But some change is inevitable, probably in the direction of concentrating the transmission of party political broadcasts around election campaigns, and reducing the number of broadcasts which take place outside campaign periods. For example, the broadcasters would like to discontinue the tradition of transmitting a ten-minute 'talking head' piece to camera by the Chancellor, after the annual Budget speech in parliament (which is by convention 'answered' by the main opposition spokespersons). This is argued to be a reasonable reform in the context of expanding live coverage of parliament, and the extended media coverage of it which now takes place. On the other hand, should not the public be permitted to hear the Chancellor explain, in his or her own words, without the mediation of journalists, what the Budget that year is about?

Here and in other features of the British PPB system, new technologies which allow more and better coverage of parliament (and the political process in general), and the force of commercial pressures on access to broadcast airtime, make some degree of change inevitable in the years to come. How much, and how quickly it will be implemented, remain to be decided. Before long, however, there will be hundreds of channels transmitting into people's homes by cable and satellite. The uses to which such channels might be put are difficult to foresee, but paid political advertising on the American model, on some of them at least, is clearly a possibility.

# 7

# PARTY POLITICAL
# COMMUNICATION II
## Political public relations

Advertising, we have noted, has one fundamental weakness as a form of political communication. To the receiver of the message it is perceived as being, if not necessarily 'propaganda' (in the negative sense of that term), then 'biased' and partial. Regardless of whether or not the audience agrees or disagrees with the message being advertised, he or she is aware that it *is* a politically loaded message, reflecting the interests, ideas and values of the sponsor. For this reason, the effectiveness of political advertising as a means of persuasion will always be limited. Knowing that a message is 'committed' allows the reader, viewer or listener, to take a distance from it – to resist and reject it. This has not, as we have seen, prevented political advertising from occupying a growing role in the political process, but it has encouraged the view that other forms of communication may be more effective in transmitting the desired messages. In particular, political actors have come to believe in the importance of 'free media' in achieving their goals, as opposed to the paid-for variety (Levy, 1989). By 'free media' we refer to those spaces and outlets in which political actors may gain exposure and coverage, without having to pay media organisations for the privilege.

Gaining access to free media is not without costs, of course. It requires a more or less professional apparatus of public relations advisers, which must be paid for by the political organisation concerned. Constructing or manufacturing the events and contexts through which politicians can acquire 'free media' access may be expensive in money and time. Nevertheless, we will use the term 'free media' here to distinguish those practices which fall under the broad headings of 'political marketing' and 'public relations' from those of the advertising world described in Chapter 6.

Politicians like free media because, unlike advertising, their role in it is not that of authorship. When a politician is reported on the

125

news, editorial responsibility for the selection of 'soundbites' broadcast, and the interpretation placed upon them, is seen to belong with the journalist. When Margaret Thatcher appeared on the BBC's live *Jimmy Young Radio Show* (as she frequently did during her time in office) the things she said were inevitably perceived rather differently than if she had addressed television viewers within the context of a party political broadcast. Such messages are 'less manufactured' than advertisements and, as such, may be thought to carry more legitimacy and credibility. Even if such a conversation is light-hearted and avoids politics entirely, the audience may still feel that a 'truer' picture of the politician emerges. The lack of control and apparent spontaneity of most free-media scenarios heightens 'believability'.

This quality of free media is a double-edged sword, however. To the extent that a politician's appearance on a news or discussion programme *is* genuinely outside his or her editorial control, the scope for mistakes (from the politician's perspective) is clear. Broadcast interviews can be hostile as well as deferential. Misjudgments can be made about the impact of a political event once it has passed into the hands of the media, as happened famously with the Labour Party's Sheffield rally during the 1992 election campaign (see p.136). When in 1983 Margaret Thatcher was questioned by a well-prepared viewer on live national television about the sinking of the *Belgrano* she revealed to millions of viewers an unpleasantly arrogant side of her personality.

The advantage of free media exposure for politicians is founded on the awareness of the audience that such appearances are 'live', or if not live in the technical sense, something more than a manufactured political advertisement. And the audience knows this because politicians frequently slip up, or encounter hostile opposition and criticism when they enter the free media arena.

Politicians, therefore, while desiring media exposure of this more 'authentic' kind, also strive to reimpose some kind of control over the output, and to achieve this requires that politicians employ professionals skilled in the workings of the media.

## POLITICAL PUBLIC RELATIONS: A BRIEF HISTORY

As the media's heightened role in the conduct of political discourse became apparent, the twentieth century witnessed the birth and

rapid growth of a new profession, devoted to the effective communication of political messages: as Stanley Kelley puts it, 'a class of
professional propagandists' (1956, p.16). Today, the members of
this profession, incorporating public relations, advertising, and
marketing, stand between the politician and the media, profiting
from the relationship of mutual interdependence which exists
between the two.

Corporate public relations, from which the professional political
communicator emerged, first developed in the United States at the
turn of the century, as big US companies encountered for the first
time the often conflicting demands of commercial success and public opinion. Twentieth-century capitalism brought with it 'an
increased readiness of the public, due to the spread of literacy and
democratic forms of government, to feel that it is entitled to its voice
in the conduct of large aggregations, political, capitalist or labour'
(Bernays, 1923, p.33).

In a political environment of expanding suffrage and public scrutiny of corporate activity, big US capital began to engage in opinion
management, employing such pioneers as Ivy Lee, who set up the
first consultancy in 1904 (Kelley, 1956), working largely for the
coal and rail industries.

Politicians quickly embraced the principles and methods of corporate PR. In 1917, US President Wilson established a federal
committee on Public Information to manage public opinion about
the First World War. The Democratic Party established a permanent
public relations office in 1928, with the Republicans following suit
in 1932 (Bloom, 1973). Since then, public relations consultants
have held 'one or more seats on the central strategy board of
virtually every presidential candidate' (Ibid., p.14).[1]

The first political public relations consultancy was established by
husband and wife team Clem Whittaker and Leone Baxter in Los
Angeles in 1933, under the name of Campaigns Inc. Dan Nimmo
attributes this to the fact that in California, more than in any other
US state in the 1930s, referenda were extensively used to resolve
political issues. Moreover, the population of California was
immigrant-based, and thus more ethnically and socially diverse
than in some parts of the United States. Traditional party organisations were weak. In this environment of particular sensitivity to
(volatile) public opinion, political consultants, Nimmo argues, in
effect filled the space occupied elsewhere by party political
machines. From Campaigns Inc. developed what Nimmo calls a
nationwide 'service industry' (1970, p.39), facilitating political

communication between parties, candidates, and their publics; designing and producing publicity and propaganda material; raising funds; advising on policy and presentation, and polling public opinion – becoming, in short, 'the stage managers and the creative writers of living-theatre politics' (Sabato, 1981, p.111).

By the 1970s there were hundreds of full-time political consultants in the United States, and their numbers were growing in Britain and other democratic countries. In Britain in the 1980s the names of Peter Mandelson, Tim Bell, the Saatchi brothers, and Harvey Thomas became inseparable from the political process. The remainder of this chapter examines the means and methods by which political parties, at times of election and in the intervals between them, with the help of their political consultants, seek to manage the media in such ways as to maximise favourable coverage, and to minimise that which is damaging to the organisations' interests.

The discussion will be organised around four types of political public relations activity. Firstly, we address forms of *media management* – those activities designed to tap into the needs and demands of the modern media and thus maximise politicians' access to, and exposure in, free media. These activities chiefly comprise the manufacture of *medialities* – media-friendly events which will tend to attract the attention of media gate-keepers, all other things being equal, and to keep public awareness of the party high. The objective of this activity is, of course, not simply to preserve a party's visibility, but to have its definition of political problems and solutions covered. In this sense, we may also think of it as *issues management.*

Secondly, we examine the practice of *image-management* in political public relations: the personal image of the individual politician, on the one hand, and how it can be moulded and shaped to suit organisational goals; and on the other, the image of the political organisation. The latter activity may also be described as *political marketing*, and will frequently incorporate the advertising techniques described in the previous chapter. But the marketing of political identity and image extends far beyond the placement of paid messages in the media, into such matters as the design of a corporate logo (a party's symbol), the language used during political interviews and in manifestos, and the general work of a party when it campaigns in the public sphere.

The success or otherwise of the aforementioned categories of activity depends to a large extent on the effectiveness of a third: the *internal communications* of the organisation. This includes the setting up of channels for transmitting information internally, co-ordinating activity, and dealing with feedback. As we shall see, some of the great failures of party political communication in recent years can be attributed to inadequate *internal* public relations. Just as modern corporations now routinely support in-house public relations departments for the purpose of maximising organisational efficiency, so must political parties develop structures of effective internal communication.

Lastly, but by no means of least importance in the study of political communication, are the activities of *information management*. We distinguish this category from media management as defined above in so far as it tends to involve open and covert methods of information manipulation by political actors in positions of power. Information is a powerful political weapon, and its selective dissemination, restriction, and/or distortion by governments is an important element in public opinion management. Organisations which are not in power may still use information to attack opponents, but this form of public relations work is inevitably most important for a governing organisation, which has all the information management resources of the state at its disposal, and which may use them to exert considerable influence on the lives of citizens.

## Media management

The term 'media management' does not, in this context, refer to those engaged in the professional work of managing media organisations, but to the wide variety of practices whereby political actors may seek to control, manipulate, or influence media organisations in ways which correspond to their political objectives. To use such a term conveys, probably accurately, the politicians' view that the media are valuable, but potentially unruly allies in the political process: essential for public exposure but unpredictable and with a tendency to display independence. As we saw in Chapter 4, even the most loyal of a party's friends in the media (such as the British 'Tory' press before it changed its loyalties in the era of New Labour) can embarrass and put unwelcome pressure on it. The relationship of mutual interdependence between political actors and media organisations described earlier does not preclude severe criticism of the former by the latter, nor the more routine monitoring of political power implied by the 'Fourth Estate' watchdog role.

In this context media management comprises activities designed to maintain a positive politician–media relationship, acknowledging the needs which each has of the other, while exploiting the institutional characteristics of both sets of actor for maximum advantage. For the politicians, this requires giving the media organisation what it wants, in terms of news or entertainment, while exerting some influence over how that something is mediated and presented to the audience.

As was the case with advertising, it would be a mistake to think that media management in this sense is new in democratic politics. Chapter 2 noted that the first newspaper interview with a public figure was conducted in the United States in 1859 (Boorstin, 1962), and that the first American news release was issued in 1907. The interview form was imported to Britain in the 1880s, as subsequently were all the techniques of influencing media coverage pioneered in America (Silvester, ed., 1993).

We have traced the development of the political public relations industry from the work of Ivy Lee and Edward Bernays at the turn of the twentieth century. But, as with advertising, media management has increased in political importance in parallel with the advance of mass communication, and television in particular, which has provided ever more opportunities (and dangers) for politicians to harness the efforts and skills of professionals, and through them seek to influence public opinion. Political parties, their leaders, and their public relations advisers, have become steadily more sophisticated in their appreciation of the implications for their media management efforts of journalistic news values, technical constraints on newsgathering, and commercial prerogatives. Since F.D. Roosevelt's live radio broadcasts in the 1930s, through Ronald Reagan's reprisal of that idea in the 1980s, to Bill Clinton's 'meet the people' broadcasts of the 1990s, and Tony Blair's live statements and news conferences, such as his description of Princess Diana in the hours following her death as 'the people's princess', politicians have become – thanks largely to the new profession of media managers – more adept at exploiting media. As we shall see, many journalists consider that the process has pushed the media–politician relationship beyond that state of mutual interdependence to one of *media dependence* on, and deference to, politicians, and that journalists should now consciously adopt a more detached, critical approach to the use of these techniques.

For many analysts of political communication, the modern era of political public relations begins with the Nixon–Kennedy presidential debates of September 1960 (Kraus and Davis, 1981). Political scientists agree that this event had a key impact in the 1960 campaign. Here we note that the live presidential debate – now an

American institution, copied in many other democracies – is the archetypal 'free media' event. In itself it guarantees the politicians extensive live coverage, since the serious broadcasting organisations must all report it fully, providing acres of follow-up coverage of the issues raised, and the respective performances of the participants. The debate *sets the agenda* in a contemporary US presidential campaign. It provides a platform for a candidate to appeal directly to the mass audience, and to demonstrate his or her superiority over the opponent. And for the politician it is, in contrast to advertising, free.

As is characteristic of free media, however, the presidential debate also carries the possibility of catastrophic failure. Live and unedited, mistakes are more difficult to cover up, and a candidate's detailed, intelligent articulation of policies can be fatally undermined by one slip. In his 1976 debate with Jimmy Carter, incumbent Gerald Ford unintentionally reinforced a growing image of him as stupid and lightweight by appearing to suggest that Poland was not part of the Soviet bloc. Ford probably knew what he was trying to say, as no doubt did most of the audience, but the verbal *faux pas* haunted him for the rest of the campaign, contributing substantially to his defeat by Carter. Carter himself, during one of the 1980 debates with Ronald Reagan, appealed to the audience's anxiety about the Republican's hawkishness by introducing the image of his daughter, Amy, losing sleep at night over the issue of nuclear weapons. Coverage of the debate tended to take the view that this was a cynical manipulation of a child, furthering the process by which Carter lost to Reagan on polling day.

The live debate format encapsulates the great dilemma of free media for modern politicians: the massive exposure which it generates can win elections (this, for example, has become the received wisdom about John F. Kennedy's narrow victory over Richard Nixon in the 1960 campaign, which he won by only 117,000 votes). It can also lose them over such a simple matter as a slip of the tongue.

Britain, in contrast to the United States, has not developed a tradition of live debating between candidates for the highest governmental office, although each passing general election campaign is accompanied by calls for such debates from the challengers. British prime ministers, Labour and Conservative, well aware of the dangers debates can throw up, have taken the view that one of the privileges of incumbency is to refuse to participate in such an uncontrolled spectacle. The assumption here is that there is more to be gained by playing the role of a dignified statesperson, rather above the glitzy presidentialism of the debate format, than could be lost by being seen as aloof and inaccessible. That said, in June 1994, following the death of Labour leader John Smith, the three candidates for the succession – Tony Blair, Margaret Beckett, and John Prescott – debated live on BBC's *Panorama* programme, the first time such a debate had ever been broadcast on British television. And in 1997, prodded by Labour's media managers (confident of Tony Blair's ability to perform well) the main parties came closer than ever before to agreement on the terms and conditions of live debates between the party leaders. In the end they backed off, for reasons which remain unclear. Some speculated that Labour, having initially supported the idea of a leaders' debate, took the view that with a huge lead in the opinion polls it was not worth risking the kind of disaster experienced by Carter, Ford, or Dan Quayle when the latter famously, and foolishly, compared himself to John F. Kennedy. Others claimed that it was the Tories, fearful of how their leader, John Major, would perform against Blair, who stymied the negotiations. For whatever reason, there was no leaders' debate in 1997, but it seems likely, given the growing ease and familiarity with which politicians accept exposure to live, free media, and the increasingly anachronistic refusal of the party leaders to submit to this new form of media scrutiny, that future elections will include live debates between them of some kind.

It should of course be remembered that in Britain, unlike the USA, the prime minister and his or her principal challengers *are* seen debating live on television most weeks of the year. Prime Minister's Question Time in the House of Commons is an event without parallel in the US political system, and may perhaps be viewed as a more than adequate substitution for the one-off presidential debate. In the House of Commons a party leader's success is not measured in terms of soundbites and slip up alone (although these are noted), but on performance over a parliamentary session, which may be thought to be a harsher and more accurate test of debating skill than the 90 or so minutes of a US presidential clash.[2]

There are in Britain, in addition, live campaign debates between more junior politicians, in which detailed policy issues are covered. The party leaders also submit themselves to set-piece interviews by the most prominent pundits of the day, such as David Dimbleby, Jeremy Paxman, and John Humphrys. These occasions compare with the live presidential debate, since they allow a measure of comparison to be drawn between candidates. The Labour leader's 'handling' of Jeremy Paxman or Jonathan Dimbleby can be compared with that of William Hague and Paddy Ashdown. Gaffes are easily made, and not as easily recovered from. One of the decisive events of the 1987 general election campaign occurred during Labour leader Neil Kinnock's interview with David Frost on the latter's Sunday morning breakfast show.[3] At that stage in the 1987 campaign Labour was doing reasonably well in the polls, and had received some enthusiastic coverage for its advertising campaign (see Chapter 6). In the course of the interview Kinnock implied, during an attempt to explain Labour's non-nuclear defence policy, that the Soviets would not invade Britain, whether it had nuclear or non-nuclear defence, because of the strategic difficulty of taking the islands against determined opposition (including, he emphasised, guerrilla warfare). This statement of an obvious military fact slipped out almost unnoticed, until Conservative campaign managers spotted it on recordings of the show and proceeded to develop a powerful public relations and advertising campaign around the theme of Labour's incompetence on defence (see Figure 7.1). Kinnock had inadvertently opened up the defence debate, on which Labour was traditionally weak, and handed the Conservatives a valuable opportunity to 'score'.

Less prone to error, but equally useful in attracting and holding media attention on a politician or organisation, are those types of activity which fall into the category of 'pseudo-event' described in Chapter 2. The pseudo-event, it was noted there, is a 'happening' which bears only a tenuous relationship to political reality. It has meaning in and of itself, primarily as a *media* event. Some would argue that the debate and interview-type events discussed above often fall into this category, since there is clearly something rather artificial and manufactured about the ways in which participants are set up, questions framed, and answers carefully constructed. On the other hand, they *are* often live, and the audience does have an opportunity to make judgments about political actors based on their performances. Closer, perhaps, to the 'pure' pseudo-event are occasions such as party conferences which, in the latter part of the twentieth century, have changed – particularly in the United States but increasingly too in Britain and other advanced democracies – from being forums of policy-resolution and decision-making into spectacles designed for the maximisation of positive press coverage.

In the United States, where this change in the role and function of the party gathering began, the Democratic and Republican conventions have embraced, with unabashed enthusiasm, the principles of show business. Meaningful political debate and manoeuvring takes place behind the scenes, while in its public manifestation the

*Figure 7.1* Labour's defence policy
*Source:* Reproduced courtesy of Conservative Central Office.

convention functions as a huge signifier of whatever it is that the party that year is selling. In Ronald Reagan's re-election campaign of 1984 the Republic convention was dominated by emotional film of Ron and Nancy, accompanied by the adulation of convention delegates and (by extension) the American people. All this was communicated, through media coverage, to the audience.

In Britain, the trend towards the conference-as-symbol was pioneered, as were so many elements of modern political marketing, by Margaret Thatcher's Conservative Party (Scammell, 1995). In the 1980s, show-business entrepreneur Harvey Thomas was employed to design the annual conferences, which he did according to the principle that 'on a political platform we only get a few seconds on BBC news [or ITN] . . . we've got to make sure that those few seconds are absolutely pure as far as the message is concerned' (quoted in Cockerell, 1988, p.325). In the search for 'purity' the stages on which conference speakers and party leaders sat were constructed with the same attention to form and colour co-ordination as a West End stage set. At the 1983 conference, the first following the Thatcher government's victory in the Falklands, the stage resembled nothing more than a great, grey battleship, on which the Tory leadership sat like conquering generals.

As Thomas recognised, mass media coverage of that conference, and most others, was limited to at most a few minutes. Although in Britain there is a tradition of live coverage of the conference debates on the minority audience BBC2 channel (now augmented by cover-age on *Sky News*, BBC24 and BBC Parliament), the main news bulletins, whose audiences the politicians are most concerned to reach, treat them merely as stories (albeit important ones) in a packed news agenda. There is therefore a tendency for journalists to look for the 'essence' of the event – a particular phrase in the leader's speech, for example – and to organise coverage around that feature. Hence, the discourse emanating from conferences is constructed in the expectation that only a small part of it will be repeated to the audience which matters. Speeches are loaded with 'soundbites' – convenient, memorable words and phrases which can become the hook around which journalists will hang a story. Mrs Thatcher's 'this lady's not for turning' speech of 1981 is an excellent example of the phenomenon. The speech and the circumstances of its delivery are long forgotten, but the phrase lingers on in the public imagination, evoking the 'essence' of Thatcherism. Similarly, the soundbite 'tough on crime, tough on the causes of crime', came to symbolise New Labour's radical centrist approach of combining a stress on law and order with concern for social justice.

Political speeches, then, delivered in the pseudo-event environ-ment of a televised party conference, attempt to satisfy the journal-ists' need for easily – reportable 'bits' of political information, in such a way as to set the news agenda in the politicians' favour.

As the previous chapter noted, the Labour Party paid little atten-tion to political public relations in the early 1980s, and paid the electoral price for that neglect in 1983. But as the decade pro-gressed, the Labour Party under Neil Kinnock successfully emulated the techniques pioneered by Thomas and the Tories. More attention was paid to the 'look' of a conference, involving everything from the choice of logo to the cut of the speaker's suit. The debates, which at Labour conferences had always been genuine exchanges of view (evidenced by their frequently rancorous, anarchic quality), often leading to media coverage of 'splits' and 'disunity' became, like those of the Tories, bland and artificial, with the real acrimony taking place behind closed doors. The Labour Party, to be fair (even in the era of Blair and Mandelson), has not travelled as far down this road as the Conservatives (whose conferences were by the 1990s organised as little more than expressions of adulation for the leader, even when the leader was John Major, a man manifestly unpopular with his party members), and in 1993 allowed the conference to engage in a potentially damaging display of ideological disagreement when it debated the party's links with the unions. On this occasion the leadership won the debate, and was thus able to present then-leader John Smith to the media audience as a commanding figure. After his election as Labour leader in 1994, Tony Blair had to face some difficult moments at party conferences, over such issues as the reform of Clause Four of the constitution, and other cherished 'old Labour' policies. Despite such moments of 'reality intrusion', nevertheless, Labour, like the Conservatives and the Liberal Democrats, had by the 1990s been persuaded of the need to apply the principles of pseudo-eventing to its public gatherings and become increasingly adept at applying them, with rare exceptions.

During the 1992 election campaign, such was the manufactured quality of the major Labour rally that its construction became a news story in itself, backfiring on the party's efforts to present itself as modern and media-literate. The Sheffield rally of April 4, 1992, has passed into British political mythology as an example of the point at which the construction of pseudo-events for media consumption crosses the line from acceptable public relations activity to cynical manipulation. Credited by some commentators as contributing substantially to the 'late swing' which is said to have deprived Labour of victory,[4] the event is a further example of the politicians' difficulty in controlling 'free media'. Designed to portray an image of the party a few days before the election as supremely confident in itself and its leader, Neil Kinnock, the Sheffield rally was instead interpreted by the (mostly Tory) media as demonstrating arrogance. Kinnock's evangelistic style at the rally seemed stilted and embarrassing, the media suggested, rather than, as had been intended, relaxed and youthful. The exact role of the Sheffield rally in Labour's 1992 defeat cannot be known with precision, but there is certainly force in the argument that it provoked in many members of the audience a sense of unease. The presumption of victory which underpinned the event was premature, and an indicator of complacency. The event gave off what were, for Labour, unwelcome connotations.

Pseudo-events can also be organised on a much smaller scale than the full conference or rally. An essential part of modern political campaigning is the setting up of *photo-opportunities* (with accompanying soundbites). In the 1979 election campaign Margaret Thatcher spent a considerable portion of her time touring factories, donning white coats and, in the most famous example, holding a calf at an agricultural enterprise. For the journalists covering the campaign these events provided excellent news material, if not information about the Conservatives' political programme. Their need for broadcastable material was satisfied, as was the aspiring prime minister's hunger for exposure and publicity.

Since Harold Macmillan's official visit to Moscow in 1959, incumbent politicians have used their status to create images of statesmanship and global power (Foote, 1991). As we saw in the previous chapter, the coverage generated by such photo-opportunities frequently resurfaces in political advertising campaigns, as did pictures of Margaret Thatcher's 1987 state visit to Moscow, and shots of George Bush meeting foreign dignitaries in his capacity as vice-president.

The prevalence of these techniques, which are now routinely used by all parties, has generated debate within the journalistic profession about the extent to which, by allowing the politicians to flood the campaign environment with pseudo-events of this kind, they are contributing to the degradation of political culture and the manipulation of the audience.[5] As a result, recent election campaigns have witnessed journalists adopting a considerably more sceptical approach to the pseudo-event. Political coverage now frequently includes, not merely an account of the event, but a critique – *meta-coverage* – of its status as an event and how it has been covered. In the case of Labour's Sheffield rally, as already noted, this meta-discourse became seriously critical. In future, it seems, politicians will have to construct their pseudo-events in ways which acknowledge their 'constructedness'.

All political news management, indeed, now operates in a context of ongoing journalistic commentary about the 'game' of politics. Journalists are aware of the efforts made to influence their coverage, and include analysis of these efforts as part of their reportage.

Political journalism, as a result, is increasingly focussed on matters of process rather than policy; on the hidden meanings behind the surface appearance of political events. Some observers are critical of this 'relentless emphasis on the cynical game of politics' (Fallows, 1996, p.31), warning that it diverts the citizens' attention from the 'real issues'. Labour home secretary Jack Straw, for example, criticised 'the quality of political journalism' in Britain at the height of the 'cash-for-contacts' scandal in 1998. In this case, the *Observer* newspaper reported that lobbyists associated with the Labour government (and at least one, Roger Liddle, in its employ at the time) were selling their (claimed) privileged access to business clients. This kind of 'process' journalism, argued Straw, was squeezing substantive coverage of policy out of the media, at the expense of trivia. On the other hand – and the frantic efforts of the Labour leadership to discredit the *Observer* story when it broke in July 1998 might be thought to reinforce this point – journalistic monitoring and deconstruction of the political process – including the behind-the-scenes efforts of the lobbyists (see below) – are arguably the citizens' best defence against the increasingly sophisticated efforts of the politicians and their media advisers to create favourable media images of their clients.

Finally, under the category of media management, we turn to the *news conference*, in which political actors make public statements before audiences of journalists, which are then transmitted by print and broadcast media to the wider citizenry. News conferences present politicians with opportunities to set media agendas and thus influence public debate during election campaigns, as in the routine pursuit of politics between elections. Since Pierre Salinger first persuaded John Kennedy to give live television news conferences in the early 1960s they have become a presidential institution in the United States. Trading, once again, on the inherent newsworthiness of presidential utterances, and of reportable soundbites and pictures, presidents seek to impose *their* reading of events on the political environment by having it reported at the top of the main news bulletins. Hart's book-length study of presidential rhetoric notes that

> the presidency has been transferred from a formal, print-oriented world into an electronic environment specialising in the spoken word and rewarding casual, interpersonally adept politicians . . . Presidents and their staff [have] become expert in [the sociology of persuasion], and much of their time is devoted to discovering the best social superstructure

for insuring that a given rhetorical event will proceed
smoothly and persuasively.

(1987, p.61)

In Britain during election campaigns each party begins its day
with a news conference, setting out its 'theme' of the day, and the
issues on which it hopes to compete with opponents. Thus, in 1997
Labour had a 'health' day, the Tories a 'tax' day, and the Liberal
Democrats a 'proportional representation' day. By setting out the
issues in this way, early in the campaign day, each party hoped to
dominate the media agenda with coverage which would highlight
(and favour) its policies, while casting a poor light on those of the
opposition.

In general, news conferences are designed with a view to maximising coverage. Hence, they will be put on in time to be reported
on key news bulletins, and at locations accessible to journalists.
None of which ensures, of course, that coverage *will* be favourable.
The débâcle of 'Jennifer's Ear' (see Chapter 6), when the Labour
Party's attempt to set the 1992 campaign agenda on health turned
into a debate about ethics and manipulation which challenged the
party's integrity (as it did that of the Conservatives), involved a
series of news conferences in which party spokespersons sought
to reclaim the initiative, largely without success. As Butler and
Kavanagh observe

> the way in which the war of Jennifer's ear captured the
> agenda was the most extraordinary episode in the cam-
> paign on the air, explicable only in terms of the mounting
> frustration amongst journalists at a boring campaign and
> the intensity of news management by the parties. Frustra-
> tions boiled over, news management collapsed, the ratpack
> soared off out of control, scenting a 'real' story at last, and
> both parties and broadcasters lurched off course.
>
> (1992, p.164)

At news conferences tears were shed, tempers lost, and recrimin-
ations made as Labour sought unsuccessfully to bring the media's
agenda back into line with its own.

Despite the dangers inherent in using 'free media', the newsworthiness of live television interviews and debates ensures that no
party leader or head of government can refuse to participate in them
to some degree. To minimise the risks politicians employ public

relations professionals, whose job it is to attempt to ensure that the interpretation of a speaker's words (or gaffes) is a convenient and desirable one. These 'spin doctors' seek to shape the journalistic agenda in making sense of their employers' discourse. This they may do by issuing press releases clarifying ambiguous or contradictory remarks; having quiet words with key journalists and pundits; or giving news conferences. Leading politicians will also employ the services of 'minders', who manage the details of media encounters and attempt to anticipate and neutralise risks. In Britain, following the rise of Tony Blair and the election of Labour into government, the most famous (and infamous) of these became Alistair Campbell, the new prime minister's press secretary. Campbell did in government what he had done in opposition – seduced, cajoled, harried and intimidated the media from behind the scenes – into giving his leader the best possible coverage in any given circumstance. Spokespersons, on the other hand, literally speak for the politician in public. In the United States the presidential spokesman or woman has a key role in maintaining daily contact between the president, the media, and the public. Where the president may give a news conference weekly, monthly, or less frequently, the spokesperson provides a constant flow of soundbites which are assumed to be authoritative. When George Stepanopolous or Dee Dee Myers spoke to US journalists about Clinton administration policy, the latter know that they were receiving the presidential perspective on events. Even when presidents and other political figures make personal appearances at a news conference, rally, or other event, the words they speak are usually not their own, but those of a speech-writer who will attempt to present the desired message in a media-friendly form, with sufficiently snappy soundbites.

## Image management

The supply by politicians of structured news events for the purposes of maximising favourable media coverage is accompanied by a heightened concern with *image*: the personal image of political actors on the one hand, and the corporate image of the party on the other. In the area of personal image, modern politicians are judged not only by what they say and do, but *how* they say and do it. In short, political *style* now counts for almost as much as substance. One could argue that this has always been an important factor in political success, and that leaders from George Washington onwards have consciously presented 'images' to their constituencies. As with so much that is part of political communication, how-ever, it is in the post-Second World War period, in the course of which television has become the predominant mass medium, that considerations of style have emerged as central to the political process.

Brendan Bruce argues that in modern Britain, where the policies of the competing parties have gradually become more alike, image has taken on added importance as a distinguishing feature. 'When the parties' ideological centres of gravity are converging rather than diverging, personality is likely to become a more important way for the voter to determine credibility' (1992, p.95).

In Michael Cockerell's view, the first British prime minister to successfully project a TV image was Harold Macmillan, who pion-eered the use of the tele-prompter, thus enabling himself to address audiences with a naturalness of style which his predecessors like Winston Churchill and Clement Attlee could not achieve. His suc-cessor as prime minister, Alec Douglas-Home, was in Cockerell's opinion unsuited for television, coming across as patrician and aloof. Labour's leader at this time, Harold Wilson, on the other hand, presented a populist, approachable image, which helped him to win and hold on to political power for much of the 'swinging sixties'.

The pre-eminent image manager in post-war British politics, until the rise of Tony Blair, was of course Margaret Thatcher. With the assistance of public relations adviser Gordon Reece, in the late 1970s Margaret Thatcher allowed herself to be 'made-over' – i.e., made more appealing to potential voters. When elected Conserva-tive leader in 1976 Thatcher, like most politicians when they first achieve senior status (Tony Blair is an exception in this respect), paid little attention to her image. She looked as she wished to look, and spoke in the way which apparently came naturally to her, with a nasal, pseudo-upper class accent. Under Reese's guidance she took lessons to improve her voice, deepening its timbre and accentuating its huskiness. Her hairstyle and clothes were selected with greater care. Thatcher had accepted the view that 'clothes convey messages, because they involve choice, and those choices express personality' (Bruce, 1992, p.55).

Personal image matters, for former Thatcher adviser Brendan Bruce, because its constituents – clothes, hair, make-up, etc. – sig-nify things about the politician. Image can, with skill, be enlisted to connote power, authority and other politically desirable attributes. All this Margaret Thatcher understood. And just as the Tories led the way with their use of commercial advertising techniques, so did their emphasis on personal image – and their readiness to *manufacture* images where necessary – predate that of their opponents. In 1983 as the Conservative government, fresh from the Falklands victory, presented its leader as the 'Iron Lady', Labour fought an election campaign led by Michael Foot. Foot's intellectual qualities were never in doubt, but his naivety and innocence in the matter of personal image made him vulnerable to being constantly satirised and subverted by the media. Most notoriously, when he attended the 1982 ceremony of Remembrance at the Cenotaph in London dressed in a duffle coat, standing as protocol demanded alongside the power-dressed figure of Margaret Thatcher, his 'fitness to govern' (always a predictable Tory allegation against any Labour leader) was publicly questioned.

In the wake of the 1983 defeat, not only did Labour transform its approach to advertising and public relations in general, it selected in Neil Kinnock a leader whom it was felt could compete with the Conservatives, on the terrain of image as well as policy. Like Margaret Thatcher, he permitted his dress-sense, hair-style, and voice to be coached and shaped. His successor, John Smith, was equally adept at image-management, although the constituents of his image (intelligent, reliable, safe) were different from Kinnock's (passionate, tough). Smith's successor, Tony Blair, was elected largely because of his perceived ability to look and sound good for the cameras, and to communicate, with his image, to the electorally crucial voters of southern England. Nick Jones argues that Blair was indeed the first UK party leader to have been chosen for his ability to say 'only what he wanted to say and what he believed to be true' (1997, p.9).

It may be, of course, that the importance of image is overstated, and that audiences have gradually learned to 'read' the practices of image-management and discount them. Thatcher's successor John Major was widely perceived as 'lacking' in image, meaning that his style was rather simple and plain. During the 1992 general election campaign Major adopted the old-fashioned practice of addressing the public from a 'soapbox' erected outside his campaign bus. Notwithstanding the occasional egg or flour bomb, Major's simple, homely style of campaigning did not prevent his victory on April 9, and may indeed have contributed to it. In the view of some commentators the ascendancy of John Major as Conservative leader and prime minister signified a retreat from – or a backlash to – the sophisticated image management techniques which characterised

British politics in the 1980s. On the other hand, Major's 'lack' of image may in itself be read as a careful construction, calculated to position him, brand-like, in the political marketplace. While Neil Kinnock displayed a slick and glossy self, John Major would be seen as the 'real thing', unadorned and transparent.

In Brendan Bruce's view, Major's image comprised the following elements: comparative youth; good looks; modest social background; courteousness; 'ordinariness' and the common touch (considered to be an advantage after eleven years of Thatcher). In short, Major was all the things which Mrs Thatcher was not. Major's image-managers also stressed his love of cricket (Bruce, 1992, p.93). Under the chairmanship of Chris Patten, the Tories' public relations strategy was to portray Major as representing 'Thatcherism with a human face'. As Patten put it, 'we are trying to achieve incremental change to fit a change of Prime Minister. In supermarket terms we want to sell an updated product, not a new brand' (quoted in Butler and Kavanagh, 1992, p.39).

The success of John Major in the election of 1992 (if not subsequently) indicates that in political image-management, as in other branches of the style industry, fashions change. The subsequent rise of Tony Blair, however, and the 'making over' of his party into New Labour (and all that has gone with that in terms of party organisation and media relations) confirm that the image managers remain, at the heart of the political process.

## Political marketing

The individual politician in a liberal democracy is, in theory at least, the representative of a political party. Even leaders as powerful and charismatic as Margaret Thatcher and Tony Blair became are ultimately subordinated to the party machine. While Thatcher came to embody the Conservative Party in a way that few politicians have ever done, when in the end she was perceived as having become an electoral liability she was removed from office. The party, then, has its own identity and character which, like the personal images of its leaders, can be shaped and moulded. As Bruce notes, 'all effective communications strategies contain what is called a positioning statement, a clear analysis of *what* the brand (or company, person, political party, etc.) is for: *who* it is for, and *why* anyone should be interested in choosing it' (1992, p.87) [his emphasis].

In designing the strategy, as we noted earlier, marketing and research consultants must first establish the 'core values' of the party's target audience, which then become the basis for selling the organisation as the one best able to defend and reflect those values.

The previous chapter examined the uses of advertising in political communication. Other techniques available to the image-maker include the design of party logos and other signifiers of corporate identity. In the mid-1970s the Conservative Party adopted its 'torch' logo. Ten years later, as part of its overhauling of communication strategy, Labour abandoned the symbolism of the red flag (viewed by the leadership as a sign with negative connotations of bureaucratic, Soviet-style socialism) in favour of the 'red rose', a logo first successfully employed by the French socialists. Both parties, as already noted, expend great efforts in the design of conference backdrops, seeking to symbolise with colour and form their core political values.

Another important marketing technique is that of 'product endorsement'. In commercial terms this is achieved by positioning the product (in an advertisement or promotional event) alongside a well-known and popular personality, usually from the worlds of entertainment and sport. In politics this approach has been used since the 1960s when Harold Wilson received the Beatles in 10 Downing Street. Whether or not Mr Wilson enjoyed the Beatles music, it was certainly clear to him that large numbers of the British electorate did. To be photographed and filmed with the Beatles was an attempt to appropriate this image and its connotations; to have his 'product' endorsed by young, trendy musicians. In the late 1980s, towards the end of her period in office, Margaret Thatcher tried a similar trick with football star Paul 'Gazza' Gascoigne. If some of his working-class 'blokishness' could rub off on her, she apparently felt, it would assist her to retain popularity. In the end she, like Gazza, was to fall from grace. In the Blair government's first year in office, the prime minister hosted several parties for celebrities from the worlds of art, entertainment and youth culture at 10 Downing Street. Meetings with Oasis' writer and manager (Noel Gallagher and Alan McGee respectively) were photographed and widely publicised (although the Gallagher brothers' fondness for cocaine and marijuana was in some contradiction to the new government's anti-drugs policy).

During election campaigns, rallies have become opportunities for parties to display the stars of stage, screen and sports arena who support them. At a rally in 1983 the Conservatives enlisted the aid of popular young comedians like Kenny Everett, as well as more well-known Conservative supporters like Cilla Black and Jimmy Tarbuck. In 1992 and 1997 Labour employed 'alternative' comedians Ben Elton, Stephen Fry and others to emphasise what its advisers hoped to present as a younger, more progressive set of values. For the Labour Party, as for the Alliance and Leicester building society,[6] endorsement from such sources was assumed to carry weight with the target audience.

## Internal political communication

The marketing techniques and promotional devices described in this chapter and the previous one are not pursued in isolation but as part of a communications strategy which will ideally be co-ordinated and synchronised. Parties, like commercial organisations, must develop channels of *internal* communication, so that members (and particularly those involved in a public capacity) are aware of the 'message' to be delivered at any given time, and to ensure that the different elements of the public relations operation are working with each other effectively. Failure to put in place such channels can result in public relations disasters and electoral failures, as the Labour Party found to its cost in the 1983 campaign. Hughes and Wintour note that 'the party [in 1983] ran an inept and disorganised campaign, led by one of the least appropriate figures ever to head either of the two dominant political parties' (1993, p.6). We have already referred to some of the problems associated with then Labour leader Michael Foot's personal image. Equally damaging, if not more so, to the party's campaign in 1983 was the general lack of co-ordination and planning in the public presentation of policy. Heffernan and Marqusee agree that the 1983 campaign was 'badly organised and its media strategy non-existent' (1992, p.28), and that defence policy in particular was mishandled. 'A spreading cloud of political double talk obscured the basic humanistic message about nuclear disarmament which, opinion polls had shown, was capable of commanding substantial public support' (Ibid., p.32).

Elsewhere I have examined in some detail Labour's handling of its defence policy in 1983 (McNair, 1988, 1989). An analysis of television news coverage of the campaign revealed that Labour's leadership failed to make a coherent statement of the policy, not least because Denis Healey, Michael Foot, Roy Hattersley and other senior figures appeared to disagree on important aspects of it. While the Conservatives in 1983 fought an incisive and aggressive campaign against Labour's non-nuclear defence programme, the public representatives of the Labour Party showed themselves to lack confidence and faith in their own approach to the issue.

This confusion, and other failures of the 1983 campaign, prompted Neil Kinnock, shortly after he became party leader, to form a 'communication and campaigns directorate' which would bring all of Labour's public relations activities within one management structure, headed by Peter Mandelson. In 1985 a Campaign Management Team was established under senior Kinnock adviser Patricia Hewitt, with responsibility for preparing and executing 'long' campaigns, well in advance of the actual election. Thus, when the 1987 campaign started, party leaders had an agenda of issues and 'theme days' to work through.

In 1985 Peter Mandelson, as communications director, recommended the creation of an apparatus which could co-ordinate the party's public relations, marketing, and advertising work. It would function within the context of an agreed communication strategy; a unified presentation of the political message, using all available media; and high-quality publicity materials.[7]

The Shadow Communications Agency, as it was called, would enlist as many sympathetic volunteers from the world of professional communication as possible. With the help of advertising professional Philip Gould, Mandelson and the SCA strove, with some success, to prevent the incoherence of the 1983 campaign from ever happening again. Hughes and Wintour argue that 'Mandelson and Gould succeeded, not because they exploited slick advertising and media management more effectively than the Conservatives, but because they forged between themselves an approach to political strategy which has never before been seen . . . They welded policy, politics and image-creation into one weapon' (1993, p.183).

In the campaign of 1987, however, even a vastly improved structure of internal communication management could not prevent Labour's defence policy from once again upsetting the strategy. We have already referred to Kinnock's disastrous interview with David Frost. In 1987, as in 1983, senior leaders' confusion about, and apparent lack of commitment to, the party's non-nuclear defence policy greatly weakened the campaign overall. Despite the efforts of Mandelson, Gould, Hewitt and the SCA 'it was hopeless to imagine that the party could successfully campaign on a non-nuclear policy, when the policy itself was internally inconsistent, and self-evidently evasive' (Ibid., p.16).

The work of the Shadow Communications Agency carried on to

the 1992 election, when it was suggested that the party should 'deal with Mr Kinnock's image problem by giving a higher profile to attractive and able front-benchers. He should be protected from hazards, particularly from contact with the tabloids, and should appear in as many statesman-like settings as possible' (Ibid., p.88). Thus, he was seen touring the country in a distinguished, 'prime ministerial' car, flanked by police outriders, and carrying himself with the bearing of one confidently on the verge of real political power. Slick, photogenic, and somewhat bland front-bench spokespersons like Tony Blair and Gordon Brown were preferred in public campaigning work to the more radical voices of John Prescott, Tony Benn, and Ken Livingstone.

Such tactics were again insufficient, however, to deliver electoral success. Labour improved its position by comparison with the results of the 1987 election, but failed once more to deprive the Conservatives of an overall majority. In the aftermath of a fourth consecutive general election defeat, an internal debate began within the party which echoed earlier ambiguities about the value of political marketing. Once again, senior Labour voices could be heard decrying the pernicious influence of the image-makers, and asserting that Labour should dispense with them, or at least downgrade their role in campaigning. The SCA was accused of robbing the party of its socialist identity, in favour of red roses and gloss.

Despite such criticisms, however, the election of Tony Blair as leader in July 1994 signalled the ascendancy of Labour's image-managers; those like Patricia Hewitt, Peter Mandelson and others who believed that a Labour victory was conditional on 'moving from a policy committee based process to a communication based exercise' (Heffernan and Marqusee, 1992, p.103). The astonishing, and unpredicted landslide election victory of May 1997 means that few will dare to challenge this approach in the forseeable future of British politics.

The Conservatives, for their part, have also had problems with internal communication. Despite the success of its political marketing since the mid-1970s the party found itself in some difficulty in the 1987 campaign. Confronted, on the one hand, by an unprecedentedly professional Labour campaign, their own efforts were hampered by a lack of co-ordination between key elements of the communications apparatus. Mrs Thatcher made a number of 'gaffes' during the campaign including, on Labour's 'health day', her insistence on her moral right to attend a private hospital. Tory difficulties culminated in 'wobbly Thursday', when it began to seem that Labour might win the election. In the end, Tory fears were misplaced, and Mrs Thatcher achieved a third election victory with an overall majority in three figures. Nevertheless, the party leadership's dissatisfaction with what it perceived to be a weak campaign led to a restructuring of the public relations organisation.

Party chairman Peter Brooke divided Central Office functions into three – communication, research, and organisation – and appointed Brendan Bruce as Director of Communications. A communication audit conducted by Shandwick PR in 1991 led to the appointment of regional communications officers to liaise with the local media in their areas. In 1991 too, after a period of cool relations, the Conservatives reappointed Saatchi and Saatchi to plan and co-ordinate communications strategy in all its aspects. The agency developed a 'long' campaign stressing the Tories' economic competence and raising anxieties about Labour's 'tax and spend' plans. 'The government was urged to seize the opportunity to dominate the news, exploiting ministerial statements, parliamentary questions, control of parliamentary time, and, ultimately, the Budget' (Butler and Kavanagh, 1992, p.81).

The 'short' campaign, when it came, was generally perceived as being much more successful than that of 1987 (although the government's majority was cut to 22). In 1992, unlike 1987:

> 10 Downing Street was to be intimately linked with operations in Central Office and there would be close relations between the Prime Minister and the party chairman; there would be a coherent communications strategy to which all party spokesmen would be expected to adhere; there would be no battle between rival advertising agencies, for advertising was exclusively in the hands of Saatchi and Saatchi; there would be a major effort to co-ordinate the content and timing of ministers' speeches, press conferences, election broadcasts, and photo-opportunities; and key ministers would accord priority to appearing on regional television.
>
> (Ibid., p.86)

In so far as this strategy resulted in electoral victory, it was undeniably successful. While, as we have seen, John Major's image was self-consciously 'unconstructed', the co-ordination and synchronisation of the Tories' overall political message was carefully planned and expertly executed.

Between 1992 and 1997, however, it all went wrong for the Conservatives. As noted above, a series of 'sleaze' scandals, and major policy differences over European union, destroyed its capacity to control and shape the news agenda, leaving the leadership helpless in the face of self-inflicted, self-destructive division and in-fighting. When the 1997 election campaign began, it was, we can see now with hindsight, already over, with the Tories reduced to their worst electoral showing for more than a century. Much of this collapse was the product of poor internal communication, as candidates failed to receive adequate leadership from the party's central office, and factions developed around contrasting approaches to Europe. In 1997 the Tories were as ineffectual in their internal communication and campaign co-ordination as the Labour Party had ever been.

## Information management

Finally, in this discussion of party political public relations, we turn to the techniques and practices involved in information management by government. By this is meant activities designed to control or manipulate the flow of information from institutions of government to the public sphere beyond. Steinberg defines governmental communication as 'those techniques which government officials and agencies employ to keep the public informed and to disseminate information about the activities of various departments' (1958, p.327). The dissemination of information is not, however, the only purpose of governmental communication. Information is a power resource, the astute deployment of which can play a major role in the management of public opinion. As Denton and Woodward note, 'information is power, and the control of information is the first step in propaganda' (1990, p.42). Information can be freely given out in the pursuit of democratic government, but it can also be suppressed, censored, leaked, and manufactured in accordance with the more particular interests of a government and the organs of state power. As former civil servant Clive Ponting puts it, writing of the British government, public opinion may be regarded as 'something to be manipulated rather than a voice that might alter government policy' (1989, p.189). In Britain, he notes, 'the tradition is that government is a matter for insiders and not something that need concern the general public. Decisions are taken in secret by a small group of ministers and senior servants and then the effort is made to sell those policies to the public through the government propaganda machine' (Ibid., p.177). Governmental communication for this observer, himself a former Whitehall 'insider', is about the control and management of information for the purpose of protecting and insulating power from the critical gaze of the public, rather than empowering the latter and drawing them into the governmental process. Cockerell *et al.* concur that 'what government chooses to tell us through its public relations machine is one thing; the information in use by participants in the country's real government is another' (1984, p.9).

The British government first established an apparatus of media management during the First World War. Known as the Official Press Bureau, the principles of secrecy to which it adhered have been retained in the governmental information apparatus ever since. In this respect British political culture may be seen as 'closed' and secretive, as distinct from the relative openness of the United States system. This is reflected in legislation such as the Official Secrets Act, and the disclosure rules which prevent some official secrets being revealed to the public for 30, 40, or even 100 years after the event. One of the key pledges of the new Labour government was to introduce, for the first time in Britain, a Freedom of Information Act. As this edition went to press, the legislation was reported to be still in preparation for eventual passage through the House of Commons. Early reports indicated that it would indeed go far in the direction of eroding the culture of closure and secrecy surrounding official information in Britain, although there would be many exceptions and loop holes, such as those necessary for law enforcement and other security matters.

## 'Pro-active' information management

Governmental information management may have a number of functions. The activities of a body such as the Central Office of Information are ostensibly about informing the public in a neutral manner, on matters of interest and concern to them, such as civil defence procedures or the activities of the British Council abroad. In recent years, however, the COI has been 'co-opted' into a more overtly political role. In the early 1980s the Conservative government employed it to counteract the activities of the anti-nuclear protest movement. Later in the decade the COI's spending on advertising tripled, largely to publicise the government's privatisation campaign. In so far as this communication activity was intended to inform the British public about the fact of privatisation, it did not breach the parameters of the COI's traditional remit.

Much of the material produced was, however, clearly promotional in function – advertising designed to *sell* the ideologically grounded policy of a particular party and government. In 1988 the head of the COI, himself concerned about the undermining of his agency's neutrality, demanded a public inquiry, which was not granted (Harris, 1991).

Other ostensibly neutral state agencies, such as the Government Information Service, have developed an equally ambiguous relationship to the political process. The GIS was established in the 1950s 'to give prompt and accurate information and give it objectively about government activities and government policy. It is quite definitely not the job of the Government Information Service to try to boost the government and try to persuade the press to' (Lord Swinton, quoted in Harris, 1991, p.113). Current guidelines state that the publicity work of the GIS should be 'relevant' to the activities and responsibilities of the government, and that it should be 'objective and explanatory, not tendentious or polemical', and 'should not be party political' (quoted in Ingham, 1991, p.368). That the GIS was accused of flouting these guidelines in recent years is largely the responsibility of Margaret Thatcher and her mould-breaking press secretary, Bernard Ingham. Tony Blair's Labour government has been just as controversial, however, subjecting the service to radical overhaul (including modifying its name to the Government Information and Communication Service [GICS]). Many of the changes can be defended as sensible responses to changes in the media environment, which no government, of whatever hue, could have avoided. Others, such as the increased role of 'special advisers' appointed from outside the civil service, and the downgraded status of traditional mandarins, have been greeted with cries of 'politicisation', and many resignations. In this respect, however, Labour is merely following the precedent established by the Tories, even if the speed of their reforms surprised many.

## Prime ministerial public relations

All prime ministers, noted a former political reporter of the *Sunday Times*, seek to 'dominate the press, radio and television as the vital precondition to their domination of Parliament, parties and public opinion. They [desire] to control and exploit the media as an arm of government' (James Margach, quoted in Cockerell *et al.*, 1984, p.8). The main means by which this domination can be secured is through the figure of the chief press secretary.

The post of Prime Minister's Press Secretary was first created by Ramsay MacDonald in 1929, in order to assist him in his dealings with the media. The work of a contemporary press secretary involves managing government-media relations as a whole: enabling journalists' access to information, communicating governmental views and decisions to the media, and 'feeding back' media reportage of, and commentary on, governmental performance.

Although a civil service appointment paid for from public funds (and thus *not* part of the party apparatus), the press secretary has frequently been strongly identified with the politics of his or her prime ministerial employer. Harold Wilson's press secretary, Joe Haines, was politically close to the Labour leader. But it was Margaret Thatcher's press secretary Bernard Ingham (now Sir) who is perceived to have truly politicised the post.

Ironically, Ingham when appointed was not an obvious political ally of the Thatcher premiership, but an ex-Labour-supporting career civil servant who found himself, by his own admission, entranced and seduced by his employer's iconoclastic radicalism (1991). As press secretary Bernard Ingham was, like each of his predecessors, at the heart of the British government's information management system. He chaired the Meeting of Information Officers, a committee comprising the senior public relations officials in Whitehall; co-ordinated the news management work of governmental departments, including relations with 'the Lobby' (see below); and in 1989 was appointed to head the Government Information Service (and with it, the Central Office of Information). In Robert Harris's view, by the close of the Thatcher era Ingham had become a *de facto* 'Minister of Information' rather than a neutral public servant (1991). In this capacity he orchestrated and directed governmental communication in conformity with the interests, not of the public as a whole, but of his government and, in particular, of his prime minister.

A key instrument of Ingham's communicative work was the 'Lobby' system, identified by Cockerell *et al.* as 'the Prime Minister's most useful tool for the political management of the news' (1984, p.33). The Lobby was established in 1884 as a means of enabling parliamentary correspondents to gain access to authoritative information about political events and governmental business. So called because journalists originally assembled in the lobby of the House of Commons, the system was institutionalised in 1921 and persists to the present day. Bernard Ingham describes the workings of the Lobby thus:

> Press officers speak as frankly as they feel able to members
> [of the Lobby], either individually or collectively, on a
> background basis: i.e., the journalist does not identify his
> source precisely in writing his story ... This method of
> communication with journalists is universally practised in
> government and other circles the world over as a means of
> opening up the relationship [between government and
> media].
>
> (1991, p.158)

Critics dispute both Ingham's optimistic reading of the Lobby's
impact on government–media relations, and his assertion of its
'universality'. In Robert Harris's view:

> by the late 1970s, most countries had a straightforward
> government spokesman – a political appointee who would
> brief the press, appear on radio and television, and pro-
> mote the official line. But in Britain, the spokesman was not
> only anonymous: he acted in accordance with quasi-
> masonic rules drawn up in Queen Victoria's time. A system
> which had been designed to preserve the quintessentially
> English atmosphere of a gentleman's club had been
> imported into the television age.
>
> (1991, p.82)

The main criticism of this system of non-attributable media briefings was that it permitted manipulation of journalists by politicians
to a degree that is unhealthy for and damaging to the democratic
process. Cockerell *et al.* argue that 'its secretiveness mirrors the
secrecy that surrounds so much of government in Whitehall and
allows the government of the day to present its own unchallenged
version of reality' (1984, p.42). This it can do simply because journalists are forced to respect the rules, or face exclusion from the
system and the valuable information it supplies. In the extremely
competitive environment of the contemporary media industry this is
not a realistic option, although the *Guardian* and the *Independent*
voluntarily withdrew for a period in the 1980s, in the hope
(unfulfilled) that change to the system would follow.

When, for example, Margaret Thatcher wished to leak damaging
information about ministerial colleagues who had fallen from
favour, she frequently employed Ingham, and the Lobby system, to
do it, in the knowledge that nothing said in briefings could be

attributed to her personally. John Biffen, Leon Brittan, and Nigel Lawson were among those ministers who in the 1980s found their credibility and positions threatened in this way. Nigel Lawson, indeed, went so far as to accuse Number 10 and Ingham of 'black propaganda' in their dealings with him (Harris, 1991, p.176).

In his memoirs and elsewhere, Ingham denies that he ever used the Lobby system, or any of the communication channels available to him, in an improper way. There can be no doubt, however, that the Thatcher–Ingham era was accompanied by an unprecedented centralisation and politicisation of the governmental communication apparatus, the potential for abuse of which was of concern to many, right and left on the political spectrum, not least, as the previous section suggested, because the even more centralised, even more ruthlessly politicised governmental information system of the Blair government could, and does claim a precedent for its approach in the Thatcher years.

As for the development of prime ministerial public relations under the Blair–Campbell regime, there have been some important positive changes in the direction of openness. Since November 1997 Lobby briefings have no longer been entirely anonymous, but can now be attributed to Campbell, as Blair's official spokesman. Lobby journalists and political commentators have generally welcomed these changes.

More worryingly, for some, Campbell brought his aggressive style of news management from opposition – where it was used to great effect to woo the hitherto Tory press (see Chapter 4) – into government where, as in the Thatcher–Ingham years, it is as likely to be used against Labour ministers as opposition politicians or the BBC. Regarding his regular spats with the latter organisation, Campbell wrote in a 1997 article that 'the media is aggressive and it often requires aggressive argument in return'.[8] In this respect he was, as this edition went to press, proving a more than worthy successor to Sir Bernard in his rough handling of the journalists.

# 8

# PRESSURE GROUP POLITICS AND THE OXYGEN OF PUBLICITY

The preceding two chapters were concerned with the communication practices of the mainstream political parties as they seek to exert influence over the political environment, public opinion, and ultimately voting behaviour. But as Chapter 1 stressed, party organisations are not the only political actors. On the margins of the political mainstream exist a huge variety of organisations which compete alongside the established parties for influence and political efficacy. These organisations, like the parties, have been required to learn the rules of the late twentieth-century media game, and to use channels of mass communication to further their objectives.

## THE SOCIOLOGY OF SOURCE STRATEGIES

By definition marginal political actors, operating outside of the established institutions, stand at a disadvantage with respect to mainstream parties, and government and official bodies. They are relatively lacking in the resources which enable the latter to make news and set public agendas. They are unlikely to have the access to the sources of finance which are available to a major political party, and thus to all the components of effective political communication which money can provide: qualified professional and skilled creative personnel, advertising and public relations material, etc. Neither will they normally have access to the 'cultural capital' held by established political actors – the credibility and authority which tends to accrue to office holders and members of recognised elite groups. They are, to use Edie Goldenberg's phrase, 'resource poor' (1984). In Philip Schlesinger's terms, they lack 'definitional power' (1989).

Schlesinger's phrase refers us back to Stuart Hall *et al.*'s work on 'primary definition' (1978), which asserts a pattern of structured, differential access to media (and the power to define issues which such access potentially brings with it), favouring those in elite or dominant positions and discriminating against marginal or subordinate groups. For Hall *et al.* the former, by virtue of their privileged access to channels of mass communication, acquire the status of 'primary definers' in public debate about current issues. Their interpretations of events, their explanatory frameworks within which events are made sense of, become consensual, while alternative explanations and accounts are excluded or relegated to the margins, denied legitimacy.

Hall *et al.*'s work is informed by a Marxist problematic which seeks to explain the relative invisibility of subordinate and oppositional accounts of social reality in the mass media, while avoiding the crude, 'vulgar' materialism of some Marxist academics. For Hall *et al.* primary definers become so not simply because journalists and editors are 'biased' towards elite groups (although straightforward ideological bias may be a sufficient explanation in some cases) but as a result of the media's structural relationships of dependence on, and deference to, recognised authority. The journalist's need for reliable sources of information; editorial pressures to meet deadlines; and elite groups' typically more developed systems for meeting these needs, gives them an inevitable advantage over the 'dissident' or oppositional group.

This *organisational* factor is reinforced by cultural assumptions on the part of news-gatherers (which are widely shared in the society as a whole) about which sources are the most reliable and authoritative on a given issue (thus the Labour Home Office Minister is automatically a primary definer on law and order issues, while the views of the working-class resident of an inner-city housing estate are not sought, unless on an occasional chat or phone-in show with a 'human interest' angle).

The primary definition thesis is a compelling one, which has proved useful in predicting and analysing patterns of access in media debate about a wide range of political issues. Schlesinger and others have pointed out, however, that it fails to account adequately for the complexity of mediated political debate, and the many cases where 'primary definers' have failed to impose their primary definitions on the public debate as a whole. Recent political history provides many examples of dominant or elite groups being, in effect, defeated in public debate, often by the activities of relatively marginal political actors, and sometimes at the cost of real political power. In other cases, a 'dominant account' or interpretation of events has had to be revised to accommodate alternative or oppositional views.

The Nixon administration's withdrawal from the Vietnam War was one such example. In this case radical change was forced on a policy sponsored by the United States politico-military establishment by a combination of pressure-group and journalistic activity (see Chapter 9). The British Conservative government's 1980s retreat on the 'poll tax' (the refusal to retreat being an important factor in Margaret Thatcher's removal from office and replacement by John Major) was occasioned not least by a groundswell of public opposition to the policy, focussed on pressure groups of greater or lesser extremism, and reported widely in the media (Deacon and Golding, 1994). The experience of the Major government after its election victory of 1992 was one of constant challenge to its policy content and style, in stark contrast to the 1980s, when 'Thatcherism' was presumed to have become consensual. In Italy, as the *tangentopoli* scandal emerged in 1993, an entire generation of politicians from all parties was brought down by popular opinion.

The causes of these political shifts, and the contexts in which they occurred, are of course very different. They all, however, highlight the weaknesses of any theoretical framework which asserts the existence of a deep structural bias on the part of the media towards 'the powerful', 'the establishment', or 'the ruling class' in modern capitalist societies. Greek sociologist Nicos Poulantzas long ago rejected, from a Marxist standpoint, the notion of a 'ruling class' as a meaningful political entity, preferring to think in terms of 'class fractions', and alliances of class fractions, whose influence rose and fell as economic and social circumstances changed.[1] Thus, one could identify the influence of 'finance capital' in 1980s Britain, and the relative political impotence of 'manufacturing capital'. Some observers have argued that the sudden political demise of Margaret Thatcher in 1990 can be viewed partly in terms of the reassertion of British manufacturing capital in the context of a government whose opposition to the concept of European union was endangering future markets and prosperity. The same Conservative hostility to European union has been cited as one explanation for the shift in business support to Labour from 1994 onwards (in addition to the political communication factors discussed already).

If economic classes (in the Marxist sense) can be divided, and have contradictory political interests, so too the members of political parties, governments, business organisations and other collectivities will often be unable to act coherently and rationally as one body. The existence of such divisions means that political elites, and others who could in Hall's terms be described as potential primary definers, circulate. Their fortunes rise and fall: as one 'faction' loses power another takes it on.

Sometimes the removal of one elite member from power, such as occurred at the end of Margaret Thatcher's premiership, is a tactical manoeuvre designed to preserve the power of a wider group, in this case the Conservative Party in government. At other times, such as the transfer of power from George Bush's Republican Party to the Democrats in 1992, or from Conservative to Labour in 1997, the shift signals a more fundamental change in the direction of a country's government. At other times still, such as the *tangentopoli* crisis in Italy, a wholesale cleansing of the political establishment takes place, with commentators speaking of 'revolution'.

In none of the above cases is the rotation of elites 'revolutionary' in the true sense of signalling a transition from one type of social system (what Marx called 'mode of production') to another, and the weakening of the primary definition thesis (and similar Marxian-structuralist accounts of how power is exercised at the cultural level) does not imply that the political arena is completely open to unlimited dissent. But the reality of recent political history has encouraged a movement away from sociological approaches which view political, economic, and cultural power as essentially static, located in relatively fixed or rigid categories of class, sex, ethnicity, etc., to one which focusses on the openness of the political communication process, and the opportunities available for subordinate groups to intervene meaningfully in the public sphere, having their alternative definitions of events reported and taken seriously by the media, at which point they are much more likely to be viewed as legitimate in public debate.

Such an approach asserts that there is no single 'primary definition' of an event or an issue circulating in the public sphere at any given time, but a multiplicity of definitions, reflecting the interests of various collectivities, within and outside the 'establishment'; that while one definition may be dominant at a particular time, challenges will continually be mounted, as opposition groups seek to advance their alternative definitions; that structures of access to the media, through which the struggle for definitional principally takes place, are not rigid but flexible, and capable of accommodating, even under certain circumstances welcoming challenges to the establishment; and that such flexibility is, indeed, an integral legitimating feature of the media in a liberal democracy.

As we noted in Chapter 4, the continuing credibility of the media's 'Fourth Estate' role requires, in conditions of liberal democracy, the maintenance of journalists' 'relative autonomy' from power elites. While we may readily agree that the majority of the media in capitalist societies are, for economic, organisational, and ideological reasons, predisposed to certain sources and viewpoints over others, we must acknowledge too that media organisations have their own institutional interests to pursue, which include being *seen* to be independent and objective and, in most cases, competitive and profitable. These imperatives create opportunities for non-elite groups to gain access to mainstream media.

The question thus arises: what are the conditions in which marginalised political actors, aspiring to participate in public debate around an issue, or to put an issue on the media's and the public's agenda, can maximise their 'definitional power' and pursue their political objectives? We must acknowledge at the outset that access to the media for a particular source is never completely open, but dependent on such factors as the degree of institutionalisation accruing to that source; its financial resources; its 'cultural capital' or status, and the extent of its entrepreneurship and innovation in media management. In 1978, Hall *et al.* argued that

> if the tendency towards ideological closure [in news media] is maintained by the way the different apparatuses are structurally linked so as to promote the dominant definitions of events, then the counter-tendency must also depend on the existence of organised and articulate sources which generate counter-definitions of the situation. This depends to some degree on whether the collectivity which generates counter-ideologies and explanations is a powerful countervailing force in society; whether it represents an organised majority or substantial minority; and whether or not it has a degree of legitimacy within the system or can win such a position through struggle.
>
> (1978, p.64)

As already noted, such groups usually start from a 'resource poor' position, relatively deprived of material and cultural capital. To compensate for their lack of institutional status and authority, strategies of media management must be deployed in order to

159

exploit the opportunities for access which exist. Sources which cannot take media access for granted must *work* to generate it, using skill, innovation and knowledge to enhance their value for media organisations. Such groups can, for example, increase their newsworthiness by careful attention to interacting with the media, cultivating contacts and responding to the organisational demands of media production (for example, issuing news releases in time for last editions and main evening news bulletins). As Edie Goldenberg suggests, 'a skilful source can build a relationship similar to that which often exists between resource rich source and beat reporter, in which the reporter depends on the source for news and, as a result, the reporter is willing to listen to and act on behalf of the source's interests' (1984, p.237).

In this sense, the group or source must cultivate *dependence*, through generating *newsworthiness*, which requires an understanding of what constitutes *newsvalues*. Goldenberg argues that newsworthiness is partly a function of *difference*. and is increased 'the more a group's political goals deviate from prevailing social norms' (Ibid., p.234). Collins's discussion of counter-cultural religious movements notes how they have frequently gained 'access to a public voice' by cultivating and generating controversy (1992, p.116). A group's newsworthiness, and thus access, is also increased if its goals parallel a currently newsworthy issue, and if they are specific and relatively easy to make sense of for the journalist and can be associated with already-established 'definers' and sources (such as the peace movement's association with retired military personnel in the 1980s).

King makes the obvious point that access to the media is strongly influenced by 'performance factors' such as 'situational credibility, perceived sincerity, and rhetorical skill in conveying the message' (1987, p.10). For groups without the culturally validated authority of elite sources, access can also be achieved by recourse to forms of 'spectacular' action – demonstrations of anger, determination, or campaigning ingenuity which provide media organisations with attractive and valuable news material and thus increase the likelihood of coverage.

Media management of this type can and frequently does generate substantial coverage for a political viewpoint or cause which might otherwise be invisible to the mainstream media audience, a fact which has led to the gradual adoption by pressure groups and other subordinate sources of the whole battery of political communication techniques (subject, of course, to resource limitations).

However, just as the British Labour Party for many years resisted this trend in its campaigning work on the grounds that it signalled a fundamental degradation of the political process, so many pressure groups, particularly those on the left of the political spectrum, remain suspicious of what they view as unauthentic, corrupting campaign methods (though, as the power of such methods becomes clear, resistance lessens). Todd Gitlin's discussion of the interaction between the US-based Students for a Democratic Society movement and the media in the 1960s acknowledges that techniques of the sort listed above allowed the SDS to be present in media coverage, but argues that by adopting them the organisation was 'incorporated' into the political process in such a way that its original objectives were lost. 'As movement and media discovered and acted on each other, they worked out the terms with which they would recognise and work on the other; they developed a grammar of interaction. This grammar then shaped the way the movement-media history developed' (1984, p.240). This development, Gitlin suggests, was one in which the SDS members came under pressure to 'legitimise' themselves and their objectives, in the interests of gaining access to the mainstream media agenda.

In any case, Gitlin adds, to receive coverage in the media is not by any means the same thing as gaining *access* to it for the effective articulation of one's definition of events. News journalism tends to trivialise and simplify the activities of subordinate groups, and to focus on the spectacular demonstrations at the expense of explanation and argument. Such 'access' may have more negative than positive consequences for an organisation.

In the remainder of this chapter we consider these issues in the context of the experience of three different types of organisation: pressure groups proper, such as the Campaign for Nuclear Disarmament and Greenpeace; illegal or 'terrorist' organisations, such as the Irish Republican Army (IRA); and, to begin, the trade unions.

## POLITICAL COMMUNICATION AND INDUSTRIAL RELATIONS

The trade unions in Britain have traditionally been among the most ardent critics of media 'bias' against their viewpoints on, and definitions of, issues in which they have an interest, such as the economy, employment rights, and industrial relations legislation. Fuelled by the work of the Glasgow University Media Group

(GUMG) in the 1970s, it was argued by trade unionists that the media – press and broadcasting – reported such issues from an inherently anti-labour, pro-capital perspective. Media accounts of the causes of industrial disputes, for example, tended to be dominated by management, while the viewpoints of the workforce were simplified and distorted.

Perceiving this to be the case trade unions, like many other left-of-centre organisations with political agendas to pursue, came to view the media as 'the enemy' in an ongoing class struggle. To gain fair media coverage, it was argued, the left would have to build and sustain its own media channels, as was attempted unsuccessfully with the *Daily News* experiment in Scotland in the early 1970s (McKay and Barr, 1976), and the *News on Sunday* in 1986 (Chippindale and Horrie, 1988).

Since the late 1970s, however, and especially since the election of the Thatcher government in 1979, trade unions have been obliged to reassess their relationship to the media, acknowledging that in addition to anti-labour biases (of which there undoubtedly were and remain many, particularly amongst the right-wing tabloids) there are also spaces and opportunities for media coverage which they can exploit.

Nicholas Jones's valuable study of the role played by the media in industrial disputes asserts that the coming of Thatcherism fundamentally transformed the environment within which they were pursued. In the period before Thatcher came to office – sometimes referred to as the era of 'social democratic consensus' – unemployment was relatively low, Labour governments were a reality (as they became again, eighteen years after Thatcher first came to power), and organised labour enjoyed a certain degree of economic and hence political power, exemplified by its role in the downfall of Edward Heath in 1974, and the 'winter of discontent' in 1978–9 which eventually destroyed the Labour government of James Callaghan. Industrial relations legislation permitted effective solidarity action, such as mass picketing, which allowed workers in dispute to believe that they had some chance of success if confrontation with employers became necessary. Employers, for their part, had incentives to seek agreement with workers in dispute, since strikes and other forms of action could be long and costly.

After 1979 all this changed. The Thatcher government pursued a policy of driving up unemployment to levels not seen in Britain since the 1930s. It introduced wave after wave of anti-labour legislation, designed to make effective combined and solidarity action increasingly difficult. Mass picketing was outlawed, compulsory ballots of members before strikes introduced, and 'sympathy' action by one union on behalf of another made illegal, with sanctions for breach of the law including the 'sequestration' (seizure by the court) of a union's assets. This shifting of the industrial balance of power away from the workforce and towards employers was accompanied by an ideological campaign which encouraged managers to 'exercise their right to manage'. Compromise and negotiation with the unions, particularly those on the left, was frowned upon by government in its own dealings with the nationalised industries, and private capital was encouraged to follow the example. Thus, the unions became weaker, and industrial disputes more brutal, as the 1984–5 miners' strike and the 1986 Wapping dispute showed.

In Jones's view these environmental changes heightened the role of the media in the pursuit of industrial disputes. As the traditional channels of negotiation and compromise were closed down, both sides in disputes were required to compete more actively for the support of public opinion. And in this competition, the mass media were the main channels of communication available. The unions, in particular, had to learn to use the media to overcome the over-whelmingly negative public image which they had acquired in the late 1970s, redefining their social and political role in the context of an unremittingly hostile government and business community. In this cultural shift they were prompted by the sophisticated news management techniques of some key business leaders, such as Michael Edwardes of the nationalised car manufacturer British Leyland.

In the 1970s British Leyland came to epitomise Britain's indus-trial relations 'problem', being the site of several bitter disputes, frequently involving strike action. The GUMG argued in their *Bad News* and *More Bad News* studies that the tendency of the media at the time to 'blame the workers' while ignoring the role of manage-ment and other factors for which the unions had no responsibility was part of the pattern of bias referred to earlier (1976, 1980). Be that as it may, by 1977 the company was in deep crisis, and the then Labour government appointed South African industrialist Michael Edwardes to rescue it on behalf of the taxpayer.

Edwardes pioneered, in the British context, a variety of media management and communication techniques which had the effect of circumventing established management–union channels, weak-ening the authority of the union leadership and the solidarity of the workforce. Edwardes and his management adopted a strategy of 'going over the heads' of union negotiators, communicating directly with the workforce and seeking to persuade them of the correctness of management's policies. Edwardes also applied public relations techniques, pursued through the media, to the mobilisation of public support.

For example, announcements of important management decisions would be timed to accommodate main news programmes, particularly the popular early evening bulletins with the largest audiences (basic public relations, of course, but innovative in the context of industrial disputes). News reports would be closely monitored by British Leyland's PR staff, and any perceived mistakes or inaccuracies in coverage immediately relayed to the media organisation concerned, for correction at the next available opportunity. Edwardes insisted on going 'live' when he appeared in broadcast interviews, thus preventing the possibility of his views being edited to his disadvantage. To protect his authority and status, he never appeared in debates with union leaders on television.

BL under Edwardes pioneered the practice of producing company newspapers which were delivered free of charge to the workforce. This allowed management to bypass the leadership of the union by disseminating its message directly into workers' homes. Management offers on pay, conditions, or other points of dispute could be made 'unmediated' by union leaders' objections and counter arguments. BL management also introduced the practice of carrying out surveys of workers' opinions, the findings of which would then be incorporated into negotiating tactics. By the use of such methods Edwardes secured from the BL workforce a vote of 7 to 1 in favour of his recovery plan, despite the vociferous objections of the union.

Where British Leyland had led, other managements followed, compelling union negotiators to accept that they, too, would have to embrace communication techniques which involved co-operation with, rather than huffy dismissal of, the 'capitalist media'. This would require an appreciation of the media's demands and news-values, and attention to the presentation, as well as the substance of a negotiating position.

During the rail strike of 1982 the National Union of Railway-workers did precisely this, making the dispute, in Jones's view, the first in which 'a substantial attempt at negotiating through the news media was made' (1986, p.4). In the 1984–5 miners' strike, notwithstanding the bitterness and violence which accompanied the dispute. National Union of Mineworkers' leaders, and Arthur Scargill in particular, pursued a determinedly pro-active communication strategy, using the media where possible to disseminate the miners' positions to NUM rank and file members, other unions, and the British public as a whole. Scargill, like Edwardes before him, appeared in television interviews only if he was 'live' and in complete control of the use made of his remarks. Indeed, his readiness to make public defences of the miners' case, and the competence with which he did so in the face of invariably hostile interviewing techniques, made a sharp contrast to the evasiveness and lack of presentational ability demonstrated by National Coal Board Chairman Ian McGregor, whose most memorable moment of the campaign was to be filmed with a plastic bag over his head as he sought to avoid the attentions of reporters.

Both the NUM and the management of British Coal broke new ground in communication terms by accepting an invitation from *Channel 4 News* to prepare contributions to the programme, over which they had complete editorial control, outlining their respective arguments. The Coal Board spent £4.5 million on advertising its case in the press.

Despite the energy and innovative flair applied by the NUM to its public relations campaign, it failed to prevent the destruction of most of Britain's coal industry, and a historic victory for the Thatcher government, still seeking retribution for the miners' role in the humiliation and downfall of the Heath government. Explanations for the miners' defeat have subsequently been sought in the NUM's failure to organise a pre-strike ballot and thus legitimise the action among those miners who, in the absence of a ballot, chose to carry on working. The strike came at a time when coal stocks were exceptionally high, and the winter of 1984–5 was unseasonally mild. These factors were undoubtedly important, though only elements in an overall environment which was much more hostile to organised labour than had been the case ten years earlier. After the Falklands conflict and its landslide election victory in 1983, the Thatcher government was near invincible, as the miners found to their cost. Nevertheless, the public relations strategies employed by Scargill and the NUM leadership demonstrated that even the 'hard left' of British politics could, and should, engage in persuasive political communication. Weakened by mass unemployment and draconion anti-labour laws, the NUM and its partners in the trade union movement were drawn more closely into the battle for public opinion.

In the years following the miners' strike, while Conservative dominance of government and continuing high levels of unemployment

kept the unions very much subordinate parties in industrial relations, skilled use of the media produced many symbolic, if rarely
actual, defeats for the government and private employees. Disputes
by ambulance drivers and nurses in the National Health Service
were characterised by the participation in media coverage of emi-
nently reasonable, sympathy-inducing public spokespersons, with
government ministers frequently being made to appear miserly and
brutal. On the other hand, the violent picketing by print workers at
Rupert Murdoch's Wapping newspaper plant in 1986 (much of it
provoked by the police) produced media images which were less
than helpful in building public support for the printers' cause.

The impact of media management on the outcome of an industrial dispute will never be as great as the environmental factors
already referred to, such as the level of unemployment, the political
strength of a government, and the nature of legal constraints on
unions' collective action. However, in so far as governments and
employers must take public opinion into account when pursuing
such disputes (and that will depend on a range of factors) unions
have learnt that there is much to gain, and little to lose, by playing
the media game.[2]

## PRESSURE GROUPS

Trade unions may be viewed as 'subordinate' political actors in
capitalist societies, because it is their duty and function to represent
the interests of labour against those of capital. This frequently
brings unions into conflict, sometimes of a violent nature, with government and the repressive apparatus of the state. Another form of
subordinate organisation is the single-issue or pressure group,
which exists to campaign on a particular issue of special importance. The pressure group, too, will often find itself confronting
established power, challenging positions which are dominant. This
they will typically do from a 'resource poor' position, compelling
them to find ways of participating in and contributing to public
debate which do not require material or cultural 'capital'. For such
groups, the use and manipulation of the media to communicate
political messages is potentially the most effective way of achieving
this intervention, though even if media access is realised, it imposes
many limitations on the form and content of that message.

Pressure groups, unlike trade unions, comprise more or less
broad cross-class coalitions of individuals, united in their readiness

to act collectively in pursuit of a limited political objective (sometimes around a single issue, such as the poll tax of the 1980s) (Simmons and Mechling, 1981). They emerge as reactions to particular historical conjunctures, and usually decline or disappear when these conditions change. Where trade union action focusses on various kinds of obstruction of the production process, with the media used as a device for communicating to and negotiating with a variety of constituencies (union membership, employers, the public, etc.) pressure groups are more concerned with symbolic demonstrations of concern about, or opposition to, what are viewed by its members as undesirable social and political trends. Thus the international peace movement, which we cite as a case study in this section, emerged in the late 1970s and early 1980s as a response to what were perceived by many citizens in the United States and Western Europe as a disturbing deterioration in the NATO–Warsaw Pact relationship, and a corresponding increase in the likelihood of nuclear war.

The 'nuclear issue', having been high on the political agenda in the 1950s and early 1960s, lay dormant for many years, reflecting the period of relatively stable relations between the United States and its allies, and the Soviet Union, which came to be known as *détente* (McNair, 1988). With the rise of the radical right in Britain and the US at the end of the 1970s, however, and the expanded military budgets and heightened anti-Soviet rhetoric which accompanied that rise, the anti-nuclear movement once again began to grow. In Britain, in the four years from 1979 to 1983, membership of the British wing of the peace movement, the Campaign for Nuclear Disarmament (CND), grew nearly thirtyfold, from 3,000 to 80,000. Like most pressure groups, CND included in its membership a politically and socially diverse mix of individuals. For some, the motivation to campaign with CND was religious; others objected ideologically to NATO's aggressive (under the leadership of Ronald Reagan) and moralising approach to the rest of the world, and its apparent readiness to countenance nuclear warfighting in Europe; others simply thought of themselves and their children, and feared for the future.

Although 'resource poor', in Goldenberg's terms, CND and the peace movement internationally possessed certain characteristics which made them more 'media-friendly' than some pressure groups. Being diverse and socially heterogeneous, they were not easily stereotyped as 'left-wing' or 'subversive', although many attempts were made by government to do so. The movement's chief spokespersons (such as Monsignor Bruce Kent and Joan Ruddock in the

UK) were well-educated members of the middle class – liberal, rather than radical, as were many of CND's ordinary members. It was able to draw on the resources of many supporters in the creative professions – musicians, designers, writers, and actors. And it was explicitly committed to a strategy of 'non-violent' opposition to nuclear weapons.

To exploit these attributes the peace movement developed a political communication strategy which saw it successfully gain access to the mainstream news agenda in Europe and the United States. Huge demonstrations were organised in London, New York, and other cities in the early 1980s, providing television news organisations in particular with highly attractive visual material. While some broadcasters deliberately excluded such images from their output (on the curious grounds that it did not contribute anything to the 'debate'[3] – a criterion of newsworthiness which, if applied consistently, would leave our television news screens blank for most of the time) the majority reported the demos, and the other spectacular events organised by the peace movement in these years. Even symbolic actions undertaken by relatively small groups of people, such as the vigils carried out by women at the Greenham Common nuclear airbase, or the 'die-ins' staged outside the London Stock Exchange, were reported on main news programmes. In their innovative design and effective execution of such events, peace movements in Britain, the United States, Germany and elsewhere 'manufactured' news and turned the media into transmission belts for a potent political message – there is a growing risk of nuclear conflict between the superpowers, and we are here to protest about it.

The perceived threat to political stability posed by the demonstrators, and growing popular opposition to a central tenet of the Western powers' strategic military policy, was sufficient to generate a sustained counter-offensive on the part of NATO governments. In Britain, the Defence Minister Michael Heseltine was frequently filmed at the Berlin Wall, warning citizens of the 'threat' against which NATO's nuclear weapons were the only protection. On one famous occasion he took part – suitably attired – in a military expedition to 'retake' the Molesworth cruise missile base from protesters who had camped outside its perimeter fence. This event, indeed, was largely responsible for Mr Heseltine's acquiring the nickname of 'Tarzan', which haunted him for the rest of his time in government.

These events, like those of the peace movement on the opposite side of the political divide, were symbolic acts of political communication, designed to highlight the nature of the Soviet threat on the one hand, and the resolution of NATO governments on the other. Their impact on public opinion at the time is difficult to ascertain, but they had the unintended effect of increasing the newsworthiness of the peace movement, adding to its 'cultural capital' and legitimising it as a definer of events. Once it became clear that members of the politico-military establishment took CND and the other anti-nuclear organisations seriously, media organisations followed suit. In one notable example of this effect, Mr Heseltine's announcement in 1983 that his government would be spending some £1 million of public money on anti-CND propaganda generated numerous headlines for the peace movement, and significantly raised its profile as a legitimate participant in the nuclear debate. While an innovative approach to communication and media management permitted the peace movement to gain access to news media, official responses to that access reinforced its visibility and authority. The Defence Secretary's 'cultural capital' was transferred, in part, to a competitor.

It would be misleading to suggest, however, that the peace movement came anywhere near to dominating the debate as mediated by broadcasting and the press. Firstly, the defence establishment used its privileged access to intervene at key moments in the peace movement's campaigning. I have described in detail elsewhere how governmental news management ensured that coverage of a major CND demonstration held at Easter, 1983 was 'framed' by stories about the Soviet threat (McNair, 1988), a rhetorical device which throughout the 'new Cold War' was routinely presented by journalists as objective fact rather than contestable assertion. The presentation of an anti-nuclear viewpoint was consistently contextualised by a wider 'reality', that of the threat nuclear weapons were supposed to protect us against.

Secondly, the content of 'peace movement news' was typically lacking in explanation and analysis of the anti-nuclear argument. While journalists undoubtedly gave extensive and often sympathetic coverage to the people involved in demonstrations, there was rarely any attempt to examine the detail of their case, or indeed its validity. As was noted earlier, the very nature of news militates against considered analysis of events in preference for coverage of the epiphenomenal, easily graspable aspects. In this respect the peace movement, like other pressure groups (and political actors in general) found it difficult to have its arguments, as opposed to its existence, reported. One should qualify this observation by noting that spaces were occasionally found in current affairs and in-depth news programmes of the type provided by BBC's *Newsnight* and *Channel 4 News*, for detailed articulation of the anti-nuclear perspective.

As the East–West confrontation eased in the late 1980s, culminating in the 'end' of the Cold War and the collapse of the Soviet Union, the peace movement withered away. In terms of governmental decision-making, historians will probably judge that the movement had negligible impact. In the end, cruise missiles were installed in Europe, Britain commissioned the Trident submarine system, and the US government pursued its desired nuclear weapons programmes. There was, however, a public debate about these crucial issues in the 1980s, where there had been practically none in the 1960s and 1970s. The communication strategies and campaigning activities of the international peace movement can reasonably take the credit for forcing that debate, and requiring NATO governments to consider public opinion, where they had not been used to doing so before.

## Pressure groups in the 1990s

As the anti-nuclear weapons movement declined in the 1990s, so the environmental movement came to prominence. Like CND in the 1980s, the rise of the 'greens' was a response to growing perceptions of a new kind of risk – away from the threat of nuclear war and towards the threat of environmental disaster caused by human intervention in, and distortion of, the natural order of things. This was the product of science, as it generated worrying new knowledge about such problems as the hole in the ozone layer, and then of politicians who began to incorporate environmental issues into their policy agendas in a unique and somewhat unexpected way (exemplified by prime minister Thatcher's pro-environment speech of September 1988).

It was also the product of effective source strategies by the environmental movement itself, which included new political parties (the Greens) and pressure groups, most successfully Greenpeace and Friends of the Earth. Using the same non-violent, direct action techniques as CND a decade before these groups organised visually spectacular, powerfully symbolic (and thus media-friendly) demonstrations against such threats to the environment as nuclear power stations, the destruction of rain forests, and the dumping of industrial waste in the sea. Celebrities like U2 and Sting were enlisted to invest cultural capital in many of these protests, and the environment became a prominent issue in the news, as it was intended to. Newspapers and broadcast news organisations recruited environmental correspondents, and the proportion of routine news coverage devoted to the subject increased.

A classic case of successful political communication by the environmental movement was Greenpeace's 1995 protest against the planned disposal of the Brent Spar oil rig off the coast of Scotland. The Shell company, whose rig it was, was eventually compelled by the pressure of public opinion across Europe, manifested in consumer boycotts of Shell products, and the occasional torching of a Shell petrol station, to call off its Brent Spar operation. This reversal had been achieved, despite vocal support for the company from the British government (in whose territorial waters the operation was taking place), entirely because of the success with which Greenpeace commanded the news agenda. Supported by a sophisticated media relations operation, Greenpeace activists boarded the deserted oil platform, moored in stormy northern waters, in the process providing great pictures for television news. The story was irresistible to journalists, and Greenpeace's propaganda (which later turned out to be false) about the environmental dangers posed by Brent Spar set the agenda and became the dominant reading. Greenpeace became, in this story at least, the primary definers of reality.

### Gay liberation

Another pressure group to achieve gains through media campaigning in the 1990s was the gay rights movement. In Britain, a variety of more or less polite demonstrations secured such long overdue advances as the lowering of the homosexual age of consent to sixteen in June 1998, and the repeal of the infamous Section 28 (introduced by the Thatcher government in the 1980s, this legislation prohibited local government from spending money on the 'promotion' of homosexuality, including simple information and education for young people about what homosexuality was, and why it was not an evil force). Although the movement was divided between those, led by such as Peter Tatchell, whose tactics included the staging of aggressive demonstrations of 'outing' and pulpit-storming to secure media coverage; and others, led by such as Sir Ian McKellen, who preferred quiet lobbying of politicians and media, in the end a combination of both approaches achieved a real shift in public

171

perceptions of gayness which, if it was less than some activitists wanted, was more than would have been achieved without skilful use of the media as a platform for articulation of the gay rights case.

## TERRORISM AND THE OXYGEN OF PUBLICITY

We turn, finally, to that category of political organisation which pursues its objectives by illegal, often violent means. As was acknowledged in Chapter 1, the word 'terrorist' is a loaded term, used to describe organisations whose own members may prefer to think of themselves as 'freedom fighters', 'guerrilla soldiers', or 'revolutionaries'. Noam Chomsky and others have developed the concept of 'state terrorism' to describe the violence which has been used by the United States and other countries against civilians. We will use it here, however, to refer to those non-state groups which pursue 'terror' tactics against governments, soldiers and civilians of their own or other countries. 'Terror', in this context, includes bombings, assassination, kidnappings, and hostage-taking – actions which will in most cases be of minor military value, being designed rather to communicate messages of various kinds. Terror, in this sense, is a form of political communication, pursued outside the realm of constitutional procedures. In the words of Thomas Thornton, the terrorist act is 'symbolic . . . designed to influence political behaviour by extranormal means, entailing the use or threat of violence' (quoted in Kelly and Mitchell, 1984, p.283). Baudrillard describes terrorism as a 'Theatre of Cruelty' which 'aims at the masses in their silence' a political message – 'in the purest symbolic form' – of challenge (1983, p.31). For Schmid and de Graaf, terrorism is a media management strategy adopted by groups whose members feel otherwise excluded from political discourse.

> We see the genesis of contemporary insurgent terrorism, as it has manifested itself in the Western World since the late 1960s, primarily as the outgrowth of minority strategies to get into the news. Since the Western media grant access to news-making to events that are abnormal, unusual, dangerous, new, disruptive and violent, groups without habitual access to news-making use these characteristics of the news value system to obtain access.
>
> (1982, p.217)

They add that terrorism is 'violence for effect. It is theatre. It is crime and it is politics. This three-fold confluence of real life-and-death spectacle, high politics and base crime fits so well into what the Western media is conditioned to cover that they cannot resist giving it full exposure' (Ibid., p.76).

Like all the other forms of political communication discussed in this book, terrorism can only have significance as a communicative act if it is transmitted through the mass media to an audience. Unless it is reported, the terrorist act has no social meaning. David Paletz observes that 'terrorists seek publicity to bring about their psychological goals . . . they use violence to produce various psychological effects – demoralising their enemies, demonstrating their movement's strength, gaining public sympathy, and creating fear and chaos. To succeed in these goals, terrorists must publicise their actions' (Paletz and Schmid, 1992, p.2). Pickard notes that terrorist acts 'have been strategically used to help turn the public's attention towards problems that aggrieved groups wish to have attention focussed upon' (1989, p.21).

In addition to the general aim of generating publicity for a political objective terrorist acts may be intended to fulfil a number of more specific purposes (Gerritts, 1992). They may, for example, be organised in such a way as to demonstrate the vulnerability of the state. The assassination by the Irish National Liberation Army (INLA) in 1978 of Lord Mountbatten was such an act, as was the bombing of the Conservative Party conference in Brighton in 1984 by the Irish Republican Army, and that same organisation's 1991 mortar attack on the Cabinet as it met in Downing Street. The casualties and narrow escapes occasioned by these acts were symbolic reminders to the British people of the reach of groups who were, according to the official line, unrepresentative criminal thugs.

Terrorist groups may use these acts to communicate to their own supporters. In the aforementioned examples of Irish republican terrorism, one may argue that non-republicans in Britain, including those with a dislike and even hatred for the then Conservative government, would not have welcomed the death and destruction caused by, for example, the Brighton bomb. To their own supporters, however, the IRA were attacking a legitimate target, with a professionalism and devastating impact which would certainly have enhanced their status within their own community. Related to this, terrorist acts may be used to signify the 'heroism' of the perpetrators. The suicide bombings carried out by Hezbollah in Lebanon in the 1980s against US and other Western targets fell into this category.

Normally, of course, terrorist activity will shock and outrage the community against which it is directed, generating a public response which may suit the organisation's objectives in so far as it radicalises and polarises public opinion. The many IRA bomb attacks against civilians in Britain were intended to generate public support for British military and political withdrawal from Northern Ireland, a strategy which has not been without success.

Terrorist activity may also be consciously designed to provoke repressive counter-measures by the state, enabling the organisation and the community whose interests it claims to represent to be portrayed as victims. The IRA bombings of pubs in Birmingham in the 1970s led both to the introduction of the Prevention of Terrorism Act, and the miscarriages of justice experienced by the 'Birmingham Six' and others. Both have generated much adverse publicity for the British police and legal system. Similarly, the 1988 ban on broadcast statements by supporters of republican violence such as Sinn Fein generated much negative publicity for the British government, at home and abroad.

To achieve these goals, terrorists must gain access to the media, and in this they are assisted by the inherent newsworthiness of their activities. Such acts are normally spectacular, providing journalists with dramatic visual material. They are explosive (literally) and often incorporate elements of great drama. The 1978 siege of the Iranian embassy in London, and the holding of an American airline at Beirut airport in 1985 are examples of unfolding dramas which commanded headline news throughout their duration.

The grammar of television news, then, means that terrorism has newsvalue, and can be used as a means of attracting media and thus public attention to a political cause. In itself, however, publicity may not further a political objective and may, for obvious reasons in the case of terrorism, present an obstacle to it.

This fact requires terrorist organisations, like other political actors, to engage in more sophisticated strategies of news management than merely setting up spectacular acts of violence. Pickard argues that 'labelling perpetrators of terrorism as seekers of publicity for its own sake is simplistic and ignores their very significant efforts to direct news coverage, to present their cause in favourable ways and to disassociate groups from acts that will bring significant negative response to the cause' (1989, p.14).

Terrorist groups, like other political actors, have developed media management systems, and gradually come to use 'most of the techniques normally employed by public relations professionals' (Ibid.) including the issuing of press statements, videos (a practice adopted frequently by the hostage-takers in Lebanon), news conferences, and the production of newspapers (such as the IRA's *An Phoblacht*). One observer notes that 'the PR skills of such as Gerry Adams and Danny Morrison are so highly reputed that the Sinn Fein press office is widely regarded as the Saatchi and Saatchi of "terrorist" publicity departments' (Ibid.). The political communication skills of Adams and the Sinn Fein leadership were such as to have led, by the time of the Good Friday agreement in April 1998, to handshakes with President Clinton in the White House, meetings with the British prime minister at 10 Downing Street, and the slow emergence in the late 1990s of Sinn Fein as a legitimate (from the British state's point of view) political force. Poor political communication by the loyalists, on the other hand, exemplified by the Orange Order's 'siege of Drumcree' and their response to the sectarian murder of three children in July 1998, steadily lowered their prestige and credibility in the eyes of the British people and the world as a whole, to the significant (if as yet unquantifiable) long-term advantage of their republican opponents.

Yasser Arafat, in the decades before the PLO achieved international diplomatic recognition, was another 'terrorist' who skilfully used the media to project and gain sympathy for the Palestinian cause.

In the vast majority of examples, however, terrorist 'public relations' – or political communication – has failed to achieve success in the pursuit of the cause. While terrorism generates publicity, because it meets many of the requirements of modern news production, it rarely bestows the groups responsible with legitimacy, far less media support. As Schmid and de Graaf point out, 'the insurgent terrorist news promoter, as source of news, has at times considerable influence on the way the media report his actions. Yet his opponents, the government and its security forces, are in fact the main sources for the media' (1982, p.98).

We have noted elsewhere in this book that news tends to eschew explanations and analyses of the events reported, a generalisation which is no less true of terrorism. The audience sees the bomb exploding or the hijacker waving his gun from the cockpit of an aircraft, but will not very often be provided with the historical background or political context to the events taking place, and their justification (if any). Kelly and Mitchell acknowledge that 'the media will help [the terrorist] attract the attention of an audience but it will not let him transmit his message. By sapping terrorism of its political content, the media turn the crusader into a psychopath' (1984, p.287). For these reasons, much media coverage of terrorism may be viewed as self-defeating.

As noted above, one goal of terrorist activity may be to provoke state repression, or to demoralise a population and force a change in policy. Media coverage *can* provide success in these terms, as the Provisional IRA and others have shown. Kelly and Mitchell are correct, however, to assert that no media system will provide terrorism against its own state with legitimation. For the establishment, moreover, even publicity is frowned upon. When in 1985 the British Home Secretary warned journalists against providing republican terrorists with the 'oxygen of publicity'[4] he was implying that *any* coverage of such activities – negative or otherwise – was harmful to the mainstream political process. In so far as coverage of spectacular terrorist acts assists the groups responsible to shape the political agenda, he was probably correct. Media organisations, however, have been reluctant to censor themselves on these grounds, arguing that denial or avoidance of the issues which generate terrorism is – apart from being an unacceptable restriction of the media's fourth estate role – ultimately counter-productive to the resolution of those issues.

# 9

# INTERNATIONAL POLITICAL COMMUNICATION

Thus far we have been concerned with the role of communication and mass media in the domestic political debates of a society. The political process, however, also has an international dimension. Nation-states have interests *vis-à-vis* each other, which frequently bring them into economic, diplomatic, or military conflict. In pursuing such conflicts governments use not only the conventional instruments of power (economic pressure and military force) but public opinion, both at home and abroad.

Before the era of mass communication, relations between states were carried on largely behind closed doors, with appropriately heavy reliance on secret diplomacy and subterfuge. Educated elites could read about them in their newspapers, but the mass of the people remained in relative ignorance of their governments' activities in this sphere. Secrecy and covert manoeuvrings are still extensively used, of course, but international relations can no longer be conducted without consideration being given to public opinion. As the mass media have expanded, and the time lag between event and reportage of it has inexorably shortened, so the foreign policies of states are pursued in the full glare of publicity. Indeed, governments and other political actors use the media to influence public opinion on foreign policy in their favour. In international politics, as in domestic, image has come to rival substance in the calculations of politicians and their advisers. The principles of news and information management described in previous chapters now apply equally to the sphere of international relations. For all governments, domestic and global public opinion has become a key factor in the formulation and execution of foreign policy.

In this chapter we consider how governments, principally those of Britain and the United States in the post-Second World War period, have sought to manage journalistic discourse about their foreign policies and international relations. The focus is on military conflict situations, from the Vietnam War of the 1960s and 1970s to the Gulf War of 1991. As we shall see, the perceived importance of public opinion in shaping the outcome of such conflicts has led their protagonists to develop sophisticated strategies of public relations and media management, often involving the same commercial companies and advisers employed to handle politicians' domestic campaigns.

In one key sense, of course, international relations *are* a domestic matter, since a government's conduct in this area can sharply affect its popularity with the voters, and hence its re-election chances. In the pursuit of a state's international relations, a government has the opportunity to perform on the world stage, before a global audience of billions. The quality of that performance inevitably has resonance for the domestic audience. Hence, the success of governmental efforts to control media image can make an important contribution to wider political success.

There is one further sense in which communication about the international political environment has consequences for the domestic debate. Throughout the twentieth century, governments and ruling elites in the business, military and media spheres have manipulated symbols and images of 'the enemy' for domestic political purposes. The nature of 'the enemy' has changed over time, but the basic principle underlying this communication has been retained: that it is possible to mobilise public opinion behind campaigns which, though ostensibly targeted on an 'alien' force, have domestic political objectives. We shall begin this chapter with a discussion of the century's most sustained example of such a use of the media: the 'Cold War'.

## EAST–WEST RELATIONS AND THE COLD WAR

Between 1917, when Vladimir Lenin and the Bolsheviks seized control of the Russian empire and the late 1980s, when Mikhail Gorbachov brought it to an end, relations between the Soviet Union and the capitalist powers were, with some exceptions which we shall discuss in this section, characterised by the term 'Cold War'. Cold War signified a state of hostility and tension which teetered on the brink of, while never quite tipping over into, full-scale military conflict, or 'hot war'. While the phrase is usually applied to the period between the end of the Second World War and the era of *perestroika*, 'Cold War' is an apt phrase for the pre-war decades too.

From the political communications perspective, the Cold War is an interesting case for two reasons. Firstly, it was a real conflict, fought over spheres of economic and political influence which at times, such as the Cuban missile crisis and the Korean Airlines disaster, could have led to the direct exchange of fire between the USA and the USSR, with unthinkable consequences for the entire world. Secondly, the Cold War furnished the US and other Western governments, for most of this century, with an 'enemy'. The 'threat' posed by this enemy – expressed in military and moral terms – was frequently invoked in the service of domestic politics, such as the undermining and eradication of socialist parties, trade unions, and as late as the 1980s, anti-nuclear protest movements. Symbols of the 'communist' or 'Red' threat were used to justify resistance to, or refusal of, social welfare improvements, workers' rights, and other 'left' causes throughout the century.[1]

There is a sense, of course, in which the 1917 Bolshevik revolution did present a real threat to the Western capitalist powers. The revolution occurred at a time when millions were dying in Europe over an imperialist struggle for territory and resources. With the help of propaganda techniques and atrocity stories young men from Britain, France, Russia and the United States were being persuaded to lay down their lives in the struggle against Germany. As hundreds of thousands died in battles for a few metres of land here and there, opposition to the war increased, spearheaded by the Bolsheviks and their socialist allies in the Third International. When they took power in Russia the Bolsheviks withdrew from the war and agitated for an international proletarian revolution to replace the imperialist conflict. This 'export' of revolution was a potent slogan, rightly perceived as threatening by the custodians of the capitalist order in Europe and America.

Faced with this threat, and a rising tide of socialist opinion, the Western powers, having defeated Germany, sanctioned the invasion of Soviet Russia by a multinational expeditionary force including troops from Britain, France, the United States, and Japan. These forces entered the civil war then raging in Russia on the side of the anti-Bolshevik 'white' forces. The intervention failed, and the Bolsheviks went on to consolidate their power in Russia, which was eventually renamed the Soviet Union. However, the attack established a state of mutual hostility between the Soviets and the capitalist powers which continued virtually unaltered until the Gorbachov era.

In the early years of the East–West conflict the governments of the capitalist powers engaged in diplomatic and economic sanctions against the Soviets. They also undertook an intense campaign of propaganda directed at their own populations in an effort to prevent them being 'seduced' by Bolshevism, or by milder forms of socialism and social democracy. In the early 1920s the British establishment manufactured the 'Zinoviev letter' in a bid to prevent the election of a Labour government. The letter, allegedly from the Soviet foreign minister, suggested that a future Labour government would be the 'creature' of the Bolsheviks, carrying out their will and overthrowing British capitalism. The letter was a forgery, but extensive media publicity of its contents contributed to the Labour Party's subsequent electoral defeat.

In America, the first 'Red scare' began shortly after the revolution in 1918, lasting until 1920. The scare, argues historian Murray Levin, was initiated by a coalition of corporate, media and governmental interests, led by the US Steel Corporation, which in 1917 experienced major industrial unrest. In response the president of the corporation, Judge Elbert Gray, organised what Levin calls 'a nationwide public relations campaign to create the stereotype of rampant Bolshevism in the steel industry' (1971, p.40). The strikes were presented by national newspapers such as the *New York Times* and the *Wall Street Journal* as prefiguring 'a Bolshevik holocaust' (Ibid., p.38). The unions were accused of being communist-led. Robert Murray observes that public opinion was initially sympathetic to the aims of the unions, and opposed to the heavy-handed strike-breaking tactics of the employers. The latter, therefore, had to 'promote a more favourable public opinion toward their own positions. Perceiving that their greatest ally was the latent public fear of the strike's radicalism, the steel interests realised that much of the current animosity to [them] would disappear and the strike would fail if the public could be convinced that "bolshevism" was the only strike issue' (1955, p.142).

The public relations campaign against 'communism' at home was complemented by tendentious and sensational reporting of Soviet Russia itself. As Levin describes:

newspapers, with rare exceptions, portrayed the revolution as an orgy of mass murder, individual assassination, rape, pillage, and slaughter. It was commonly claimed that nuns were raped, monasteries burned, and it was reported that the Bolsheviks in Petrograd used an electrically operated

guillotine to behead five hundred victims per hour.
Bolshevik rule was described as a compound of slaughter,
confiscation, anarchy, and universal disorder.

(1971, p.95)

Using unchecked rumours, word-of-mouth gossip, and the kind
of atrocity stories employed against the Germans in the 1914–18
war the US media, supporting the chairman of US Steel and its allies
in business and the Congress, created a climate of political hysteria
within which to frame domestic industrial relations problems. For
Levin 'the hysteria was an attempt – largely successful – to reaffirm
the legitimacy of the power elite of capitalism and to further weaken
workers' class consciousness' (Ibid., p.90).

Despite the lack of empirical foundation for the Red Scare of
1918–20, its success as a public relations campaign may be judged
by the fact that by 1923 one million workers had left the American
trade union movement, and that by 1920 the American Communist
Party's membership had fallen from 70,000 to 16,000. More significantly, perhaps, the Red Scare established 'militant anti-
communism' as 'a core American idea . . . The idea that the ultimate
aim of the USSR was, and always would be, the violent overthrow
of the American government took root at this time' (Ibid., p.89).
Robert Murray asserts that 'the net result [of the campaign] was the
implantation of the Bolsheviks in the American mind as the epitome
of all that was evil' (1955, p.16).

Throughout the 1920s and 1930s this 'core' idea was reflected in
the output of Hollywood's 'dream factory'. Films such as *Comrade
X* and *Ninotchka* advanced a picture of Soviet Russia as inferior,
morally and economically, to the United States. Bolshevik characters were stereotyped as cold, austere ideologues who, in Greta
Garbo's case, needed nothing more than a firm hand to loosen them
up and awaken them to the joys of American capitalism. These
films complemented journalistic accounts of Bolshevik atrocities
and contributed to the consolidation of anti-Bolshevik, anti-left
ideology at the heart of American culture and politics.

## The grand alliance

By the 1930s, of course, Stalinism had been established in the Soviet
Union and the atrocity stories of earlier years had acquired a degree
of substance. Show trials, famine, and mass executions of political
dissidents led to millions of Soviet casualties between 1934 and the

outbreak of the Second World War. It is not without irony, then, that precisely when the evils of Soviet communism were becoming evident even to socialists, the content of Western media images of the country began to change, in accordance with changing perceptions of political and military requirements.

Between 1939 and 1941, while the Soviet Union maintained an uneasy distance from the war with Nazi Germany, anti-Bolshevism remained highly visible in the Western capitalist countries. Following Hitler's Operation Saragossa and Russia's entry into the war on the Western allies' side, it became necessary for governments to mobilise public opinion behind the war effort in general, and that of the Soviet Union in particular, locked as it now was in a fight to the death with Germany. From being the pre-eminent enemy of and threat to capitalism the Soviet Union was recast in the Western media as a valued and brave friend and ally. Philosophical and political disagreements with the Communist Party of the Soviet Union were placed on one side in the interests of defeating a common and far more dangerous enemy.

The political objective of mobilising support for the Soviet Union was achieved by a propaganda and public relations campaign designed to overturn the negative images of the preceding two decades. A new, more positive picture emerged of the Soviet Union as a welcoming, friendly place inhabited by noble, hard-working proletarians, honest communists and peace-loving armies. Stalin became 'Uncle Joe', as Western populations were exhorted to donate food and money to the starving Russians in the siege of Leningrad.

All of these positive images were included in Warner Brothers' 1943 movie *Mission to Moscow*, in which Hollywood star Walter Huston played the part of the real-life US ambassador to Moscow. The film gave an 'account' of events in the Soviet Union leading up to the outbreak of war, including lengthy courtroom scenes in which state prosecutor Vyshinsky dealt firmly but fairly with Bukharin, Radek, and other 'Trotskyite' conspirators. Vyshinsky, Soviet President Kalinin, even Stalin himself, were all depicted in the film as kindly, sympathetic figures, for whom no sacrifice would be too great for the cause of humanity. In America, as in Britain and other countries, the media were given the task of building an international political environment in which, contrary to the pre-1939 period, Nazism was the enemy and Bolshevism the friend of the West.[2]

## The Cold War

The Second World War ended in 1945, and with it this brief period of East–West harmony. Little changed in the Soviet Union (Stalin remained firmly in control, as he had done since 1934) but its image in the Western media quickly reverted to that of the earlier 'Red Scare' phase. The United States had emerged from the war as the dominant global power, and wished to extend its economic and military influence throughout the world. In this regard the notions of 'Soviet expansionism' and 'communist subversion' were found to be useful pretexts with which to justify sending military forces at various times in the post-war period to South-East Asia (Korea, Vietnam, Cambodia), central America (the Dominican Republic, Guatemala, El Salvador), the Middle East (Lebanon), and the Caribbean (Cuba, Grenada).

Noam Chomsky and Ed Herman have described the close relationship between post-war US economic and military interests and the development of the concept of the 'Soviet Threat' in its various manifestations (1988). For these authors, in a pattern which was repeated in the Gulf War of the 1990s, the concept served chiefly as a device for the mobilisation of public support behind what might otherwise have appeared to the American people as costly and unnecessary military adventurism. To intervene abroad the United States (in some cases accompanied by key allies like Britain) required an enemy. Although the Soviet Union was never in a position to pose the threat suggested by Cold War propagandists (even assuming that it wished to do so) the secretive, posturing nature of its Communist government made it a convenient object for such propaganda.

In the 1940s the notion of the Soviet Union as a global threat to freedom and democracy was complemented by the 'threat' of internal communist subversion. In 1948 the US Congress established the House Un-American Activities Committee to investigate alleged communist infiltration of the US political, military and cultural establishment. The committee hearings developed into 'witch-hunts', led by Senator Joseph McCarthy and supported by Hollywood stars such as Ronald Reagan, James Stewart, John Wayne and Bing Crosby, who lent their reputations and artistic resources to the anti-communist cause.

These were the years of the 'Cold War' proper. Stalin died in 1953, to be replaced by Nikita Krushchev, while John F. Kennedy became President of the United States. Kennedy continued the anti-communist theme in US government policy and propaganda, sanctioning the failed Bay of Pigs invasion of Cuba, and authorising the first dispatches of troops to Vietnam. He also brought the world to the brink of nuclear war in the Cuban missile crisis. Throughout these tense and anxiety-ridden years, anti-communism was a given in Western politics and culture.

By the late 1960s and the arrival of Richard Nixon as US President, it seemed that the worst years of the Cold War were over, with both sides embracing the policy of *détente*, amounting to a mutual acceptance of each other's differences and legitimate interests. In the Western media anti-Sovietism softened, as Nixon and Brezhnev signed historic arms control, economic, and cultural agreements.

By the late 1970s, however, *détente* was under strain. In the United States and Britain radical right-wing politicians were coming to power, who included in their ideological armoury a fierce anti-Sovietism. Between them, Ronald Reagan's Republican administration and Margaret Thatcher's Conservative government revived the Cold War and initiated a decade of East–West hostility. These were the years of the Korean Airlines disaster; the boycotts, by West and East respectively, of the Moscow and Los Angeles Olympic games; of public discussion by senior NATO figures of the possibility of limited nuclear war in Europe; the Soviet invasion of Afghanistan and the US invasion of Grenada.

I have written elsewhere about the causes and cultural consequences of the 'second' Cold War (McNair, 1988). Here, we note that a renewed US and British commitment to economic, military and ideological struggle with the Soviet Union and its allies was reflected in journalistic and entertainment media. To justify and win support for the huge increases in arms spending that the new Cold War required, the Soviet Union was depicted in official statements, policy documents and Hollywood movies alike as a menacing, evil power, bent on world domination. Herman and Broadhead document the way in which the attempted assassination of the Pope in 1982 by a Turkish neo-fascist became the occasion for a wave of manufactured anti-Soviet propaganda (1986). The Korean Airlines disaster of 1983 was presented by the Reagan administration as clear evidence of the USSR's 'terrorism' and innate 'barbarism' (Herman, 1986; McNair, 1988).

Such campaigns were not prepared in isolation from the surrounding political environment. To the surprise of the Thatcher and Reagan governments, millions of people in the US and Western Europe refused to endorse many of the assumptions of NATO's

Cold War policies. They rejected NATO's view of the USSR as a uniquely evil and threatening power, and resisted the nuclear expansion being pursued by the US and Britain. The rise of the peace movements in the 1980s (see previous chapter) threatened to undermine public support for the pursuit of the new Cold War. In this context, governments hoped that anti-Soviet propaganda would help to reinforce public opinion. The Korean Airlines disaster, for example, was a key moment in NATO's efforts to convince Western European public opinion that it should permit the installation of Cruise missiles at bases in Britain and Germany. In America, the disaster and the propaganda use made of it by the administration smoothed the way for Congressional endorsement of hitherto controversial weapons programmes such as the MX missile system and binary nerve gas production (McNair, 1988; Edelman, 1988).

In so far as partial, distorted, and exaggerated information about the Soviet Union and 'communism' emanated from and was disseminated by official sources through the mass media it was 'political communication', intended to influence the political environment and mobilise public opinion behind certain specific policies. As such, the years of the new Cold War are illustrative of the pattern, observed since the first red scares of the early twentieth century, in which 'the twists and turns of media anti-communism and alarmism largely parallel similar shifts in official policy' (Parenti, 1986, p.135). Communication about the Soviet Union in the 1980s was, as it had been in the 1920s, 1930s, and 1940s, communication with politico-ideological motivations and objectives.

The success of such communication cannot be taken for granted, as the persistence of the peace movement in the 1980s showed. The effectiveness of messages about the evil and threatening nature of Soviet communism was largely dependent, like the other aspects of political communication with which this book has dealt, on the strategies of persuasion adopted by their senders. In this respect, Ronald Reagan was a powerful and effective performer, surrounded by a public relations and news management apparatus which frequently enabled him to seize media attention and set the public agenda (McNair, 1988). In sharp contrast, Soviet public relations remained, until the emergence of Mikhail Gorbachov as CPSU General Secretary in 1985, a contradiction in terms. While Reagan communicated directly to the populations of the NATO countries using satellite and other advanced technologies, presenting the US case in deceptively simple and compelling terms, the Soviet government hid behind a veil of defensiveness and secrecy. Soviet accounts of events such as the KAL 007 disaster or the war in Afghanistan were never effectively communicated on the international stage. If the 1980s were years of sustained propaganda warfare between NATO and the Warsaw Pact, in which international public opinion was the prize to be won, the USSR fought with two hands tied behind its back. Only when Mikhail Gorbachov came to power, armed with an appreciation of news management and public relations techniques, did the Soviet position on events and issues begin to emerge with some accuracy in the Western media. At the Reykjavik summit of 1988, for example, the Soviet side supplied a news-hungry media with a rich diet of briefings (on and off the record) and photo-opportunities. Raisa Gorbachov made herself available for the cameras, while at the end of the summit her husband mounted a two-hour *tour de force* news conference for the assembled media. Reagan, by contrast, appeared hesitant and ill-briefed (McNair, 1991).

The years between 1985 and 1991, when Gorbachov led the Soviet Union, illustrate the fact that source strategies are of profound importance in political communication. As the previous chapter argued, the Western media, by virtue of their dependence on sources and attraction to certain types of news material, will provide spaces for views not those of the 'ruling elite' to be reported. While the pro-establishment biases of the media as a whole are amply documented, Gorbachov's successful advocacy of the Soviet perspective in the years of *perestroika* provide further evidence of the potential of skilful public relations in challenging these biases. It hardly seems an exaggeration to state that the end of the 'new Cold War', and decades of East–West tension, were greatly facilitated by the source strategies of Gorbachov and his media advisers and spokespersons. The changes in presentation were accompanied, of course, by major developments in Soviet foreign and domestic policy, which might have rendered the 'Soviet threat' concept untenable in any case. Of major importance, however, is the fact that Gorbachov, as the public face of the Soviet Union during these years, effectively communicated to the world a vision of Soviet society, and an account of Soviet government policy, which undermined the Cold War propaganda of the NATO allies and eventually made it appear anachronistic. In this sense, one might say, skilful political communication brought an end to the Cold War.

The experience of the Cold War is perhaps the most significant example of the fact that contemporary international relations are, like domestic election campaigns and political debates, focussed on and projected from the channels of the mass media, and television in particular. Inter-state relations are negotiated by appeal to domestic and global public opinion, from which governments and international organisations such as the United Nations seek to draw legitimacy. As was noted in the introduction to this chapter, much diplomacy continues in secret, but the immediacy and scale of modern reportage of diplomatic affairs requires political actors always to consider the impact of their actions, and communications, on public opinion.

## INTERNATIONAL CONFLICT AND POLITICAL COMMUNICATION

The Cold War was so termed because, thankfully, it did not involve direct military confrontation between the Western powers and the Soviet Union. However, many 'proxy' wars were fought in the post-Second World War period, in which allies of East and West respectively were pitted against each other. In the Angolan civil war, for example, the Marxist government was supported for many years by the Cuban and Soviet governments, who provided diplomatic and military assistance. The Angolan government's opponents, UNITA, were, on the other hand, funded by apartheid South Africa and a rather murky coalition of Western intelligence and military bodies. Wars in the horn of Africa, central America and South-East Asia were also fought, with Western and Soviet involvement as 'sponsors'. In addition to these proxy wars, in which the superpowers (and their respective allies, like Britain, France, Czechoslovakia and East Germany) more or less openly stood behind their favoured factions, many military conflicts were provoked by the fear, real or otherwise, of the other's advance into jealously guarded spheres of influence. The Reagan administration's support for the contras in Nicaragua, and its endorsement of death squad activities in Chile, El Salvador, Guatemala and elsewhere, was justified with reference to alleged Soviet 'subversion' of the region, directly or through its Cuban communist and Nicaraguan Sandinista allies. Grenada was invaded in 1983 on the grounds that American citizens on the island were at risk from Cubans. In this sense, many of the 'hot' wars of the post-war decades were rooted in underlying tensions between East and West; capitalism and Soviet-style socialism. There were also wars rooted in colonialist hangovers, such as the 1982 Falklands conflict; national liberation struggles such as the Israeli–Palestinian conflict; and the expansionist ambitions of maverick national leaders, such as the Gulf War of 1991.

In the days before the emergence of modern electronic media military conflicts were covered by press correspondents, whose dispatches sent from the front lines inevitably lagged behind events by weeks and even months. By the time the public got to hear about a battle being fought in its name in a foreign country, it was in all probability over. Nevertheless, the exposure given to war by newspapers, limited as it was, meant that governments had to formulate strategies for managing domestic opinion. Thus, during the First World War, governments engaged in intensive propaganda campaigns to convince their populations of the inhumanity and immorality of the other side's soldiers (Knightley, 1972). As the speed and efficiency of international communication channels improved in the twentieth century, news became more contemporaneous with the events being reported, and the importance of public opinion increased. By the 1980s, one military expert could observe of modern conflict that 'what really matters is its effect on public opinion at home and around the world' (Hooper, 1982, p.215).

In military conflict, as in the less violent forms of conflict which normally comprise the domestic political process, public opinion is a factor which cannot be ignored. When Western television viewers can watch on their evening news bulletins as Iraqi missiles fall on Tel Aviv, or US cruise missiles weave their contour-guided path through downtown Baghdad; when military casualties and atrocities against civilians in Bosnia or Burundi are reported almost as soon as they occur; and when one side's victories or defeats cannot be hidden from the eyes and cameras of the thousands of correspondents present in the modern conflict zone, those who wage war know that they must include the impact of media coverage on public opinion in their calculations. In liberal democratic countries like Britain and the USA, a supportive public opinion is just as important in the pursuit of military conflict as well-resourced armies.

In some conflicts, of course, governments can take such support for granted. During the Second World War it was not necessary to highlight evidence of German atrocities against Jews and other groups in the countries they controlled for the populations of the allied countries to recognise the menacing nature of Nazism. In this case, national survival was perceived to be at stake.

Wars of national survival are rare, however. Indeed, it may be argued that the Second World War was the only such conflict of the twentieth century for the advanced capitalist world. War against the USSR, had it ever been allowed to break out, would have been another. But most conflicts are fought over issues of territoriality, strategic resources, or economic self-interest. In such wars defeat may involve national humiliation and the downfall of a government, but not the collapse of the society. Citizens, therefore, are less likely to support them, and may actively campaign against them, as occurred in both the Vietnam and the Falklands conflicts. Mercer *et al.* note that 'in a limited war, the relationships between politicians and the media will be particularly sensitive; the government's interest will not necessarily be construed as identical to the national interest. [In] a time of tension preceding a war, the potential power of the media to sway public opinion is even greater' (1987, p.6). In these situations governments have to 'manufacture' consent for the pursuit of war, and manage opinion in such a way that the war aims are achieved.

Opinion also matters on the international level. To embark on a major military campaign like Operation Desert Storm, the US and its allies required not only the support of their own people, but that of the United Nations in its capacity as the collective voice of the world community. Wars *have* been fought by big powers in the absence of international endorsement, but the current political environment is such that no country, no matter how powerful politically, can pursue major military objectives in isolation. Early in 1998, when it appeared that the Saddam regime was refusing to comply with UN resolutions on weapons of mass destruction, a huge public relations effort was organised by the United States and British governments to prepare domestic opinion in both countries for another military campaign against the Iraqi dictator. Like the first Gulf War (see below) this was a necessary prerequisite for military action (which on this occasion, fortunately, turned out not to be necessary).

In short, then, modern wars are as much about communication as armed aggression. In a liberal democracy, where government must submit itself to periodic electoral judgment, wars, to a greater extent than any other aspect of policy, must be legitimised in the eyes of the people. In recognition of this fact defence ministers, generals, and others responsible for the planning and execution of warfare have been joined by public relations professionals, whose job it is to ensure that the media's image of a conflict is such as to maximise the degree of popular support for it. Military public relations has become an important sector of the opinion management industry, without an understanding of which no analysis of modern warfare would be complete. In the rest of this chapter we examine the pursuit of military public relations in three conflicts, chosen because of their importance in establishing the rules of 'the game', as it were, and because they have been extensively researched and written about. We deal, firstly, with the Vietnam War, often viewed as the 'first media war'. We then examine the media management tactics of the British government during the Falklands conflict. And finally, we consider the experience of the Gulf War of 1991, in which many of the public relations lessons of previous conflicts were applied with considerable success by the United States, Britain, and their allies.

## Vietnam

By the 1960s newsgathering technologies had advanced to the point that relatively 'live' coverage of military conflict was possible. There was still likely to be a gap of a day or two between scenes being shot and the film flown back to the news organisation's headquarters, but by comparison with the Second World War and before, military events could be reported more or less as they happened. The availability of such technology meant that the conflict in Vietnam between communist and anti-communist forces, the latter supported by the United States, became the first 'open' war. So open was it perceived to be, indeed, that the victory of the North Vietnamese, and the corresponding humiliation of the US armed forces, was and continues to be blamed by many Americans on the media which reported it.

If the conflict in Vietnam became what Mercer *et al.* call 'the first television war' (1987, p.221), it began in secrecy and disinformation. During the Kennedy administration troops were sent to South-East Asia without the knowledge of Congress or the American people, and their numbers increased incrementally in order to avoid political controversy. When larger scale involvement was required the Johnson administration manufactured the Gulf of Tonkin incident, in which a 'threat' to US forces became the pretext for stepping up US military activity. The threat never existed, but the objective of winning domestic and international consent for a heightened US role in the conflict was achieved.

Disinformation is, of course, a form of military public relations which has been pursued in many conflicts since the Vietnam War. In 1984 the Reagan administration used the (illusory) threat of Soviet MiG fighter jets being exported to Nicaragua to prepare US public opinion for an escalation of military aggression against the Sandinista government (the escalation never came, but the US media and those of other countries reported the MiG story as if it was true) (McNair, 1988). The bombing of Tripoli in 1986 was justified by alleged Libyan involvement in a terrorist bomb attack on US servicemen in Berlin, even though the US government was aware that the most likely culprits were in fact the Syrians.

In so far as the escalation of the Vietnam War began with the Gulf of Tonkin incident the Johnson administration may be seen as pioneers in the use of this type of political communication. It was, indeed, an enthusiastic exponent of the whole range of military PR techniques in its efforts to convince public opinion at home and abroad of the legitimacy of US policy on Vietnam. The Americans were hampered, however, by the fact that their ally in Vietnam, the South Vietnamese government, was hostile to the media. As Mercer *et al.* put it

> they did not see the need to provide the international news media with necessary working facilities and were uneasy with the tradition of granting journalists access to troops and top civil and military officials. The South Vietnamese armed forces had no concept of public relations. Their official military spokespersons were usually difficult to find, and military communiques appeared well after the event.
>
> (1987, p.221)

The South Vietnamese authorities were not, unlike the Americans, operating within the context of liberal democracy, and therefore had no need to concern themselves unduly with matters of public opinion. The US administration, on the other hand, could not pursue what had by the late 1960s become a bloody and intense military campaign without at least the passive consent of the population, who had routine access to television images of the war. The conflict became, therefore, the 'Madison Avenue war', in which 'the authorities attempted to put a gloss on US efforts in the field and promote an image of progress at the expense of all else' (Ibid., p.235). The government embarked on an effort 'to sell the war through a high-powered public relations campaign' (Ibid., p.254).

AN INTRODUCTION TO POLITICAL COMMUNICATION

In 1967 the Johnson administration launched 'Operation Success', setting up a 'Vietnam Information Group' in the president's executive office with the specific remit to supply good news stories to the media. Propaganda and disinformation about the successes of the South Vietnamese, and the failures of the North, was constantly disseminated.

Despite the public relations effort, as is well known, the intervention of the United States in Vietnam failed, and President Nixon ordered the first withdrawals of troops in the early 1970s. Moreover, military failure was attributed by many in the US political establishment to a failure in political communication: specifically, to the excessively rigorous journalism of the US media corps as it recorded the horrors of the conflict for daily transmission on prime-time news. From this perspective, shared by conservatives such as Ronald Reagan and George Bush, who applied it to their own pursuit of military public relations when they came to power in the 1980s, the rise of the anti-war movement amongst the young people of America, and the widespread revulsion which accompanied growing awareness of US military brutality in South-East Asia, was the product of a media out of control, and running loose on the battlefield.

As was noted in Chapter 4, this 'common sense' view of the media's relationship to public opinion about the Vietnam War has been challenged by a number of authors (Hallin, 1986; Williams, 1993). Bruce Cummings asserts that between 1961 and 1968 the US media, including television, enthusiastically performed their patriotic duty on behalf of the government's war efforts, and that after 1968 'television brought into the home not the carnage of war, but the yawning fissure in the American consensus that underpinned this war in the previous period' (1992, p.84). Reportage of the war in its latter stages was not 'anti-government' so much as reflective of the divisions which afflicted the politico-military establishment on policy. Daniel Hallin's detailed study has established that Vietnam coverage was at its most diverse, critical and negative during periods of political conflict around the issue, but that journalists never challenged the fundamental legitimacy of US war aims (1986). Even the My Lai massacre was virtually ignored by the US media for two years after it happened.

While, however, reportage of the Vietnam War does not merit the charges of subversion made against it by some US politicians as they sought to find explanations for their country's humiliation at the hands of the North Vietnamese, the information environment in

192

which journalists found themselves *was* relatively unrestricted. While the administration pursued its public relations activities, journalists in the field were permitted a degree of latitude with which to film often shocking images of death and destruction. Television viewers in the US and elsewhere saw pictures of children being burned to death by (US) napalm; of villages being torched by US troops; of summary executions of suspected communists by South Vietnamese officers; and, most significantly in the view of contemporary commentators, US troops in disarray as the North mounted its 'Tet offensive'. These images were the product of the US administration's view, in accordance with the strongly liberal tradition of American democracy, that 'the public have a right to information' (Mercer *et al.*, 1987, p.5). There *were* substantial and largely successful efforts made to manage news and public opinion, as we have noted, but control over journalists was far from complete. The belief of some, essentially pro-war, journalists that they had the right and indeed the duty to report the conflict in its totality, and the reluctance of the government to censor on anything but security criteria, *did* generate disturbing images, which cannot fail to have influenced many of those who became active opponents of the war.

## The Falklands

Whether the Vietnam War was lost on television or not (and a scientifically conclusive answer to that question may never be forthcoming), the *perception* that it had been remained strong in the 1970s, and when a new generation of political leaders came to power in Britain and the US in the 1980s they allowed that perception to govern their approach to information management in the conflicts of that decade.

When Argentinian forces invaded the Falkland Islands in April 1982 they triggered a conflict which, if relatively small-scale in military terms, was of immense symbolic importance to the British government. At that time the government of Margaret Thatcher was suffering the lowest popularity ratings ever recorded. Britain was deep in economic recession, and unemployment was over three million. 'Thatcherism' had not yet established pre-eminence in the British political landscape. The Argentine aggression against a piece of British territory overseas, however, permitted the Thatcher government to undertake a late post-colonialist military expedition, and to demonstrate its patriotism and resolve in the face of the upstart

193

dictator Leopold Galtieri. In this sense, the conflict became in itself an act of political communication, loaded with symbolic resonance and echoes of Britain's imperial past. It was also a limited war, as defined above, in which no less important than military success was the battle for public opinion at home and abroad.

The military option was not the only one available for dealing with the Argentinians. Economic and diplomatic sanctions could have been used more aggressively by the British government, as they have been used against many other countries in recent history. Once the military option had been decided upon, however, the Falklands conflict became a war of news and opinion management, as much as one of armed force. Throughout, the British government, like the Americans in Vietnam, had to counter domestic and international opposition to its preferred means of resolving the conflict. That Margaret Thatcher and her ministers succeeded where the Americans failed was due not least to the degree of control which they exercised over public images of the war. Few observers would dispute the view that media coverage was among the most restricted of all post-Second World War conflicts. Journalists were confronted with censorship, disinformation, misinformation, and political intimidation in the course of the government's efforts to ensure a favourable (from its perspective) portrayal of the conflict. Despite the limited character of the war, government information policy was to treat it as a matter of national survival, and to manipulate and constrain coverage accordingly.

Its ability to do this was greatly facilitated by the fact that the Falklands conflict was fought 8,000 miles away from Britain (and from most of the rest of the world) on territory and in conditions relatively inaccessible to media organisations. Although the availability of electronic newsgathering technology could have permitted live coverage of the conflict (of the type which later that year accompanied the Israeli invasion of Lebanon) the geographical isolation of the Falkland Islands was an obvious obstacle for media organisations. Electronic newsgathering, if it is to be truly 'live', requires the use of communication satellites. Access to these was not easy in the Falklands. Robert Harris's study of media–government relations during the conflict notes that 'the special circumstances of the Falklands campaign ensured that the government had unique control over how the war appeared on television. Because there were no satellite facilities, the MOD could regulate the flow of pictures and deodorise the war in a way that few other democratic governments – especially recent administrations in the USA – have been able to get away with' (1983, p.61).

Technical constraints would always have influenced coverage of the conflict, then, even if the political environment had been more favourable to the media.

As it was, however, technical problems in the communication of news about the conflict were only the least of the journalists' difficulties. From the outset, the British government pursued an information policy heavily influenced by the US experience in Vietnam, and the perception that excessive openness on the part of the authorities had contributed to a loss of morale on the 'home front'. Thus, the British authorities opted for a policy of tight control of information and imagery, often justified in terms of the aforementioned technical constraints. In terms of content, the policy amounted to restricting images of British military failures, while allowing positive images of success.

The fundamentally political logic of this approach was reinforced by the traditional secrecy of the British Civil Service and Defence Ministry. Military public relations in the Falklands conflict were handled in the first instance by the navy which, unlike the army in Northern Ireland, had relatively little experience of information management. The army's PR operation in Northern Ireland was sophisticated and (at least on the surface) 'open' to journalistic requirements (Miller, 1993). The navy, on the other hand, 'lacked awareness of the media's role in war and often appeared [in the Falklands] oblivious of the political need to win popular support at home and abroad' (Mercer *et al.*, 1987, p.92). Naval PROs' treatment of the journalists who accompanied the British expeditionary task force to the Falklands was often dismissive and uncooperative, to the extent indeed that it frequently came into conflict with the political requirements of the government, leading to a struggle of wills between competing public relations departments.

For example, when it was announced that the government would be dispatching a task force to retake the disputed islands, the naval authorities decided that *no* journalists would be permitted to travel with it. Only the personal intervention of Margaret Thatcher's press secretary, Bernard Ingham, and the pressure which he put on her to recognise the negative publicity a complete ban on journalists would attract, persuaded the navy to reconsider. In the end, after heated negotiations between British media organisations, the government, and the military, 28 journalists travelled with the task force.

No non-British journalists were included in the pool, a fact cited by some observers in attempting to explain the frequently critical attitudes of the international community to the British position in the dispute (Harris, 1983). Although the international community in the end tolerated Mrs Thatcher's military solution to the crisis, support was rarely wholehearted, and had the conflict been more protracted and bloody than it eventually turned out to be this could have become a serious political problem for the UK government. Had foreign journalists been involved in the media contingent, it has been argued, coverage of the British position might have been more sympathetic.

The military authorities' reluctance to include journalists, even British, in the task force was an illustration of the impact of the Vietnam experience on Western attitudes to military public relations. In 1977 the Ministry of Defence had prepared a secret paper on 'Public Relations Planning in Emergency Operations' which stated that 'for planning purposes it is anticipated that twelve places should be available to the media, divided equally between ITN, the BBC and the press . . . The press should be asked to give an undertaking that copy and photographs will be pooled' (quoted in Harris, 1983, p.149). The Falklands conflict saw this policy being applied for the first time although, as noted, the intervention of Ingham secured the availability of 28, as opposed to 12 places.

When the pool had been assembled and the task force departed on the long journey to the Falklands, the military's unease with the journalists was further reflected in a general lack of co-operation, even obstruction, in the latter's efforts to produce material for their organisations back in Britain. While all the journalists accepted the legitimacy of censorship on security criteria, it soon became clear that they were also under pressure not to report things which could be construed as 'damaging' to the morale of the troops, and that could show the forces in a negative light to the public as a whole (such as brawls between soldiers on board ship).

When the task force reached the islands and the conflict proper began, reports were censored on grounds of taste and tone (the deletion of expletives, for example, or what were regarded by the military as potentially morale-damaging accounts of British setbacks). Most notoriously, television pictures were prevented from being shown – on the grounds that satellite facilities were unavailable – for several weeks after being taken. Robert Harris's study of the media's role in the conflict notes that 'without satellite facilities, film from the task force simply had to be put on the next ship heading back to Ascension [the military base where facilities were available for television transmission]. In an age of supposedly instant communication, what were perhaps the most eagerly awaited television pictures in the world travelled homewards at a steady 25 knots' (1983, p.59).

Back in London Ministry of Defence briefings, conducted by the department's deputy chief of public relations, Ian MacDonald, were minimalistic in the extreme, often failing to clarify important information such as the name of a sinking battleship, or details of casualties. Off the record briefings were not provided, preventing journalists from producing reports which, if they did not reveal very much of a specific nature, would at least have enabled the country as a whole to know what was happening. One observer suggests that the government's 'closed' information policy on the Falklands was counter-productive, in this respect:

> the failure to brief the media off the record led to all sorts of difficulties. Unable to check on a number of facts and lacking any form of in-confidence briefing, the media reported all they saw and heard. Worse still they speculated. The result was a mass of information about ship movements, the composition of the task force, weapons capabilities and continuous comment about the various options open to the task force.
>
> (Alan Hooper, quoted in Adams, 1986, p.8)

Official reticence in this respect led to the famous observation by Peter Snow on BBC's *Newsnight* programme, 'if the British are to be believed'.[3] This in turn led the government, and Margaret Thatcher in particular, to mount a campaign of political pressure on the BBC, targeted against its 'impartiality' in coverage of the conflict. As the Glasgow University Media Group showed in their study of war reporting, the impartiality of television news was debatable (1985). Coverage in general was normally deferential to, and supportive of, dubious official claims of military success. The war was sanitised for television viewers, and the non-military possibilities of a resolution to the conflict marginalised. Criticism of the government's policy, as in the infamous *Panorama* special of May 11, 1982, was rare.[4] For the government, however, all this amounted to a kind of subversion, as if the BBC should have accepted that on this issue the government's interests and views were synonymous with those of 'the nation'.

Throughout the Falklands conflict there was a fundamental tension in official information policy. Ministry of Defence advice issued to journalists on the task force included the recognition that 'the essence of successful warfare is secrecy. The essence of successful journalism is publicity' (quoted in Harris, 1983, p.16). This is not strictly true, however. Publicity, as we noted above, is now viewed as an instrument of war, particularly by the politicians who must take responsibility for its execution in a democracy. Thus, while the military authorities and the Defence Ministry pursued a policy of non-cooperation with the media, the government as a whole required media publicity for its symbolic campaign.

Mercer *et al.* note that 'from the outset the Prime Minister sought to rally party, national and international opinion' (1987, p.18) through such displays as the departure of the task force. In the words of a serving admiral at the time, 'it was very important to give tangible evidence of military power to back up the diplomatic effort. It was very much a PR show – to show the Fleet leaving, both for British opinion, to rally them behind the ships and as an expression of power for world opinion and, of course, the enemy' (Ibid., p.19).

For the reporting of good news, then, the media were most welcome, and treated accordingly. Beyond this role as transmitters of symbolic demonstrations of military power, the media were also used to confuse and 'disinform' the enemy. When, for example, landings on the Falklands were being prepared, misleading information was leaked to the media, thence to the public and, of course, the Argentinians.

Whether or not one agrees with the 'justness' of the Falklands War and the government's information policy during it, there is no doubt, as Robert Harris concludes, 'that in many respects the British people were not given the facts during the Falklands war. Information was leaked out slowly and often reluctantly by the Ministry of Defence; rumours were allowed to circulate unchecked; and the British authorities frequently used the media as an instrument with which to confuse the enemy' (1983, p.92). Such tactics may or may not have contributed to British military success in the Falklands, but they certainly helped to revive the political fortunes of the Thatcher government, which went on to win landslide general election victories in 1983 and 1987. In this sense, the conflict – and media reportage of it – had major political ramifications.

Harris also notes that 'the Falklands conflict may well prove the last war in which the armed forces are completely able to control the movements and communications of the journalists covering it. Technology has already overtaken the traditional concepts of war reporting' (Ibid., p.150). This prediction has turned out to be wrong. In the next section we consider a succession of conflicts, culminating in the Gulf War of 1991, which demonstrate that the control of media coverage of military conflict for political purposes has increased, rather than decreased, since the Falklands War. The success of the Thatcher government in controlling media images of the Falklands War was not an anachronism, but the beginning of a trend.

## The Gulf and other wars

For the US government of Ronald Reagan, still smarting from the perceived mistakes of the Vietnam War, British media policy in the Falklands provided important lessons in how to manage public opinion in times of military conflict. In sharp contrast to the relative ease with which media organisations gained access to the fighting in Vietnam, when US forces invaded the Caribbean island of Grenada in 1983, and the central American republic of Panama in 1989, journalists were almost entirely excluded from covering the action.

In the first instance, internal disputes within an avowedly Marxist regime gave the Reagan administration the opportunity to remove what had been a thorn in its side for some time. On the pretext of protecting the security of Grenada's neighbours, and the lives of American students on the island, and with much public relations emphasis on the presence of Cuban troops there (who turned out to be mainly construction workers), US marines landed and quickly installed a regime favourable to the US. Since no journalists were permitted to accompany the troops, official accounts of what was happening and why went unchallenged. The deaths of civilians, including those killed during the bombing of a hospital, were passed off by the military as regrettable mistakes, and generally represented as such by the media, both within the United States and abroad.

Just as victory in the Falklands had rescued the Thatcher government from potential electoral failure in 1983, the 'success' of the Grenadan operation substantially boosted Ronald Reagan's popularity in the run-up to the 1984 presidential election, which he won by a landslide. It also appeared to confirm the value of retaining strict control of the media in military conflict situations, as opposed to allowing journalists to roam freely around the war zone, seeing and reporting what they liked. Consequently, George Bush's first military crisis as president, the invasion of Panama, was characterised by the same approach to information management.

When US troops entered Panama in search of the fugitive dictator Manuel Noriega, they too were free of the constraining influence of the independent media. Martha Gellhorn's account of the events in Panama reveals the extent of civilian casualties in the effort to apprehend Noriega, and suggests that many of them were unnecessary (1990). At the time, American and international public opinion was simply not told of these facts, and encouraged to believe that the operation had been relatively bloodless. When the true nature of the invasion began to emerge, media and public attention had moved on to other matters.

Like the Falklands War for Britain, the invasions of Grenada and Panama were, from the US military's point of view, relatively minor conflicts. Although important events in shaping the fortunes of domestic political actors (hence the attention devoted by the authorities to media management) they were in no sense wars of national survival. The Gulf War of 1990–1, on the other hand, while still far short of 'total war', was a major conflict, involving several countries, hundreds of thousands of troops, and some of the largest military manoeuvres in history. Its pursuit and outcome were matters of intense international concern, with consequences for the global economy and the delicate balance of power existing in the Middle East. The decline and changed ideological nature of the Soviet Union meant that the Gulf conflict was unlikely ever to have become a 'world war' as that term is commonly understood, but there is no doubt that it represented an extremely dangerous moment for the Middle East, and the international community as a whole.

The major protagonists in the conflict – the United States, Britain, Iraq, and Kuwait – all pursued vigorous media management campaigns. For Britain and the US, military public relations policy was strongly influenced by the experiences of the smaller 1980s conflicts discussed above. This resulted in a policy of minimising journalistic access to the fighting, while maximising official control of those images which did emerge.

The objectives of the policy were, firstly, military, in so far as 'the news media can be a useful tool, or even a weapon, in prosecuting a war psychologically, so that the operators don't have to use their more severe weapons' (Arthur Humphries, quoted in Macarthur, 1992, p.145). They were also political, in that the populations of the countries in the anti-Iraq alliance had to be convinced of the justness of the coming conflict, with its unpredictable and potentially enormous consequences. This task was of course complicated by the fact that Saddam Hussein's Iraq had been the friend of the West for most of the 1980s, and had been in receipt of sophisticated military equipment from Britain, France and other countries in the pursuit of its war with Iran. Now Iraq was the enemy, and explanations were required before a military solution to the invasion of Kuwait could be pursued with confidence. As John Macarthur puts it in his study of US media management during the conflict, 'on August 2, when Hussein grabbed Kuwait, he stepped beyond the imaginings of the practitioners of real-politik. Suddenly more was required than manipulation by leak. Convincing Americans to fight a war to liberate a tiny Arab sheikdom ruled by a family oligarchy would require the demonisation of Hussein in ways never contemplated by human rights groups. It called for a frontal assault on public opinion such as had not been seen since the Spanish–American war. The war had to be sold' (Ibid., p.42).

Pursuing these objectives in the Gulf was never going to be as easy as had been the case in the Falklands, Grenada, or Panama. The geographical location of the conflict, and its international dimension, inevitably increased its media accessibility and newsworthiness. Media organisations, particularly the television crews of CNN, the BBC and others, had access to more sophisticated communications technology, such as portable satellite transmission equipment, than had been the case even a few years before. Furthermore, many Western journalists located themselves in Iraq, beyond the reach of allied military censors, before hostilities proper began.

Despite these environmental factors, the allies could still have prevented journalists reporting the conflict, had they been inclined to do so. As Macarthur points out, however, the war had to be 'sold' as well as fought and won. Indeed, as noted earlier the two procedures were, by the end of the twentieth century, closely related. It was not therefore in the interests of the anti-Hussein coalition to block all coverage, and to antagonise international public opinion by denying it information. Better by far to ensure that the information about, and images of, the conflict which made it into the public domain were compatible, as far as possible, with the allies' military and political objectives. This resulted in the Gulf War, and its build-up, being conducted against the backdrop of a sophisticated information management and public relations campaign.

From the onset of the crisis journalistic access to the crucial areas was restricted, with the US and its allies co-operating in the establishment of a 'pool' system. As the *New York Times* put it, 'the Gulf war marked this century's first major conflict where the policy was to confine reporters to escorted pools that sharply curtailed when and how they could talk to the troops' (quoted in Macarthur, 1992, p.7). One hundred and fifty US military 'public affairs' officers were assigned to shepherd the journalists of the 'National Media Pool' around the desired locations, and to keep them away from sensitive areas. The British army deployed its apparatus of public relations officers to perform the same function.

At the front, journalists were formed into 'Media Reporting Teams', closely watched over by the military PROs who accompanied the troops during their training and, when the time came, into battle. With the exception of a few 'unilaterals' (Taylor, 1992) such as Robert Fisk of the *Independent*, who broke away from the pool system and attempted, with varying degrees of success, to gain unsupervised access to stories, the vast majority of journalists present at the scene were subject to the 'protection' of the military.

While the journalists were thus constrained from moving freely around the war zone and reporting what they saw there, the allies fed the media with a diet of information which, on the one hand, sanitised the conflict for domestic consumption, and on the other contributed to the ongoing psychological battle against Hussein and the Iraqis.

In Dhahran, where the allies were preparing their military offensive, a Joint Information Bureau was established to supply journalists with material. When hostilities began, this amounted largely to video film of aircraft undertaking aerial strikes against Iraqi targets. The material appeared to demonstrate the success of the allies' military tactics, while avoiding coverage of Iraqi casualties. As many observers have noted, the media war had the appearance of a computer game. Visuals were often accompanied by exaggerated claims of success in bombing raids, taking out Iraqi missiles, and so on.

The Gulf War was, of course, a spectacularly successful military operation from the allies' point of view, presenting an awesome demonstration of the destructive power of modern technology, and resulting in very few allied casualties. The conflict, unlike that in Vietnam, was quick and clean, by the standards of the military, serving to justify the restricted information policy which accompanied it. As John Macarthur and other observers have pointed out, however, if we as citizens are to 'take seriously the concept of informed consent in a democracy' (1992, p.150) do we not have the right to expect a fuller, more complete picture of an event of such importance as the Gulf conflict?

Those who argue that we do have such a right criticised the Western media – and those of Britain and the United States in particular – for so meekly embracing the pool system, the sanitised information and disinformation coming out of Dhahran and Riyadh, and the frequent censorship of journalistic material which occurred, as in the Falklands, for reasons of 'taste and tone' rather than military security. The media, it is argued, should have applied its Fourth Estate, watchdog role to the event with more vigour, giving citizens a genuine opportunity to judge the rights and wrongs of allied policy, and the appropriateness of the military response to the Iraqi invasion of Kuwait. Thankfully, the argument continues, allied casualties were not on the scale of Vietnam, but if they had been, or if the conflict had sucked in Israel, Syria and the other Arab states, would we have been able to give or withhold our 'informed consent'?

The media's general acceptance of the military's close management and control of their newsgathering was a product, firstly, of straightforward commercial criteria. The experience of the early 1980s conflicts discussed above had shown the capacity of the military to exclude journalists from the field of operations, and their readiness to use this power. Media organisations accepted the pool system in the Gulf, and the restrictions which it entailed, in the knowledge that the alternative was exclusion. None of the US networks, or the major US newspapers, was prepared to pay this price and see its rivals gain access and commercial advantage. In Britain, too, organisations like the BBC and ITN willingly co-operated with the military and its demands, on the grounds that, if they did not, someone else would.

In addition to commercial considerations, media organisations were undoubtedly influenced in their editorial policies by the nature of the conflict, and the relatively unambiguous distinction between right and wrong which it presented. Many have noted correctly the hypocrisy inherent in the allies' position: it was they who armed and supported Saddam Hussein as he engaged in a murderous war with Iran, and gassed his civilians at Halabja and elsewhere. Despite the cries of moral outrage against Hussein's behaviour during the invasion and occupation of Kuwait, he was behaving more or less as he had always done. This time, unfortunately for him, he had chosen to challenge the strategic interests of the US and its allies by threatening Arab oil reserves.

While many questioned the allies' motivations for going to war with Iraq, once it had begun there were few in the West prepared to take Hussein's side. Iraq was not Vietnam, or Nicaragua, a fact reflected in the media's enthusiastic adoption of the allies' perspective on events. As Bruce Cummings observes of media coverage: 'the Gulf War sequence reversed Vietnam: whereas television served [US] state policy in the first phase of the war and questioned it in the second (after Tet), Gulf coverage interrogated the war in the months before Desert Storm, and served the state once the storm broke' (1992, p.103).

There was, in short, an exceptionally high degree of consensus around the legitimacy of allied war aims, shared even by those who criticised the sanitisation and voluntary censorship of coverage exhibited by the main media. To an extent not seen since the Second World War, operation Desert Storm was viewed as a 'just' war.

The allies' carefully controlled account of the conflict was not entirely unchallenged, however. Earlier we noted that throughout the conflict there were Western journalists present in the Iraqi capital, Baghdad. CNN's Peter Arnett, in particular, provided information which, if not hostile to the allies' cause, frequently contradicted the public relations emanating from Riyadh. When, for example, US bombs destroyed an air-raid shelter in Baghdad, killing hundreds of civilians and shattering the concept of a 'clean' war, CNN and other Western television organisations were present to film the aftermath, disseminating images of death and destruction to the global audience. Hussein's administration of course welcomed such coverage, and tolerated the presence of Western journalists in Baghdad in the belief that they could, by their focus on civilian casualties, cause greater damage to the allies' military effort than to Iraq's. Fortunately for the Iraqis (if not for Hussein) civilian casualties were low, given the ferocity of the allies' bombing, and the effort to have Iraq portrayed as the wronged party was unsuccessful. Eventually, most of the Western journalists were expelled from the country, with the exception of CNN and a handful of other organisations.

Hussein also used Western media to pursue a more 'pro-active' public relations campaign. Before hostilities began Hussein was filmed greeting the foreigners who had been trapped in Kuwait by his invasion. Most notoriously, he attempted to use British children to portray himself as a kindly 'Uncle Saddam' figure, but succeeded only in sickening international public opinion with his implied threat of what might happen to the hostages should his invasion of Kuwait be resisted.

After operation Desert Storm had commenced, images of captured allied airmen, visibly brutalised, were shown on Iraqi television and then through Western television organisations to the rest of the world. As Philip Taylor notes, these and other efforts to influence international public opinion through the use of media were 'ill conceived and badly researched' (1992, p.90), alienating rather than attracting support for the Iraqi cause. 'If Saddam had been attempting to exploit the Vietnam Syndrome to create public dissatisfaction with the [allied] war effort, the apparently brutalised nature of the pilots merely caused fury and resentment' (Ibid., p.107). Hussein failed to understand the social semiotics of his communicative efforts, and thus to predict how his messages would be decoded.

## Babies, incubators and black propaganda

If the allies and Iraq controlled and manipulated the media to pursue their respective objectives, the Kuwaiti government in exile also engaged in public relations of the type frequently used in wartime – what is sometimes referred to as 'black propaganda'. Saddam Hussein's forces in Kuwait routinely committed atrocities against civilians, as they had done for years in Iraq itself, and some on the Kuwaiti side believed that if serious United Nations and Western support in the struggle to evict Iraq was to be forthcoming, these atrocities should be highlighted and, if necessary, exaggerated or even invented. Thus, in the period of build-up to Desert Storm, when public opinion in the United States and elsewhere was divided, and domestic political support for military action uncertain, a public relations campaign got underway to portray Hussein as an enemy of such evil that he could not be allowed to get away with his invasion.

In the United States, where reinforcing support for the Kuwaiti cause was most important, exiles formed Citizens for a Free Kuwait. This body then hired the public relations firm Hill and Knowlton, at a cost of some $11 million, to disseminate atrocity stories connected with the Iraqi occupation of Kuwait. Special 'information days' were held, videos produced, and US congressmen enlisted to lend their weight to the appeal for military intervention.[5]

Many of the atrocity stories were true, as already noted, while others appear to have been manufactured for the specific purpose of mobilising public opinion behind Kuwait. Most notable in this connection was the tale of how Iraqi troops in Kuwait City had entered a hospital, removed 312 babies from the incubators in which they were placed, and shipped the incubators back to Iraq, leaving the infants to die on the hospital floor. In October 1990, Hill and Knowlton sent a Kuwaiti eyewitness, a young woman named as 'Nayirah', to the US Congress's 'Human Rights Caucus' before which she gave a detailed and emotional account of the incubator story.

The story spread quickly, appearing in the media of several countries as 'true'. In the US Congress, shortly afterwards, the resolution to pursue a military solution to the Gulf crisis was passed by a mere two votes. US observers are in little doubt that 'Nayirah's' story, and others of a similar type which were circulating at this time, contributed substantially to swinging political support behind the military option and thereby setting in motion the subsequent Desert Storm (Macarthur, 1992). In the event, 'Nayirah' turned out to be the daughter of the Kuwaiti ambassador to the United States, and the incubator story to be false. When Amnesty International inspected the scene of the alleged atrocity after the cessation of hostilities, the organisation found no evidence to substantiate the story.

## CONCLUSION

The incubator story is probably the most extreme example of the pursuit of media management and manipulation, public relations and propaganda, which characterised the Gulf War. In this respect the Gulf was not unique, since such techniques have become commonplace in military conflict in the course of the twentieth century. But the combination of new communications technologies, sophisticated public relations, and geo-political significance which provided the context of this particular conflict gave media management a heightened role. In the Gulf, messages of various kinds transmitted through the media had real political and military consequences, in so far as they served to outrage public opinion at one moment, reassure it at another, and provide legitimation for official allied accounts of the conflict, its genesis, and its preferred outcome.

To draw attention to the 'hyperreal' quality of the Gulf War as experienced by those not in the front line, and the extent of media management from all sides, is not necessarily to criticise these features. Few would deny that there are circumstances in which such techniques are appropriate; in which manipulation, distortion, and even deception may be legitimate instruments of warfare. There *are* just wars, and the Gulf conflict may be the closest the world has come to one since the defeat of the Nazis. One might also argue, however, that in the history of post-Second World War conflicts, the same or similar techniques have been used by the Western powers in military expeditions of far more dubious legitimacy – Grenada, Nicaragua, the Israeli invasion of Lebanon in 1982, to name but three. In each of these situations, 'enemies' were created, and 'threats' manufactured by military public relations specialists, while journalists were prevented or dissuaded from presenting alternative accounts of the 'truth'.

Perhaps the most disturbing feature of the Gulf War as *political communication* was its demonstration of how readily such messages as the incubator story were accepted and passed on by journalists eager for materials to confirm their image of Hussein as a tyrannical violator of human rights. When 'Gulf War II' threatened to break out in 1998, lurid and frightening images of the biological and nerve gas weapons which Saddam Hussein was allegedly building, and which could wipe out a Western European city, were reported by the media as uncontestable truths, rather than what they were – unsubstantiated speculations which were being used to whip up public opinion behind another military campaign against Iraq. Few observers doubt that Saddam Hussein was in 1991, and remained afterwards, a murderous individual, heading a genocidal, fascist regime. This does not excuse journalists from the responsibility of reporting his government's activities, and those of the Western powers ranged against him, with a degree of emotional distance and objectivity, especially if this could mean the difference between peace and war. In future conflicts the issues may not be so clear cut as they have been in relation to Iraq, the moral and military choices more ambiguous. As media management techniques advance and grow ever more all-encompassing, how are we as citizens of the twenty-first century to give 'informed consent' to our governments' military policies, and prevent unjustified military adventures?

# 10

# CONCLUSION

## Performance politics and the democratic process

This book has described the growing involvement of mass communication in a variety of political arenas, and the pursuit of what we might call *performance politics* at all stages in the process by which issues emerge in the public sphere to be debated, negotiated around and, on occasion, resolved. We have examined the use of public relations, marketing and advertising techniques by political parties in campaigning and governmental mode (sometimes, of course, the two are indistinguishable). We have noted the enhanced role of opinion and media management in disputes between states, between workers and their employers, and between governments and insurgent organisations. We have considered the role of journalists and their media as political reporters, interpreters, commentators and agenda-setters, observing how their relationship of inter-dependence with politicians has shaped the behaviours and professional practices of both groups. And we have reviewed the debate about the impact of these phenomena on citizens, on behalf of whom, finally, politics, the media and the democratic process as a whole are supposed to function.

While many of the processes described in the preceding chapters are matters of fact, debate about the effects of political communication continues to occupy all those involved in the processes of public debate, election and government, whether as protagonists, mediators or voters. I would like to end, therefore, with some remarks on the current state of that debate, before identifying some of the key outstanding issues.

We began with an epigraph from the pen of Walter Lippmann, identifying a 'revolution' in the 'art of creating consent among the governed', which would 'alter every political premise'. More than seventy years after those words were written, their accuracy is self-evident. They apply, moreover, not simply to those 'in control of affairs', but to those groups of greater or lesser marginality whose political objectives are to challenge, subvert, or capture that control.

The revolution in the 'persuasive arts' is the consequence, as we noted above, of far-reaching political and technological developments leading to universal suffrage on the one hand, and ever more efficient media of mass communication on the other. For as long as democratic principles underpin advanced capitalism and communications technologies develop further towards simultaneity and inter-activity, the revolution can be expected to continue. Political fashions may change, but the need to fashion political messages will not.

Most participants in the political communication debate will agree with these assertions, and with the further point that, as political actors and media have grown dependent on each other, politics has become not only a persuasive but a performance art, in which considerations of style, presentation and marketing are equal to, if not greater in importance than, content and substance. It is here, of course, that the arguments begin.

Chapter 3 identified two broad perspectives on the democratic significance of modern political communication. One might be said to be *pessimistic*, in so far as it asserts that our culture is degraded and democracy undermined by the intrusion of the 'persuasive arts' into politics.

A liberal variant of the argument is founded on adherence to the notion of the rational citizen, the importance of choice in democracy, and the role of the media in promoting material which makes that choice meaningful. In the liberal critique, mediated or performance politics lack rationality and substance, breeding voter apathy and shallow populism. They are more a means of 'self-promotion [for politicians] than of information for the public' (Denton, 1991a, p.93).

Pessimists on the left of the ideological spectrum share many of these objections, but add that the pursuit of performance politics is inconsistent with a coherent, radical left message. Thus, Greg Philo has criticised the post-1985 Labour Party (and blamed its 1992 defeat) on its reliance on 'the shallow science of Imagistics' (1993b, p.417). For much of the post-war period, as Chapters 6 and 7 indicated, such views drove the British Labour Party's communicative strategy, and despite the scale of the 1997 victory, they remain influential amongst the left in Britain and elsewhere.

One might view both variants of this pessimism as 'romantic' in their tendency to unfavourably compare contemporary realities with idealised pasts. The liberal concern for the health of present-day democracy presumes that there was such a thing as *true* democracy beyond the elite circles of John Stuart Mill's educated men of property. But if democracy is, as Bobbio suggests, principally about the legitimation of government by drawing more citizens into the political process, then its expansion in advanced capitalism is precisely coterminous with the development of mass media and, through them, mass political communication.

The left pessimists, on the other hand, continue to presume that there is a natural constituency of left-wing voters, from whom an 'authentic', clearly delivered, left-wing message – as opposed to 'shallow' image-making – can produce an electoral majority. If such a constituency exists, why should the presentational skills of a Tony Blair or a Peter Mandelson prevent a socialist message from getting through to it, if that indeed is what the Labour Party wishes to promulgate?

In short, then, the 'romantic pessimists', as we shall call them, might be argued to make the mistake of confusing form and content in political communication, and of contrasting – unfairly – the current reality of mass, albeit mediatised political participation, with a mythical golden age when rational, educated citizens knew what they were voting for and why. However imperfect modern mediatised democracy may be, it is surely preferable to that state of public affairs which existed not so long ago when political power was withheld from all but a tiny minority of aristocrats and the bourgeoisie.

The 'pragmatic optimists', by contrast, invite us to embrace without reservation a new age of electronic, inter-active, 'town-hall' democracy, peopled by a media-wise, culturally-knowing electorate immune to such blunt instruments as propaganda and brain-washing. Adherents to this perspective, many of whom have a vested interest in the industry which manages and directs it, argue not only that performance politics are here to stay, but that we are stronger as democracies for it. This perspective challenges the view that what one says is more important than how one says it, asserting instead that the voter can learn as much from a politician's more or less spontaneous performance than from his or her rational debate of the issues. The enhanced use of mass communication has made the political process more open, rather than less.

One can have sympathy with this position. While politics has indeed become, for the first time in human history, a mass spectator sport, it is nevertheless one in which citizens have real power to decide outcomes. Politicians employ a wide array of manipulative communication management techniques but, as we have seen, these are subject to mediation, comment and interpretation by the meta-discourse of political journalism, to which voters are relentlessly exposed. Politics in the age of mediation may have the character of a complex game, but it is one which media commentators and citizens alike have become increasingly adept at playing.

There are, however, important qualifications which must be made to the optimists' arguments. Most obviously, access to the resources required for effective political communication is neither universal nor equitable. The design, production and transmission of political messages costs money. In a capitalist system, this simple fact inevitably favours the parties and organisations of big business. Who could state with confidence that the dramatic electoral success of Berlusconi's Forza Italia movement in April 1994 owed nothing to his control of so much of the Italian media system? Chapter 8 argued strongly that innovation and skill in the techniques of media management can partially offset this resource imbalance for marginal political organisations but, to the extent that good political communication *can* influence citizens' attitudes and behaviour, economic power translates into political power.

For that reason, it is crucial to the health of the democratic process that the financing of political communication be monitored and regulated, just as certain restrictions on the ownership and cross-ownership of media organisations are insisted upon in most liberal democracies. It should not be possible, now or in the multi-channel, relatively unregulated media system of the future, for the political representatives of big capital to monopolise communication channels or to bribe their way to communicative advantage. If the optimistic perspective described above is to have validity, there must be a 'level playing field' for all those competing in the game.

Another weakness of the optimists' perspective is the continuing existence of secrecy and manipulation in the sphere of government communication. We discussed in Chapter 7 how the government of Margaret Thatcher, like others before and since throughout the capitalist world, was accused of cynically using the information apparatus at its disposal to further its own, limited political objectives. As communication becomes still more important in the political process, it becomes essential for citizens to have some power and control over which information their elected representatives choose to release into the public domain. This is especially true of international politics, in which citizens may be asked to endorse and participate in conflict with other countries. Such conflicts may have justification, or they may not. In deciding which is true in any given case, we are almost entirely dependent on information passed through mass media by government and national security establishments. The degree of accuracy of, and public access to, this information is itself a matter of (our) national security. In the matter of governmental information, as was noted above, New Labour in power has made some significant progress, promising freedom of information legislation for the first time in British history, and allowing TV documentary-makers unprecedented access to the decision-making process of such key ministers as the Chancellor of the Exchequer and the Foreign Secretary. The 'fly-on-the-wall' documentaries transmitted on British television in the first year of the Labour government, as well as constituting excellent public relations, offered a valuable insight into the thinking of politicians and their communication advisers as they went about their daily business.

Looking beyond the direct control of politicians and their spin doctors, both Britain and America in the late 1990s saw the power of the Internet as a liberalising, even destabilising force in political communication manifest itself. The exposure in 1998 of Bill Clinton's 'problems' with Monica Lewinsky on the Drudge Report website, and the Internet-led disclosure of the British Home Secretary's son's embarrassing tangle with marijuana and a tabloid journalist, were emblematic of the increasing difficulty politicians face in controlling the spread of information which they would prefer to remain secret. In both of the above cases one can have sympathy with the 'victims' of Internet exposure, and in the end neither emerged with serious damage. Bill Clinton was more popular with the American people after Monicagate than before, and Jack Straw's predicament in relation to his son's youthful experimentation with an illegal vegetable did not harm his image as one of the most effective Labour ministers of the first Blair term. The speed with which the news spread, however, and the politicians' inability to prevent its public consumption and discussion, give grounds for some optimism about the future development of democracy. It is certain that, as the new millennium begins and new communication technologies evolve further, elites in all spheres of public life will become more exposed to democratic scrutiny through the media, and that cannot be a bad thing.

In the end, however, the merging of politics and mass

communication described in this book is not a process which can legitimately be viewed as unambiguously 'good' or 'bad' in relation to its implications for democracy. The roots of the phenomenon – universal suffrage and advancing communication technology, in the context of a dynamic and expanding market for information of all kinds – cannot be seen as anything other than positive. Without doubt it has the potential to bring into being, to an extent unprecedented in human civilisation, something approaching real democracy, as defined by radical progressive thinkers from Marx onwards. The contribution of mass media to our political life will, of course, continue to be determined by the legal, economic, and social contexts in which they are allowed to function. Vigilance will be required if those contexts are to be shaped by the views and votes of the citizens as a whole, and not the particular interests of the Berlusconis and Murdochs, the Campbells and the Mandelsons, or the Wirthlins and Morrises of this world.

# NOTES

## 1 POLITICS IN THE AGE OF MEDIATION

1 For a recent book-length discussion of how the environmental issue became a news story in the late 1980s and 1990s, see Anderson, 1997.

2 Work undertaken by the Glasgow University Media Group in the 1970s and 1980s claimed to show anti-labour, pro-business bias in broadcast news coverage of key industrial disputes which took place in those years (1976, 1980). 'Bias' was also argued by the Group to have accompanied coverage of the left–right split which dominated the affairs of the Labour Party in the 1980s (1982). On the subject of Northern Ireland, several writers have presented accounts of how coverage of 'the Troubles' was slanted towards the interests of the British state (Schlesinger, 1987; Curtis, 1984).

3 Hall *et al.*'s *Policing the Crisis* (1978) explored the role of the 'public voice' of British newspapers in defining law and order issues during the 'mugging' panic of the early 1970s.

4 For a discussion of broadcast talk shows, including those which cover non-party political themes, see Livingstone and Lunt, 1994.

## 2 POLITICS, DEMOCRACY AND THE MEDIA

1 See Mill's essay 'On Representative Government', contained in his *Three Essays* (1975).

2 Robert Worcester's survey of attitudes after the 1992 general election shows that this continues to be the case in Britain, although there is evidence that, as Worcester puts it, 'the boredom factor is increasing' (1994, p.12). Worcester finds that 'a growing proportion of the [British] public now feels that the media generally, and television specifically, have provided too much or not the right coverage of election[s]'.

3 For Baudrillard, writing in the early 1980s, the masses experience mediatised politics principally as an entertainment experience, like television football. 'For some time now', he writes, 'the electoral game has been akin to TV game shows in the consciousness of the people . . . The people even enjoy day to day, like a home movie, the fluctuations of their own opinions in the daily opinion polls. Nothing in all this engages any responsibility. At no time are the masses politically and

214

historically engaged in a conscious manner. Nor is this a flight from politics, but rather the effect of an implacable antagonism between the class which bears the social, the political culture – master of time and history, and the un(in)formed, residual, senseless mass' (1983, p.38).

4 For an account of the 1997 general election campaign, by someone who participated in it as a political reporter for the BBC, see Jones, 1997.

5 Duncan Campbell, the British investigative journalist who made his reputation from the exposure of facts which government and the security services would rather keep secret. Campbell's notable successes include his publication of the details of *War Plan UK* (1983), the British government's civil defence plans in the event of nuclear war. These facts were revealed at a time when the rise of the anti-nuclear protest movement, CND, gave them heightened political sensitivity.

## 3 THE EFFECTS OF POLITICAL COMMUNICATION

1 For an overview of the issues, see McQuail, 1987. For a more readable summary of the problems, and the different approaches which they have generated, see Morley, 1980.

2 Hall's three decoding positions, which he argues to have been empirically tested, are: (a) the *dominant-hegemonic* position, when a message is decoded entirely within the encoder's framework of reference; (b) the *negotiated* position, which 'acknowledges the legitimacy of the hegemonic definitions to make the ground significations, while, at a more restricted, situational level, it makes its own ground rules', and (c) the *oppositional* decoding, 'the point when events which are normally signified and decoded in a negotiated way begin to be given an oppositional reading' (1980, p.138).

3 In 1992 the final 'poll of polls' indicated a Labour lead of 0.9 per cent. In fact, the Conservatives won the election by 7.6 per cent, giving a polling error of 8.5 per cent, the largest ever in British polling history. Butler and Kavanagh believe that 'there is no simple explanation for this massive failure in what had become a trusted instrument in election analysis' (1992, p.148), but propose the following explanations for the size of the error: (a) the sample of those polled was disproportionately working class (thus skewing the outcome in favour of Labour); (b) due to such factors as poll tax evasion, many of those polled were not included on the electoral register; (c) Tory voters were less likely to reveal their voting intentions; (d) fewer Labour than Tory voters actually voted; (e) there was a late swing to the Conservatives in the final few days of the campaign.

4 Butler and Kavanagh suggest that polls taken on April 1 indicating Labour leads of between 4 and 7 per cent were implicated in the party's electoral defeat, because they 'encouraged the triumphalism of the Sheffield rally and it helped to waken the public to the real possibility of a Labour victory' (1992, p.139).

5 So named because of its high production values, and artistic direction by award-winning feature film-maker Hugh Hudson.

6 For a recent discussion of the implications of these trends for the democratic process see McNair, 1998a.

7 The American political scientist Roderick Hart, for example, in his discussion of contemporary US presidential speech-making, argues that 'the mass media have caused presidents to seek security in discourse, not challenge, and have made the perception of assent, not assent itself, the valued commodity. What used to be a broad, bold line between argument and entertainment, between speech-making and theatre, now has no substance at all' (1987, p.152).

8 The political cartoon created by American artist Garry Trudeau.

9 The satirical puppet show produced by Central Television for the ITV network.

## 4 THE POLITICAL MEDIA

1 For a detailed discussion of the current state of the British journalistic media, press and broadcasting, national and regional, see McNair, 1999, especially Chapters 5–9. See also Watts, 1997.

2 Woolacott, M., 'When Invisibility Means Death', *Guardian*, April 27, 1996.

3 Robert Worcester's study of the 1992 election indicates that, at the time, only 32 per cent of the *Star*'s readers supported the Conservatives, as opposed to 53 per cent who supported Labour (1994, p.25).

4 Lord McAlpine stated his view that 'the heroes of this campaign were Sir David English, Sir Nicholas Lloyd, Kelvin MacKenzie and the other editors of the grander Tory press. Never in the past nine elections have they come out so strongly in favour of the Conservatives. Never has their attack on the Labour Party been so comprehensive . . '. This was how the election was won' (quoted in Butler and Kavanagh, 1992, p.208).

5 Linton, M., 'Sun-powered Politics', *Guardian*, October 30, 1995.

6 In which a senior British police officer commissioned to investigate 'shoot to kill' allegations against the Royal Ulster Constabulary in Northern Ireland claimed to have been the victim of a 'dirty tricks' campaign by the security services to discredit him.

7 *The Future of the BBC: Serving the Nation, Competing Worldwide*, London, HMSO, 1994.

8 For a discussion of 'soundbite' news see Hallin, 1997.

## 5 THE MEDIA AS POLITICAL ACTORS

1 James Curran and his colleagues at Goldsmith's College, London, detailed examples of press coverage of the 'Loony Left' in their documentary *Loony Tunes* (BBC2, 1988).

2 Sebastian, T., 'Dialogue with the Kremlin', *Sunday Times*, February 2, 1992.

3 The *Sun*, October 28, 1993.

4 Martin Jacques was throughout the 1980s a leading figure in the British Communist Party, and editor of its theoretical journal, *Marxism Today*.

5 In October 1998, the Parliamentary Channel was taken over by the BBC.

## 6 PARTY POLITICAL COMMUNICATION I: ADVERTISING

1 Kaid defines it as 'the process by which a source (usually a political candidate or party) purchases the opportunity to expose receivers through mass channels to political messages with the intended effect of influencing their political attitudes, beliefs, and/or behaviour' (1981, p.250).
2 The ad was directed by Ridley Scott for Collett, Dickinson and Pearce.
3 The general functions of political advertising are listed by Devlin as: (a) increasing the public's identification of a candidate; (b) swaying the small, but crucial segment of the voters who are 'floating', or undecided; (c) reinforcing support for a party or candidate; (d) attacking opponents, and; (e) raising money (1986).
4 Richards, S., 'Interview: Clare Short', *New Statesman*, August 9, 1996.
5 *Three-Minute Culture*, BBC2, January 29, 1989.
6 For an account of Livingstone's political development and emergence as GLC leader, see Carvel, 1984.
7 *The Local Government Act 1986*, London, HMSO, 1986.
8 *Consultation paper on the reform of party political broadcasting*, p.3.

## 7 PARTY POLITICAL COMMUNICATION II: POLITICAL PUBLIC RELATIONS

1 For details of the most important of the American political public relations specialists, see Chagall, 1981.
2 On coming to power in 1997, the Labour government reformed the operation of prime minister's question time, reducing its frequency from twice per week to once, while increasing the duration of sessions. As this edition went to press, opinion remained divided as to whether this had improved the opportunities for the prime minister to be questioned by opposing members of parliament (by allowing for more sustained and detailed questioning), or restricted them by reducing his exposure.
3 ITV, May 24, 1987.
4 Butler and Kavanagh, for example, write of the 'triumphalism' of the Sheffield rally (1992, p.139).
5 At the outset of the 1992 general election campaign Channel 4 broadcast a documentary, presented by *Guardian* columnist Hugo Young, in which a succession of journalists and analysts made clear their concerns about the democratic implications of intensifying media management by politicians (*Danger to Democracy*, Channel 4, 1992).
6 For whom Stephen Fry and Hugh Laurie have performed in television advertisements.
7 As Eric Shaw observes: 'this involved creating product recognition through the use of trademarks and slogans; differentiating the product from others by creating a unique selling proposition; encouraging the audience to want the product by enveloping it in a set of favourable associations; committing the audience to the product and its associated promises by inducing it to identify with all the advert's symbolised meaning and ensuring that the audience recalls the product and its need for it by repeated messages' (1994, p.65).
8 Campbell, A., 'We Will Survive', *Guardian*, December 22, 1997.

## 8 PRESSURE GROUP POLITICS AND THE OXYGEN OF PUBLICITY

1 In *Classes in Contemporary Capitalism* (1975), for example, Poulantzas argues that in addition to social classes defined by the exploiter/exploited relationship, each social formation also includes fractions or strata *within* classes, and what he terms 'social categories', such as intellectuals and bureaucrats, members of which may belong to several different social classes.

2 Business organisations, of course, use public relations techniques to influence the political environment in more general ways, particularly if, as is the case with the nuclear power industry, the product is politically controversial (Dionisopoulos, 1986; Tilson, 1994). For a detailed discussion of the use of source stategies in industrial relations in 1990s Britain see Negrine, 1996.

3 This argument was used in Britain by ITN's Alistair Burnett, when questioned by a critical viewer as to the reasons for the relative invisibility of CND on that organisation's bulletins (McNair, 1988).

4 In his letter dated July 29, 1985, then Home Secretary Leon Brittan stated: 'Recent events elsewhere in the world have confirmed only too clearly what has long been understood in this country. That terrorism thrives on the oxygen of publicity. That publicity derives either from the successful carrying out of terrorist acts or, as a second best, from the intimidation of the innocent public and the bolstering of faltering supporters by the well publicised espousal of violence as a justifiable means of securing political ends' (quoted in Bolton, 1990, p.161).

## 9 INTERNATIONAL POLITICAL COMMUNICATION

1 Michael Parenti notes that the 'red-baiting' of left-wing political movements has been a feature of the Western media since the nineteenth century, but that its frequency and intensity increased after the Bolshevik revolution. For him, the 'Red Peril theme' played a major part throughout the twentieth century in '1) setting back and limiting the struggles and gains of labour; 2) distracting popular attention from the recessions and crises of capitalism by directing grievances towards interior or alien forces, and; 3) marshalling public support for huge military budgets, Cold War policies and Third World interventions to make the world safe for corporate investments and profits' (1986, p.126).

2 For examples of pro-Soviet propaganda produced in Britain during the Second World War, see the documentary *Comrades in Arms* (Channel 4, 1988).

3 *Newsnight*, BBC2, May 3, 1982.

4 The programme gave voice to critics of government policy from the military and the Tory back-benches, leading to the accusation that it was an 'odious and subversive travesty' (Sally Oppenheim, MP, quoted in the Glasgow University Media Group, 1985, p.14).

5 For a documentary account of these events see *To Sell a War*, broadcast as part of ITV's current affairs strand on February 6, 1992.

# BIBLIOGRAPHY

Adams, V.: *The Media and the Falklands Campaign*, London, Macmillan, 1986.

Anderson, A.: *Media, Culture and the Environment*, London, UCL Press, 1997.

Ansolabehere, S., Iyengar, S.: *Going Negative*, New York, Free Press, 1995.

Arterton, F.: 'Campaign Organisations Confront the Media-Political Environment', in Graber, ed., *Media Power in Politics*, Washington, CQ Press, 1984, pp.155–63.

Baerns, B.: 'Journalism Versus Public Relations', in Paletz, ed.; *Political Communication Research: Approaches, Studies, Assessments*, Norwood, Ablex, 1987, pp.88–107.

Bagdikian, B.: 'Journalist Meets Propagandist', in Graber, ed., *Media Power in Politics*, Washington, CQ Press, 1984, pp.331–7.

Baudrillard, J.: *In the Shadow of the Silent Majorities*, New York, Semiotext, 1983.

Baudrillard, J.: *Selected Writings*, Cambridge, Polity Press, 1988.

Bernays, L.: *Crystallizing Public Opinion*, New York, Boni and Liveright, 1923.

Bloom, M.: *Public Relations and Presidential Campaigns*, New York, Thomas Crowell, 1973.

Blumler, J.: 'Election Communication and the Democratic Political System', in Paletz, ed., *Political Communication Research: Approaches, Studies, Assessments*, Norwood, Ablex, 1987, pp.167–75.

Blumler, J., Gurevitch, M.: 'Politicians and the Press', in Nimmo and Sanders, eds, *Handbook of Political Communication*, Beverly Hills, Sage, 1981, pp.467–93.

Bobbio, N.: *The Future of Democracy*, Cambridge, Polity Press, 1987.

Bolland, E.J.: 'Advertising v. Public Relations', in *Public Relations Quarterly*, vol. 34, no. 3, 1989, pp.10–12.

Bolton, R.: *Death on the Rock and Other Stories*, London, W.H. Allen, 1990.

Boorstin, D.J.: *The Image*, London, Weidenfeld & Nicolson, 1962.

219

Bruce, B.: *Images of Power*, London, Kogan Page, 1992.

Butler, D., Kavanagh, D.: *The British General Election of 1987*, London, Macmillan, 1988.

Butler, D., Kavanagh, D.: *The British General Election of 1992*, London, Macmillan, 1992.

Campbell, D.: *War Plan UK*, London, Paladin, 1983.

Carvel, J.: *Citizen Ken*, London, Chatto & Windus, 1984.

Chagall, D.: *The New Kingmakers*, New York, Harcourt Brace Jovanovitch, 1981.

Chippindale, P., Horrie, C.: *Disaster: The Rise and Fall of the News on Sunday*, London, Sphere, 1988.

Chomsky, N., Herman, E.: *Manufacturing Consent*, New York, Pantheon, 1988.

Cockerell, M.: *Live from Number 10*, London, Faber, 1988.

Cockerell, M., Hennessey, P., Walker, D.: *Sources Close to the Prime Minister*, London, Macmillan, 1984.

Collins, C.A.: 'Ma Anand Sheela: Media Power through Radical Discourse', in King, ed., *Postmodern Political Communication*, London, Praeger, 1992, pp.115–29.

Cooper, M.: 'Ethical Dimensions of Political Advocacy from a Postmodern Perspective', in Denton, ed., *Ethical Dimensions of Political Communication*, New York, Praeger, 1991, pp.23–47.

Cummings, B.: *War and Television*, London, Verso, 1992.

Cundy, D.: 'Political Commercials and Candidate Image: The Effect Can be Substantial', in Kaid *et al.*, eds, *New Perspectives on Political Advertising*, Carbondale, Southern Illinois University Press, 1986, pp.210–34.

Curran, J.: 'The Boomerang Effect: The Press and the Battle for London, 1981–6', in Curran *et al.*, eds, *Impacts and Influences*, London, Methuen, 1987, pp.113–40.

Curran, J., Smith, A., Wingate, P., eds: *Impacts and Influences*, London, Methuen, 1987.

Curran, J., Seaton, J.: *Power Without Responsibility*, London, Routledge, 1997.

Curtis, L.: Ireland: *The Propaganda War*, London, Pluto Press, 1984.

Dahlgren, P., Sparks, C., eds: *Journalism and Popular Culture*, London, Sage, 1992.

Deacon, D., Golding, P.: *Taxation and Representation*, London, John Libbey, 1994.

Denton, R.E.: *The Primetime Presidency of Ronald Reagan*, New York, Praeger, 1988.

Denton, R.E.: 'Primetime Politics: The Ethics of Teledemocracy', in Denton, ed., *Ethical Dimensions of Political Communication*, New York, Praeger, 1991a, pp.91–114.

Denton, R.E., ed.: *Ethical Dimensions of Political Communication*, New York, Praeger, 1991b.

Denton, R.E., Woodward, G.C.: *Political Communication in America*, New York, Praeger, 1990.

Devlin, L.: 'An Analysis of Presidential Television Commercials, 1952–1984', in Kaid *et al.*, eds, *New Perspectives on Political Advertising*, Carbondale, Southern Illinois University Press, 1986, pp.21–54.

Diamond, E., Bates, S.: *The Spot*, Cambridge, Mass., MIT Press, 1992 [1st edn 1984].

Dionisopoulos, G.: 'Corporate Advocacy Advertising as Political Communication', in Kaid *et al..* eds, *New Perspectives on Political Advertising*, Carbondale, Southern Illinois University Press, 1986, pp.82–106.

Drummond, P., Paterson, R., eds: *Television in Transition*, London, BFI, 1985.

Edelman, M.: *Constructing the Political Spectacle*, Chicago, University of Chicago Press, 1988.

Eldridge, J., ed.: *Getting the Message: News, Truth and Power*, London, Routledge, 1993.

Entman, R.: *Democracy Without Citizens*, New York, Oxford University Press, 1989.

Ericson, R.V., Baranek, P.M., Chan, J.B.L.: *Representing Order*, Milton Keynes, Open University Press, 1991.

Ernst, J.: *The Structure of Political Communication*, Frankfurt, European University Studies, 1988.

Fallon, I.: *The Brothers*, London, Hutchinson, 1988.

Fallows, J.: *Breaking the News*, New York, Pantheon Books, 1996.

Ferguson, M., ed.: *Public Communication*, London, Sage, 1989.

Fiske, J.: 'Popularity and the Politics of Information', in Dahigren and Sparks, eds, *Journalism and Popular Culture*, London, Sage, 1992, pp.45–63.

Foote, J.S.: 'Implications of Presidential Communication for Electoral Success', in Kaid *et al.*, eds, *Mediated Politics in Two Cultures: Presidential Campaigning in the United States and France*, New York, Praeger, 1991, pp.261–70.

Franklin, B., Murphy, D.: *What News? The Market, Politics and the Local Press*, London, Routledge, 1991.

Franklin, B., ed.: *Televising Democracies*, London, Routledge, 1992.

Franklin, B.: *Packaging Politics*, London, Edward Arnold, 1994.

Garnham, N.: 'The Media and the Public Sphere', in Golding *et al.*, eds, *Communicating Politics*, Leicester, Leicester University Press, 1986, pp.37–55.

Gellhorn, M.: 'The Invasion of Panama', in *Granta*, no. 32, Summer 1990, pp.205–29.

Gerrits, R.: 'Terrorists' Perspectives: Memoirs', in Paletz and Schmid, eds, *Terrorism and the Media*, London, Sage, 1992, pp.29–61.

Gerstle, J., Davis, D., Dubanel, O.: 'Television News and the Construction of Political Reality in France and the United States', in Kaid *et al.*, eds,

*Mediated Politics in Two Cultures: Presidential Campaigning in the United States and France*, New York, Praeger, 1991, pp.119–43.

Gitlin, T.: 'Making Protest Movements Newsworthy', in Graber, ed., *Media Power in Politics*, Washington, CQ Press, 1984, pp.239–50.

Glasgow University Media Group: *Bad News*, London, Routledge & Kegan Paul, 1976.

Glasgow University Media Group: *More Bad News*, London, Routledge & Kegan Paul, 1980.

Glasgow University Media Group: *Really Bad News*, London, Writers & Readers, 1982.

Glasgow University Media Group: *War and Peace News*, Milton Keynes, Open University Press, 1985.

Goldenberg, E.: 'Prerequisites for Access to the Press', in Graber, ed., *Media Power in Politics*, Washington, CQ Press 1984, pp.231–8.

Golding, P., Murdock, G., Schlesinger, P., eds: *Communicating Politics*, Leicester, Leicester University Press, 1986.

Graber, D.A.: 'Political Language', in Nimmo and Sanders, eds, *Handbook of Political Communication*, Beverly Hills, Sage, 1981, pp.195–223.

Graber, D.A.: *Mass Media and American Politics*, Washington, CQ Press, 1984a.

Graber, D.A., ed.: *Media Power in Politics*, Washington, CQ Press, 1984b.

Greenaway, J., Smith, S., Street, J.: *Deciding Factors in British Politics*, London, Routledge, 1992.

Gripsund, J.: 'The Aesthetics and the Politics of Melodrama', in Dahlgren and Sparks, *Journalism and Popular Culture*, London, Sage, 1992, pp.84–95.

Habermas, J.: *The Structural Transformation of the Public Sphere*, Cambridge, Polity Press, 1989.

Hall, S., Crichter, C., Jefferson, T., Clarke, J., Roberts, B.: *Policing the Crisis*, London, Macmillan, 1978.

Hall, S.: 'Encoding/decoding', in Hall *et al.*, eds, *Culture, Media Language*, London, Hutchinson, 1980, pp.128–38.

Hall, S., Hobson, D., Lowe, A., Willis, R: *Culture, Media Language*, London, Hutchinson, 1980.

Hallin, D.: *The Uncensored War*, Oxford, Oxford University Press, 1986.

Hallin, D.: 'Hegemony: The American News Media From Vietnam to El Salvador: A Study of Ideological Change and its Limits', in Paletz, ed., *Political Communication Research: Approaches, Studies, Assessments*, Norwood, Ablex, 1987, pp.3–25.

Hallin, D.: 'Sound Bite News', in Iyengar and Reeves, eds, *Do the Media Govern?* London, Sage, 1997, pp.57–65.

Harris, R.: *Gotcha: The Media, the Government and the Falklands Crisis*, London, Faber & Faber, 1983.

Harris, R.: *Good and Faithful Servant*, London, Faber & Faber, 1991.

Harrop, M., Scammell, M.: 'A Tabloid War', in Butler and Kavanagh, *The*

*British General Election of 1992*, London, Macmillan, 1992, pp.180–210.

Hart, R.P.: *The Sound of Leadership: Presidential Communication in the Modern Age*, Chicago, University of Chicago Press, 1987.

Heffernan, R., Marqusee, M.: *Defeat from the Jaws of Victory*, London, Verso, 1992.

Herman, E.: 'Gatekeeper versus Propaganda Models: A Critical American Perspective', in Golding *et al.*, eds, *Communicating Politics*, Leicester, Leicester University Press, 1986, pp.171–95.

Herman, E., Broadhead, F.: *The Rise and Fall of the Bulgarian Connection*, New York, Sheridan Square Publications Inc., 1986.

Hetherington, A., Ryle, M., Weaver, K.: *Cameras in the Commons*, London, Hansard Society, 1990.

Hooper, A.: *The Military and the Media*, Aldershot, Gower, 1982.

Hughes, C., Wintour, P.: *Labour Rebuilt: The New Model Party*, London, Fourth Estate, 1993.

Ingham, B.: *Kill the Messenger*, London, Fontana, 1991.

Irwin, C.L.: 'Terrorists' Perspectives: Interviews', in Paletz and Schmid, eds, *Terrorism and the Media*, London, Sage, 1992, pp.62–85.

Iyengar, S., Reeves, R., eds: *Do the Media Govern?*, London, Sage, 1997.

Jamieson, K.: 'The Evolution of Political Advertising in America', in Kaid *et al.*, eds, *New Perspectives in Political Advertising*, Carbondale, Southern Illinois University Press, 1986, pp.1–20.

Jamieson, K.: *Dirty Politics*, New York, Oxford University Press, 1992.

Johnson, K., Elebash, C.: 'The Contagion from the Right: The Americanization of British Political Advertising', in Kaid *et al.*, eds, *New Perspectives on Political Advertising*, Carbondale, Southern Illinois University Press, 1986, pp.293–313.

Jones, N.: *Strikes and the Media*, Oxford, Basil Blackwell, 1986.

Jones, N.: *Soundbites and Spin Doctors*, London, Cassell, 1995.

Jones, N.: *Campaign 97*, London, Indigo, 1997.

Joslyn, R.: 'Political Advertising and the Meaning of Elections', in Kaid *et al.*, eds, *New Perspectives on Political Advertising*, Carbondale, Southern Illinois University Press, 1986, pp.139–83.

Kaid, L.: 'Political Advertising', in Nimmo and Sanders, eds, *Handbook of Political Communication*, Beverly Hills, Sage, 1981, pp.249–71.

Kaid, L., Nimmo, D., Sanders, K., eds: *New Perspectives on Political Advertising*, Carbondale, Southern Illinois University Press, 1986.

Kaid, L.L., Johnston, A.: 'Negative versus Positive Television Advertising in U.S. Presidential Campaigns, 1960–1988', *Journal of Communication*, vol. 41, no. 3, 1991, pp.53–64.

Kaid, L.L., Gerstle, J., Sanders, K.R., eds: *Mediated Politics in Two Cultures: Presidential Campaigning in the United States and France*, New York, Praeger, 1991.

Keeter, S.: 'The Illusion of Intimacy: Television and the Role of Candidate

Personal Qualities in Voter Choice', *Public Opinion Quarterly*, vol. 51, 1987, pp.344–58.

Kelley, S.: *Professional Public Relations and Political Power*, Baltimore, John Hopkins University Press, 1956.

Kelly, M., Mitchell, T.: 'Transnational Terrorism and the Western Elite Press', in Graber, ed., *Media Power in Politics*, Washington, CQ Press, 1984, pp.282–9.

Kepplinger, H.M., Dombach, W.: 'The Influence of Camera Perspectives on the Reception of a Politician by Supporters, Opponents, and Neutral Viewers', in Paletz, ed., *Political Communication Research: Approaches, Studies, Assessments*, Norwood, Ablex, 1987, pp.62–72.

Kieran, M., ed.: *Media Ethics*, London, Routledge, 1998.

King, A.: *Power and Communication*, Illinois, Waveland Press, 1987.

King, A., ed.: *Postmodern Political Communication*, London, Praeger, 1992.

Knightley, P.: *The First Casualty*, New York, Harcourt Brace Jovanovitch, 1975.

Kraus, S., Davis, D.: 'Political Debates', in Nimmo and Sanders, eds, *Handbook of Political Communication*, Beverly Hills, Sage, 1981, pp.273–96.

Leiss, W., Kline, S., Jhally, S.: *Social Communication in Advertising*, London, Routledge, 1986.

Levin, M.B.: *Political Hysteria in America*, New York, Basic Books, 1971.

Levy, D.: 'What Public Relations Can Do Better Than Advertising', *Public Relations Quarterly*, vol. 34, no. 4, 1989, pp.7–9.

Lippmann, W.: *Public Opinion*, New York, Macmillan, 1954 [1922].

Livingstone, S., Lunt, P.: *Talk Show Democracy*, London, Routledge, 1994.

McAllister, I.: 'Campaign Activities and Electoral Outcomes in Britain: 1979 and 1983', *Public Opinion Quarterly*, vol. 49, 1985, pp.489–503.

Macarthur, J.R.: *Second Front: Censorship and Propaganda in the Gulf War*, New York, Hill & Wang, 1992.

McCombs, M.: 'The Agenda-Setting Approach', in Nimmo and Sanders, eds, 1981, *Handbook of Political Communication*, Beverly Hills, Sage. pp.121–40.

McKay, R., Barr, B.: *The Story of the Scottish Daily News*, Edinburgh, Canongate, 1976.

McNair, B.: *Images of the Enemy*, London, Routledge, 1988.

McNair, B.: 'Television News and the 1983 Election', in Marsh and Fraser, eds, *Public Opinion and Nuclear Weapons*, London, Macmillan, 1989, pp. 124–42.

McNair, B.: *Glasnost, Perestroika and the Soviet Media*, London, Routledge, 1991.

McNair, B.: 'Journalism, Politics and Public Relations: An Ethical Appraisal', in Kieran, ed., 1998a, pp.49–65.

McNair, B.: *The Sociology of Journalism*, London, Arnold, 1998b.

McNair, B.: *News and Journalism in the UK*, 3rd edition, London, Routledge, 1999.

Macpherson, C.B.: *The Life and Times of Liberal Democracy*, Oxford, Oxford University Press, 1976.

McQuail, D.: *Mass Communication Theory*, London, Sage, 1987.

Marsh, K., Fraser, C., eds: *Public Opinion and Nuclear Weapons*, London, Macmillan, 1989.

Martineau, P.: *Motivation in Advertising*, New York, McGraw-Hill, 1957.

Mauser, G.: *Political Marketing: An Approach to Campaign Strategy*, New York, Praeger, 1983.

Mercer, D., Mungham, G., Williams, K.: *The Fog of War*, London, Heinemann, 1987.

Michie, D.: *The Invisible Persuaders*, London, Bantam Press, 1998.

Miliband, R.: *The State in Capitalist Society*, London, Quartet, 1973.

Mill, J.S.: *Three Essays*, London, Oxford University Press, 1975.

Miller, D.: 'The Northern Ireland Information Service and the Media: Aims, Strategy and Tactics', in Eldridge, ed., *Getting the Message: News, Truth and Power*, London, Routledge, 1993, pp.73–103.

Miller, D., Kitzinger, J., Williams, K., Beharrell, P.: *The Circuit of Mass Communication*, London, Sage, 1998.

Miller, D., Williams, K.: 'Negotiating HIV/AIDS Information: Agendas, Media Strategies and News', in Eldridge, ed., *Getting the Message: News, Truth and Power*, London, Routledge, 1993, pp.126–42.

Miller, W.: *Media and Voters*, Oxford, Clarendon Press, 1991.

Molotch, H.L., Protess, D.L., Gordon, M.T.: 'The Media–Policy Connection: Ecologies of News', in Paletz, ed., *Political Communication Research: Approaches, Studies, Assessments*, Norwood, Ablex, 1987, pp.26–48.

Morley, D.: *The Nationwide Audience*, London, BFI, 1980.

Morris, D.: *Behind the Oval Office*, New York, Random House, 1997.

Murphy, D.: *The Stalker Affair and the Press*, London, Unwin Hyman, 1991.

Murray, R.: *Red Scare: A Study of National Hysteria, 1919–20*, Westport, Greenwood Press, 1955.

Myers, K.: *Understains*, London, Comedia, 1986.

Negrine, R.: *Politics and the Mass Media*, London, Routledge, 1993.

Negrine, R.: *The Communication of Politics*, London, Sage, 1996.

Nimmo, D.: *The Political Persuaders*, New York, Prentice-Hall, 1970.

Nimmo, D., Sanders, K.: 'The Emergence of Political Communication as a Field', 1981a, in Nimmo and Sanders, eds, *Handbook of Political Communication,*, Beverly Hills, Sage, pp.11–36.

Nimmo, D., Sanders, K., eds: *Handbook of Political Communication*, Beverly Hills, Sage, 1981b.

Nimmo, D., Combs, J.: *Political Communication*, New York, Longman, 1983.

Nimmo, D., Combs, J.: *Political Pundits*, New York, Praeger, 1992.

Nimmo, D., Felsberg, A.: 'Hidden Myths in Televisual Political Advertising', in Kaid *et al.*, eds, *New Perspectives on Political Advertising*, Carbondale, Southern Illinois University Press, 1986, pp.248–67.

Paletz, D.L., ed.: *Political Communication Research: Approaches, Studies, Assessments*, Norwood, Ablex, 1987.

Paletz, D., Schmid, A., eds: *Terrorism and the Media*, London, Sage, 1992.

Parenti, M.: *Inventing Reality: The Politics of the Mass Media*, New York, St Martin's Press, 1986.

Patterson, T.: *The Mass Media Election*, New York, Praeger, 1980.

Philo, G.: 'From Buerk to Band Aid: The Media and the 1984 Ethiopian Famine', 1993a, in Eldridge, ed., *Getting the Message: News, Truth, and Power*, London, Routledge, pp.104–25.

Philo, G.: 'Political Advertising, Popular Belief and the 1992 British General Election', *Media, Culture and Society*, vol. 15, 1993b, pp.407–18.

Pickard, R.G.: 'Press Relations of Terrorist Organisations', *Public Relations Review*, vol. XV, no. 4, 1989, pp.12–23.

Ponting, C.: 'Defence Decision-Making and Public Opinion: A View from the Inside', in Marsh and Fraser, eds, *Public Opinion and Nuclear Weapons*, London, Macmillan, 1989, pp.177–91.

Popkin, S.: *The Reasoning Voter*, Chicago, University of Chicago Press, 1991.

Poulantzas, N.: *Classes in Contemporary Capitalism*, London, New Left Books, 1975.

Pusey, M.: *Jurgen Habermas*, London, Tavistock, 1978.

Robins, K., Webster, F.: ' "The Revolution of the Fixed Wheel": Information, Technology and Social Taylorism', in Drummond and Paterson, eds, *Television in Transition*, London, BFI, 1985, pp.36–63.

Rosenberg, S., McCafferty, P.: 'The Image and the Vote: Manipulating Voters' Preferences', *Public Opinion Quarterly*, vol. 51, 1987, pp.3l–47.

Sabato, L.: *The Rise of Political Consultants*, New York, Basic Books, 1981.

Scammell, M.: *Designer Politics: How Elections are Won*, London, Macmillan, 1995.

Scannell, P., Cardiff, D.: *A Social History of British Broadcasting, vol. 1*, Oxford, Basil Blackwell, 1991.

Schiller, H.: *Information and the Crisis Economy*, Norwood, Ablex, 1984.

Schlesinger, P.: *Putting 'Reality' Together*, London, Methuen, 1987.

Schlesinger, P.: 'Rethinking the Sociology of Journalism', in Ferguson, ed., *Public Communication*, London, Sage, 1989, pp.61–83.

Schlesinger, P., Tumber, H.: *Reporting Crime: The Media Politics of Criminal Justice*, Oxford, Clarendon Press, 1994.

Schmid, A., de Graaf, J.: *Violence as Communication*, London, Sage, 1982.

Seymour-Ure, C.: 'Prime Ministers' Reactions to Television', *Media, Culture and Society*, vol. 11, no. 3, 1989, pp.307–25.

Shaw, E.: *The Labour Party Since 1979: Crisis and Transformation*, London, Routledge, 1994.

Shyles, L.: 'The Televised Political Spot Advertisement', in Kaid *et al.*, eds, *New Perspectives on Political Advertising*, Carbondale, Southern Illinois University Press, 1986, pp.107–38.

Silvester, C., ed.: *The Penguin Book of Interviews*, London, Viking, 1993.

Simmons, H., Mechling, E.: 'The Rhetoric of Political Movements', in Nimmo and Sanders, eds, *Handbook of Political Communication*, Beverly Hills, Sage, 1981, pp.417–44.

Sparks, C.: 'Popular Journalism: Theories and Practices', in Dahlgren and Sparks, eds, *Journalism and Popular Culture*, London, Sage, 1992, pp.24–44.

Steinberg, C.: *The Mass Communicators*, Westport, Greenwood Press, 1958.

Taylor, P.: *War and the Media: Propaganda and Persuasion in the Gulf War*, Manchester, Manchester University Press, 1992.

Tiffen, R.: *News and Power*, Sydney, Allen & Unwin, 1989.

Tilson, D.: 'Eco-Nuclear Publicity: A Comparative Study in Florida and Scotland', Unpublished Ph.D. Thesis, University of Stirling, Stirling, March 1994.

Watts, D.: *Political Communication Today*, Manchester, Manchester University Press, 1997.

Weaver, D.: 'Media Agenda-setting and Elections: Assumptions and Implications', in Paletz, ed., *Political Communication Research: Approaches, Studies, Assessments*, Norwood, Ablex, 1987, pp.176–93.

Williams, K.: 'The Light at the End of the Tunnel: The Mass Media, Public Opinion and the Vietnam War', in Eldridge, ed., *Getting the Message: News, Truth and Power*, London, Routledge, 1993, pp.305–28.

Williamson, J.: *Decoding Advertisements*, London, Marion Boyars, 1978.

Woodward, G.C.: 'Political News: Narrative Form and the Ethics of Denial', in Denton, ed., *Ethical Dimensions of Political Communication*, New York, Praeger, 1991, pp.199–223.

Worcester, R.M.: *British Public Opinion*, Oxford, Basil Blackwell, 1991.

Worcester, R.M.: 'Demographics and Values: What the British public read and what they think about their newspapers', Paper presented to The End of Fleet Street Conference, City University, February, 1994.

Wright, P.: *Spycatcher*, New York, Viking, 1989.

# INDEX